To JOSEPH—

THE HARDY BOYZ

[signatures]

DARE 2 DREAM!

THE HARDY BOYZ EXIST 2

 ReganBooks
An Imprint of HarperCollins*Publishers*

INSPIRE

MATT & JEFF HARDY

with Michael Krugman

HarperCollins books may be purchased for educational, business, or sales promotional use. For information please write: Special Markets Department, HarperCollins Publishers Inc., 10 East 53rd Street, New York, NY 10022.

FIRST EDITION

Designed by Joel Avirom and Jason Snyder
Design assistant: Meghan Day Healey

Printed on acid-free paper

Library of Congress Cataloging-in-Publication Data

Hardy, Matt
    The Hardy Boyz : exist 2 inspire / Matt & Jeff Hardy with Michael Krugman. —1st ed.
      p. cm.
    ISBN 0-06-052154-6
     1. Hardy, Matt, 1973 or 4– 2. Hardy, Jeff. 3. Hardy Boyz (Wrestlers) 4. Wrestlers—United United States—Biography. I. Hardy, Jeff. II. Krugman, Michael. III. Title

GV1196.A1H32 2003
796.812'092'2—dc21
[B]

                                        2002037121

03 04 05 06 07 ❖/RRD 10 9 8 7 6 5 4 3 2 1

*We would like to dedicate this story
to our mother in heaven and our father on earth*

H-A-R-D-WHY   JEFF HARDY

This is for you who thought we couldn't cut it . . .
H-A-R-D-Why are we so—
H-A-R-D-Hard to swallow
We've got our asses kicked—
And we'll get them kicked again.
We have made you so sick—
And we will make you sick again.
You have suffered from say
That we will never see this day
You've made us this way.
Anti-Hardy fans
Snap out of your trance
Define the word Chance
Never again douht our ABILITY.
Semiwars we've been though
Obstacles that we've passed
All the naysayers that we've passed
Mountains that we've climbed—
And holes that we've jumped
Oceans we've swum and bullets we've ducked.
Roads that we've drove and paths that we've made
Leading over walls and though caves
Under water or in the sky—
Matt and Jeff Hardy
Inspire until they die—

CONTENTS

ACKNOWLEDGMENTS

We would like to thank our mother in heaven for all of her inspiration; our father for his tough but supportive love, God, Shane Helms, Shannon Moore, Scott Matthews, Marty Garner, Aaron Decker, Joey Matthews, Christian York, Thomas Simpson, David Johnson, and Betty Miller.

We would like to thank all the guys that helped make the OMEGA, NFWA, and ECWF shows become reality, especially Tracy Caddell, Ted Hobgood, and Jason Ahrndt. Our entire family, including Mama Moore, Little Jim, Daniel, Shirley, Kelly, Lucy, and all our other cousins, aunts, and uncles.

The entire WWE—including the McMahons, the boys, the office personnel, Stacey Pascarella, the writers, the agents, Michael Hayes, and especially Edge & Christian and the Dudleyz for helping us create so many moments that will never be forgotten in the industry.

All of our fans, in particular those from day one, dating back to the days of the Southern Pines and Sanford National Guard Armories.

And finally, Mike Krugman and the staff at ReganBooks, especially Louis Morin, for helping us piece together our incredible trip up to this point in our lives.

MATT

I would like to thank Amy for always being there for me, and Jeff for helping me fulfill our lives' dream. They are the two best people anyone could be blessed with in life.

JEFF

Special thanks to Beth Britt for being the final piece in my completed puzzle of happiness. Thanks to Matt for everything . . . it's far from over, brother.

MICHAEL KRUGMAN

First and foremost, my thanks to Matt and Jeff Hardy, whose remarkable memories, extensive knowledge, and old-fashioned Southern hospitality made it a pleasure to work alongside them.

My gratitude and respect go to WWE's Stacey Pascarella, and ReganBooks' Louis Morin and Dana Albarella.

A number of folks made contributions that proved invaluable during the writing of this book—thanks to Adam "the Brain" Bridge at Dell Canada Technical Support, Otis Ball (a.k.a. Hoboken's own Otis Brawl), and the great Dr. Carl Berg. In addition, my friends at Atlantic Records: Patti Conte, Bob Kaus, Nick Stern, Tracy Zamot, and Jeff Murcko.

This book would not have been possible without the assistance of two top-notch gentlemen: superagent Dave Dunton at Harvey Klinger, Inc., and the one-and-only Keith Lyle, both of whose hard work and attention to detail made it all come together with ease.

Big love to my family, David, Cynthia, and Michele Krugman. And of course, a major pop must go to the many members of the MK5 clique— Jonathan Gordon, Mike Flaherty, Jason Cohen, Ken Weinstein, Nevin Martell, Deb Bernardini, Bobbie Gale, Trent Buckroyd, Amy Wan & Donovan Finn, and Richard & Kristy Martin—for their ceaseless love and patience.

EXIST 2 INSPIRE

INTRODUCTION
Autobiography in Motion

EVERY TIME WE STAND ATOP A TWENTY-FOOT LADDER and hear fifteen thousand people taking one collective gasp before we jump, then burst out in screaming excitement, we think about how far we've come.

Dreams don't come true just by dreaming them. It takes passion, hard work, and determination, a total devotion to the goal, and a willingness to sacrifice everything—including your body—to make those dreams come alive.

Since the first time we wrestled on our backyard trampoline, we've known what we wanted to do with the rest of our lives. Our goal back then was to wrestle at our school, Cameron Elementary, but in our hearts we both knew that we wouldn't be satisfied until we were WWE Superstars.

We worked on our bodies, and we worked on our skills. We drove up and down the East Coast, wrestling for no money, just to gain experience and knowledge. We busted our asses night after night to defy the odds and make our dreams a reality.

Every time our lives were confronted by something negative, we sucked it up and turned it into a positive. When people told us that we were setting unattainable goals, we just laughed it off and worked harder to make them eat their words. The word *can't* is simply not part of the Hardy Boyz vocabulary.

They say you've only got a certain amount of bumps on your "bump card"—the amount of punishment a wrestler can take over their career—and we took those bumps like nobody's business in order to entertain the fans and create the most exciting and breathtaking wrestling matches imaginable.

We've tried to do things that express who we are to this business. The high-risk maneuvers and fearless attitude—those aren't things we just bring to the squared circle. It's how we live our lives every single day. The truth is, life is full of danger and of consequences. We face those fears in and out of the ring, and that's one of the reasons so many people connect to what we do.

The professional wrestling business is one of the most intense and difficult lifestyles that you can think of. It's a life spent mostly on the road, in rental cars and cheap hotels, always on the move to the next show. The thing that's always kept us going is the love of what we do and the knowledge that when we get to the next city or town, there's going to be an arena full of people—many of them wearing Hardy Boyz T-shirts—who can't wait to see us do our thing.

After a while, people start to see a tag team as one person, *Matt-and-Jeff*. But there are two Hardy Boyz, and each of us is very different in how we see the world, and how we live our lives. We are united by blood and by a common vision, but we are two distinctly unique people—Matt Hardy and Jeff Hardy.

We want people to feel our passion and to understand the sacrifices we've made in order to get to where we are. No one ever said the journey was going to be an easy one, but the journeys worth taking never are.

Nothing of worth is ever handed to you in this life. You have to study and fight and work to make opportunity come to you. And when it does, you have to study and fight and work that much harder to make sure that you take every advantage of it.

From our backyard in Cameron, we've traveled around the world doing what we've always known we're were meant to do. We've lived for the moment in the truest sense. Every day we've climbed the ladder to our dreams.

PART 1
BOYZ LIFE

THE HARDY BOYZ

MATT: Jeff and I have met a lot of brothers who told us how they were jealous of each other, but we were close immediately. I was tickled that I had a little brother. We were best friends.

JEFF: We were partners in crime. Everything we did, we did together. The age difference wasn't that great—three years really isn't that much—and so we always got along just famously.

MATT: Growing up where we did, we were pretty much forced to be friends. We were pretty much all we had. Our home is on land that has been owned by the Hardy family since 1919—a hundred acres of beautiful pinewoods in the heart of Cameron, North Carolina.

JEFF: Our daddy—Gilbert Hardy—was a tobacco grower. His attitude toward life was that you get up at five in the morning and go to work. When the sun goes down, you go to bed. The next day, you do it all again.

MATT: Because we were so isolated, Jeff and I had to entertain ourselves. It's amazing how much time we spent in the woods. We would sneak around our land, hiding out all over the place. For some reason, we never thought our dad would find us, but somehow, he always knew where we were.

JEFF: We used to get so excited when we went to visit our grandma Moore. We had a big brown station wagon and we'd jump in the back of that sucker and go to Grandma's for a Sunday trip. That was great for us, because we had a couple of cousins that would be there, and anytime there were other kids for us to play with was always fun.

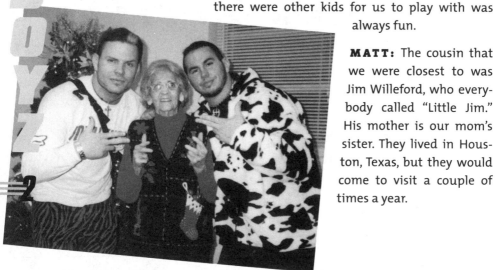

MATT: The cousin that we were closest to was Jim Willeford, who everybody called "Little Jim." His mother is our mom's sister. They lived in Houston, Texas, but they would come to visit a couple of times a year.

2

Whenever Jim would come around, we would hang out and have a good time, doing the things that boys do. Which usually involved getting into trouble.

JEFF: One of our other cousins, Daniel Freeman, would also visit and we'd go out and trespass through the woods, exploring around the rivers, looking for crayfish, things like that. We even had a name for our little group—the Adventurers.

From as early as I can recall, Matt and I created a very active fantasy life for ourselves. It wasn't just, "Hey man, we're the Adventurers." We built a clubhouse, we sketched little comic books where we were like the Fantastic Four, with each of us having different strengths and abilities.

Matt was the super-powerful leader, he could lift twenty tons, and I stretched like Reed Richards. Jim was real fast, like Quicksilver in the Avengers, and Daniel was super-strong, even stronger than Matt. Of course, we all wanted to fly.

MATT: Jeff and I always envisioned a clubhouse that would be so nice, you could actually live in it.

Our dad had these big twenty-by-ten-foot sheets of plastic that he'd use to cover up tobacco after he'd cured it and brought it into the barn. We'd steal a few pieces, then go out into the woods and nail them up to build little places to hide. We knew we shouldn't nail them to the pine trees, because it would ruin them, but occasionally we did it anyway.

JEFF: We'd go out to the far corners of the woods, thinking, *Dad'll never find us.* Two weeks later, Daddy would get angry with us: "I thought I told you guys not to be nailing in those trees!"

It was incredible, like, "How did he know?"

MATT: Just down the road from our property is the Cameron Boys' Camp. It's a huge piece of land, more than nine hundred acres, run by the Baptist Children's Homes of North Carolina. They offer an alternative education for troubled kids.

They had a big lake down there, and a very cool trolley gimmick. It was kind of like a ski lift, where you'd start at the top of a hill and ride down on a wire into the ravine. We loved it because you'd start out high up in the air, then drop off real easy at the bottom. Whenever the camp was closed, we'd sneak down and ride that thing.

One time when I was ten and Jeff was seven, Little Jim came for a visit. We were running around, playing in the woods, and Jim said, "Hey, let's go ride that trolley."

"Cool," I said, "we haven't been down there in a while."

The boys' camp would clear out a path on the hillside so that you could ride the trolley down with nothing in the way. This time we discovered that they hadn't kept it up. The rope had gotten saggy, and they had let everything grow wild, so there were little trees and shrubs and briars in the way. Still, we decided to do it anyway.

Jim and I rode down together, with him holding on close to the rope and me under him. We were starting to go down, and between the weight and the rope getting all slack, we hung down to where Jim's knees were just above the bushes. Since I was under him, I went directly through all the briar patch. It was unbelievable! It ripped my clothes to shreds, then my skin. I was screaming, "Awwwwwwww!" I must have had two hundred slashes on me. It just sliced me up.

JEFF: I watched them riding down, thinking, *Where'd Matt go?* He just vanished into the shrubs. It was like in cartoons, where some guy goes through a wall, and you see his silhouette. Afterward, he was bleeding all over. I said, "I think I'm gonna just head back."

MATT: "Go ahead, man," Jim and I said. "Try it. It'll be fine with just one of us on there!"

JEFF: It'll be great if somebody from the boys' camp reads this and finds out about how much trespassing we did. There was an amazing high dive over the lake. It must've been twenty feet up, and we loved jumping into the water from there. It's funny when you look at some of the things we do now, because we've always had this fearless attitude. I was more scared of getting caught.

MATT: That's what we were worried about. We were real sneaky about going down there. But as far as doing dangerous things, we'd never hesitate. If we had fallen, we could have killed ourselves, but we never hesitated.

JEFF: In school, I was always the guy who wanted to see who could jump off the highest landing. I remember the first time I jumped off the back of our house. For the longest time it seemed so huge, but as we grew, inch by inch, it didn't seem so scary. When I finally jumped off, it wasn't that big a deal.

MATT: There's something about both of us—I think Jeff even more than me—we're adrenaline junkies. We always loved to do dangerous stuff. There's a tree out in our woods that's got a big flat space up in the branches. For the longest time we looked up at that tree, thinking it would be cool if we could get up there and hang out. We nailed pieces of wood on the tree so we could climb up. Then we reached a point where we couldn't nail any more pieces, so we took a rope and tied it up so we could climb up the rope and get up there. It must've been a good forty-five feet high, but it didn't frighten us one bit.

JEFF: I know people think we're fearless, that we're crazy daredevils, but I still have fear in me. It's about getting past the fear and actually doing whatever it is that you're afraid of. I'm always scared when I jump off of something because I think of the possibilities. But once it's over and I'm not hurt—that's the payoff.

MATT: Unlike Jeff, my willingness to try dangerous things is not based on fear. I'm just up for a challenge. The very worst thing someone can do is tell me that I can't do something. That makes me insane and I won't quit. Ever. If someone says, "You can't do this because you're afraid," my reaction is, "Bullshit. Watch this." It's about pride, in a lot of ways. Because I love to prove people wrong.

DISCIPLINE

MATT: Jeff and I had separate rooms, but we always wanted to stay together. We were that close. My bed was smaller than Jeff's, so we always wanted to stay in his bed. I can't remember the amount of times we'd be sitting there giggling—"Tee hee hee"—and we would hear Daddy coming, so we'd act like we were asleep, making snoring noises.

"Hey, you better shut up and go to sleep! Stop laughing in there!"

JEFF: Daddy used to keep his leather belt by the doorbell, where we couldn't reach it. *The* leather belt.

We weren't bad kids, but if we would get out of line, there wasn't a lot of warning shots. There wasn't a lot of, "Hey, you better not do that again." If the lights came on and he made it out of his bedroom and went down the hall heading toward the leather belt, we were through. *Wah-poosh!*

MATT: Daddy definitely kept us on a short leash. We knew if we screwed up we were going to be punished for it. Looking back, I think it really did give us a sense of self-discipline. We learned the difference between what's right and what's wrong. Or else.

JEFF: I think that just prepared me for getting paddled at school. I used to get whupped at school all the time. Every teacher had a paddle, and they'd beat the shit out of kids. If they caught you doing something, like chewing gum or whispering, it was just *bam!*

MATT: When we weren't in school, or out playing in the woods, Daddy would put us to work in the tobacco fields. We'd do simple things, like covering seeds with the hoe. Whenever we would do a little "injustice"—like horseplaying instead of doing our jobs, or running around the tobacco, straightening up the plants—and Daddy couldn't get to his leather strap, he'd take out his knife and cut a switch off a tree.

JEFF: I hate to say it, but he definitely cut quite a few switches.

MOM

MATT: Our mom, Ruby Moore Hardy, was a great lady. She didn't smoke, she didn't drink. She was just an incredibly sweethearted woman, who raised us to believe in traditional values, like doing unto others.

JEFF: She was like a perfect person. She loved going to church on Sunday, she was very athletic—a big softball fan and a championship bowler. I think that's where we got our love of physicality.

MATT: When we were very little, our other grandma—Daddy's mother— got sick and couldn't be on her own, so we brought her to live with us. Our old man made a room for her and she stayed with us for a while.

Both him and our mom took care of her. It was such a big personal sacrifice. To take time out of your life to care for somebody else. So many people do that, but as a kid, you don't realize until you get older how valuable time is.

JEFF: In 1986, when I was nine and Matt was twelve, Mom was diagnosed with a brain tumor. I couldn't understand why something like that would happen to such a wonderful woman. If anybody was going to get cancer, why pick her?

MATT: When she first got sick, I didn't believe that she would die. Because that kind of thing certainly couldn't happen to us. We were a good family. At that age, when you don't have a great grasp of how the real world is, you

just think your mom and dad will always be there. Even as her health deteriorated, I figured things would be cool. But they weren't, obviously.

JEFF: I remember how bad I hated going to see her in the hospital. To this day, I hate the stench and smell of the hospital. As much good as they do, it's such a bad vibe for me. I just wish everybody on earth could be healthy all the time. We've been so fortunate, and when we meet people that are terminally ill, like the Make-A-Wish kids, it reminds us that there's nothing more precious in life than your health.

MATT: It was almost a year to the day from when she was diagnosed with cancer that she died.

JEFF: All three of us were there with her when she died. Looking back, it's good that we were with her on her last physical moments on earth. I remember watching the monitor she was hooked up to, and seeing the lines getting further and further apart. When it eventually went into a flat line, we just all broke out in tears.

MATT: That was the first time we had ever seen our father cry. He had always been so strong. Mom was the sweet nice parent and Daddy was the enforcer. That's how an old-style Southern family is, and we were definitely the epitome of that family. If there was something that we were worried about, or something that we knew we were going to get in trouble over, we would always go to her first before him.

JEFF: We were so much closer to her than we were with our dad. Just because he was so hard. With Mom, there was just a simple bond of love.

MATT: It didn't fully hit me until I saw the open casket at the church. That was when it really set in, that Mom was gone. I was walking backward out of the church, staring at her silhouette, the side of her face in the casket, and I realized, *This is the last time I'll ever see her.*

Her death was real tough on me, especially because I was at the point where I was starting to develop a real relationship with her. It's really cool when you grow older and start becoming an adult, and instead of your parents just being your parents, they also become like your friend and you can really communicate with them. Neither one of us really got that with our mom, which really sucks.

JEFF: When I look back on how everything has turned out, I don't know if it would've happened the same way had she lived. In a lot of ways, our whole craziness began after our mom died.

MATT: Maybe facing death at such an impressionable age did desensitize us a little bit. We lost the closest person in the world to us, and we dealt with it. After an experience like that, death just wasn't as scary and as shocking as it is for people who aren't forced to deal with it.

JEFF: Both Matt and I feel like Mom's watching down on us. She sees all we've accomplished, all the things we're doing, and she's real proud of us. Knowing that she's watching our lives has always been a great inspiration for us both.

MATT: We still try to carry all those good qualities she had. We both want to make her proud. One thing about us that we think our fans connect with is that we're both good people, and her influence is definitely a big part of that. In a world where there's probably more shitty people than there are good people, I'm proud to be one of the good ones.

SCHOOL DAYZ

MATT: Jeff and I both went to the same schools—Cameron Elementary School, then New Century Middle School, then Union Pines High School. Our house wasn't too far from the actual town, so we were always among the last kids to get picked up by the school bus. But coming home, we were on the wrong end of the route, so we wouldn't get back most days until after four.

I was an okay student, but I found school to be extremely boring. I tend to get bored with stuff real easy if there's not something to hold my attention. I was always thinking about building a new hideout or building a half pipe for our dirt bikes.

JEFF: I hated school. My grades were always for shit. There were a few things I really enjoyed, like U.S. history and, of course, art. That was always my number one thing. I'd do artwork for extra credit, drawing pictures of presidents and wars and things.

Mostly I just wanted to come home and do whatever crazy project Matt and I were doing at the time. We both had a lot of creative juices, and if there was something we wanted to try but couldn't get access to, we'd try and create it ourselves.

MATT: I did fine in high school. I was even one of the nominees for the Morehead Award. That's the most prestigious scholarship you can get in North Carolina, where you get a free ride to the University of North Carolina school of your choice.

Looking back, I wish that I would've applied myself a little harder, because it's important to learn all you can when you have the chance. But of course, you don't realize that until you're older.

JEFF: When I graduated high school, I had the opportunity to go to an art institute, but by then, we were doing pretty good as wrestlers. I know that I'm lucky the way it's all worked out. There were so many people saying, "You'd better have something to fall back on."

MATT: People always say, "You have to go college. That's the only way to succeed."

To be honest, I'm not a big advocate of that philosophy. In a lot of ways, college doesn't mean anything. You can get all the good grades in the world, but that doesn't guarantee you a career in the real world.

ATHLETES

MATT: Both of us really loved baseball when we were little. We played on teams from the time we were seven years old. Our dad was our coach from seven to nine, and then I went on and played in the next league up, the Midget League, which was for ten to twelve. When I was in Little League, I did so well I made it to the local all-star game. The final score was three to two against the other team and I was responsible for all three runs—I hit two home runs and one RBI.

JEFF: We were both pretty good ballplayers, so we thought, man, one day we could play professional baseball. Before wrestling, baseball was definitely the dream.

MATT: When I got to high school, I was blown away by how seriously sports are taken. I thought about going out for football, but I was a lot smaller back then. And some of the places where you'd go play, it was real sticky. Like in East Montgomery, there would be these fourteen-year-old country boys with big beards. Man, I didn't want anything to do with those East Montgomery boys!

Mostly I played baseball, but it was just a little too "political" for my tastes. They were really serious about winning and it totally took the fun out of it. The coaches try to change everything about you, from your swing to your overall attitude. I quickly lost my passion for the game, and by my senior year, I was completely disinterested in it.

In my junior year, I made the decision to become a wrestler, so I started to spend most of my life in the gym. I was getting bigger and stronger, so the next year, I decided, *What the hell?* and went out for football.

That was an experience! I wanted to be a running back, but I wasn't nearly as fast as some of the other boys. I was real strong and hard to pull down, so I ended up playing defense. I was a linebacker and a defensive end.

M. D. Guthrie was the football coach/athletic director at Union Pines. He was a big man, like six-five, three hundred pounds. He was a good guy but a bit of a tyrant out on the field. He said something to the team one practice that I still quote this day. "We gotta improve," he said, "because if you're not getting better, you're getting worse."

I believe that. You always have to strive to improve and modify yourself.

JEFF: I played football all through high school. I was always either a fullback or a linebacker. In my junior year, we went to the first round of the state play-offs and I got drafted up to the seniors just to sit on the sidelines. I went in for a kickoff, but that was pretty much it.

One day I went to practice and I was sick as a damn dog, so I told one of the other coaches. Coach Guthrie came up to me and said, "Go run a couple of miles, Hardy, you'll burn it out. You'll sweat all of that badness."

And he was serious! But the ability to work sick has come in handy. Lord knows, we'd have to have broken legs or something to not work in WWE.

MX

JEFF: I got very into biking when I was twelve. I would go with my buddy Alan Thomas and his family to the races. His family had more money than we did.

I loved riding dirt bikes—the speed and the danger were such a turn-on for me. There were places on the land where there were natural half pipes and we'd go out there and do jumps and tricks. I wanted a motorcycle for the longest time, but we really couldn't afford one. I used to put leaves in the back tire of my bicycle to make it sound like a motorcycle!

When I was thirteen, Daddy bought me a used Yamaha YZ-80. It was old and beat-up, but he knew how bad I wanted to ride. We fixed up that YZ and I got so into it—I was on that bike constantly, riding around the property, doing jumps. Daddy saw how much I loved riding and he broke down and bought me a brand-new Suzuki RM-125, which is one of the best motocross bikes available. It was crazy expensive, like thirty-five hundred dollars, but worth every penny.

I started going out to all the local tracks, places like Montrose Motocross and Devil's Ridge Motocross, Black Ankle Raceway and Hangtime Motocross Park.

I learned how to jump all by myself. I'll never forget the first time I did a massive hundred-foot triple. It was crazy! It was so high! It's such a scary feeling, but it's an incredible rush, throwing it down and going over the edge. Woo hoo!

In ninth grade, I decided I wanted to start racing. My first race was so much fun, but in the second one, I crashed and broke my shoulder and my collarbone. That totally messed up my pitching arm, and really put an end to any hope of a career in baseball.

Before my accident, I had only considered two professions—baseball and being a professional motocross racer. I had three bikes—two 250s and that 125. I loved it, but it was killing me financially. You have to have a lot of money to make it in the racing business. And then Matt and I started getting more and more successful as wrestlers and it became hard to fit both things into my schedule.

These days, I don't ride as often as I used to, but I'll always have dirt bikes. Getting on a motorcycle is still my favorite stress reliever.

JUST A-SWINGING

MATT: Growing up in the South, it was natural that the first music Jeff and I heard was country western. Daddy made a little extra money playing guitar in bars, mostly country and bluegrass. Sometimes, on Friday or Saturday nights, him and some of the guys he played with would come down to the house. Jeff and I would be in our pajamas, because we were supposed to be getting ready for bed, but Daddy would let us hang out and listen.

There's an old country song, "Just A-Swinging." That used to be my specialty. I'd go down there and everyone would say, "Come on, Matty, you're so cute. Sing 'Just A-Swinging.' "

JEFF: We were real sheltered, though. It wasn't until I was in the fifth grade that we actually owned our own radio. Daddy took us down to Eckerd's and got us a radio and a cassette player. That's when we first started learning about music.

Before that, the only music we'd hear was in the car, and it was always country music. Once we got that radio, a whole world opened up to us. We discovered pop and rock and roll and rap. We both thought, *Wow, this is pretty cool stuff.*

This was when MTV was the biggest thing around, and we didn't have a clue! We didn't get cable at the house until 1994, when we first started to do stuff with WWE. When we finally saw MTV, it was like, "Whoa, look what we've been missing!"

MATT: The first music that I really liked, that I formed my own opinions about, was stuff like Debbie Gibson and Tiffany and Belinda Carlisle— remember "Heaven Is a Place on Earth"? I started recording everything I could. I would wait all night for a song to come on so I could record it onto a cassette tape.

As time went on and I got older, I started getting more into hip-hop. I really liked DJ Jazzy Jeff and the Fresh Prince, I thought that was cool as hell.

JEFF: I know it's not cool to admit it, but Vanilla Ice was a huge inspiration on me. It was because of him that I started dancing. I had some friends at school that were very into hip-hop, and they showed me all kinds of cool moves. At first I was goofy as hell, but I got pretty good at busting a move.

MATT: Remember that Public Enemy song "Can't Truss It"? I cut those words into the back of Jeff's hair when he was in six grade. I don't know what he was thinking! He just had a little hair on the top and then it said "Can't Truss It" on the back.

JEFF: We would have never gotten away with that if our mom was still alive. I remember going to Daddy: "Look, Matt cut a checkerboard around my head."

Daddy was pretty damn cool, though. He always let me do whatever I wanted to do to my hair. When earrings started getting popular, he even let me do that. I guess he had bigger things to worry about.

MATT: As we got older, Daddy was probably more open than our mom would've been. He would just roll his eyes—times were changing and his kids were crazy! His attitude was pretty simple: "Just go to bed on time and don't screw up."

WRESTLEMANIA
SETS IN

JEFF: Growing up, we didn't have cable or even a VCR. The only wrestling we saw back then was NWA, because it was on regular TV, and *WWE Superstars* and *WWE Wrestling Challenge,* which were on the local station.

I just thought it was so colorful and exciting. I loved Ric Flair, he was just so cool. We were also huge fans of tag teams like the Fabulous Freebirds and the Rockers.

MATT: We used to go to a friend's house to watch WWE Pay-Per-Views, and we officially caught the wrestling bug after *WrestleMania IV,* when "Macho Man" Randy Savage won the first-ever WWE World Title Tournament. I was only fourteen years old, but I knew right then and there what I wanted to do for the rest of my life. I wanted to be a professional wrestler.

When I graduated high school, everybody in my yearbook wrote things like, "Good luck in WWE." I was so cocky; the thing I signed in their yearbooks was, "Have a good life—you'll see me before I see you." Meaning, of course, that they were going see me wrestling on TV before too long.

JEFF: Matt and I kept begging Daddy for a trampoline, and he finally bought us one for Christmas 1988. That next spring, we took a ramp I had built for my bike and painted it up like an actual wrestling entrance. We'd run down the ramp to the trampoline and wrestle.

After a while we thought, what if we actually choreographed it like they do on TV? So we started copying all the spots we saw on television. Friends like Billy and Wade Hall would come over and we'd wrestle. Because we weren't able to do all the pro moves, we mostly mat-wrestled. It was more like shoot-fighting than anything else.

MATT: In 1990 we made friends with a guy named Tracy Caddell. He was a few years older than us, but we knew him from our school. Tracy was a big wrestling fan, and one day he came over to me and said, "I hear you guys have a wrestling ring in your backyard. Is that true?"

"Yeah, man."

"Well, remember how I used to look out for you on the school bus when you were little?"

I didn't, but I said, "Sure, man," because he was a big guy.

"How about if I came over and wrestled with you some?"

Tracy started coming over with another guy, Robert Nattie—also known as the Devastator. A couple of Jeff's friends, like Shannon Moore, would also come by to wrestle. That's how the TWF—the Teenage Wrestling Federation—was born.

THE TWF ARENA

MATT: As we started figuring more and more things out, we decided to start taping our matches. We rented a video camera—it cost twenty-five dollars for a weekend—and filmed as many matches as we could over those two days.

Eventually we decided to make our trampoline into a legit wrestling ring. We cut down trees to use as ring posts, then we took some garden hose and ran it around like ropes.

JEFF: From there, we started making all kinds of changes. We put aprons up around the ring. We dug holes all the way around and made tent poles out of trees, then hung big plastic sheets—the same kind we used to make our hideouts—and built an arena around the whole thing.

One afternoon, Tracy came down to help us do some modifications on the ring. He was using a hole digger, and he ended up cutting off the phone line to our house. Needless to say, Daddy was real excited about that one.

MATT: After we dug through the telephone line, Daddy told us we had to move the ring. So me and my friend Mike Clouse went out in the woods with an ax and a rake. We cleared out some trees and made a big open area for our arena. It was a July day, hot and sunny. It wasn't especially windy, so after I raked all the leaves and branches and stuff into a big pile, we decided to light it on fire. It was burning nicely and then, all of a sudden, a gust from the heavens came down.

Whoosh!

The fire went everywhere! I was out there in shorts and no shirt, and the woods were on fire! It was maybe six hundred feet from our house. I grabbed a big pine-tree branch and started swatting at the fire, trying to knock it out.

"I'll go get water," Mike said, and ran back to the house. He got one bucketful, threw it on the fire, and said, "I'll go get some more." Then he ran back and got another bucketful. The fire just kept getting bigger and bigger and Mike was trying to douse it, one bucket at a time!

Meanwhile, I'm out there, swatting away with the pine-tree branch, getting all burned up. Finally I gave up and called the fire department.

JEFF: I was at baseball practice when the fire started, but I got dropped off just as the fire trucks arrived. I showed up and there was Matt, bright red all over, yelling at the firemen, "You gotta get this fire out before my dad gets home!"

MATT: When Daddy came home, there were fire trucks everywhere. They were spraying the fire with these high-powered water hoses, while I stood there right beside them—all singed up, swatting away with my branch. And Mike was still running back and forth, getting buckets of water!

JEFF: Oh boy, was Daddy hot!

MATT: The good news was that we cleared a nice-sized space for the TWF Arena. A lot more than we had intended. We almost cleared the whole property!

JEFF: Once the TWF Arena was set up, we started putting on shows on a regular basis. We would dress up in baseball pants and socks, with Matt and me playing any number of characters—mostly I was Wolverine and Matt was High Voltage. Those were our main identities.

I also created an early version of Willow the Whisp. We couldn't afford to buy a real mask, so I'd wear a box on my head with a face drawn on it! Then during the matches, my opponent would tear the box off to reveal . . . a ski mask!

Pretty soon, more and more guys started showing up, like Marty Garner—the one and only Cham-Pain. He was five years older than Matt, who knew him from when he was an assistant baseball coach in high school. He was even my football coach for a little while. He's one of those guys who's into everything.

MATT: I ran into Marty at the gym. I was very into rap at that time. I used to write lyrics, then take instrumental tracks from other hip-hop songs and rap to them. Marty was also very into rap and we got to talking.

"We'll have to get together and do some music," he said. "Maybe I'll try some of that crazy wrestling stuff you guys are doing."

He started coming out and became one our TWF Superstars. He hadn't come up with Cham-Pain yet—back in those days, he called himself Sub-Zero.

JEFF: We would do a big show every other Sunday. After a while we put together a couple of videotapes—one was one of our "Pay-Per-Views," and the other was a "Best of TWF" collection.

MATT: I edited the tapes with two VCRs, but all things considered, they weren't bad. Then I went to our local video stores and said, "Hey, could you put this in here?"

JEFF: People actually rented them, which was just so cool. Over the next few years we made about fifty videos, which is pretty damn impressive for a couple of kids.

HARDY WORKING

MATT: Daddy worked part-time carrying the mail for the post office, but his main way of making ends meet was farming tobacco. All through our growing up, both Jeff and I earned money by helping Daddy farm and cure tobacco.

The first part of the tobacco-curing process is harvesting the leaves by hand, which they call "priming." Then it's put on a trailer and driven to the barn, where there's a machine called a tobacco stringer. You lay the tobacco leaf down, you put a stick on it, and then you put another layer of tobacco on top of that. Then it goes through the stringer, which is like a big sewing machine. The stringer stitches it all together and then you hang it all up from the rafters to be cured.

When I was real little, as little as I can remember, I laid out the sticks. The truth is, the most idiotic person in the world could lay sticks. It's real easy to do. You have your little station, you put your stick on, and it goes on through the stringer. As we got older, we drove the tractor and we primed and basically did every little task there was.

JEFF: The tobacco is very heavy when it's green, but after it's cured, it's real light. Once it was cured, they would need somebody to get up there and hand it down. That was always fun to do. Sometimes we would sneak into the barns and climb up the poles into the rafters, playing Spider-Man.

MATT: Once I got my driver's license, I got a job working down at Harbour's Car Wash down in Southern Pines. Daddy's best friend, Paul Stewart—God rest his soul—was the manager and he set it up. I'd wash the tires and the undercarriage and the windows before they went through the machine. It wasn't a bad job for a sixteen-year-old.

Another way I earned money was raking pine straw from around all the trees on our property. It's called pine needles some places—pine straw is more of a Southern term.

It's basically processed the same way as regular straw with hay. So I'd rake up a little pine straw and sell it for anywhere from eighty to a hundred dollars a load. Once Jeff and I figured out that we wanted to be professional wrestlers, raking pine straw was a good, easy way for us to make a few dollars without having to commit to a real job.

JEFF: I worked at Goodyear right after I graduated high school. I was a gofer, running errands, things like that.

My friend Johnny Yow ran a landscaping business, so I worked for him, which was great because I could get off at any time. We'd get a call saying we needed to go somewhere and wrestle for four days, and Johnny always said, "No sweat."

When you have a good job with good benefits and good pay and you say to your boss, "Hey I need to split for five days so I can wrestle," they're going to say, "Just go forever."

Johnny was always cool. I'd go on the road and wrestle, then come back and cut grass. Every time I would get back on that mower, I'd be thinking, *Maybe next time WWE is going to sign us up.*

SHANNON

JEFF: I first met Shannon Moore right around the time when our mom died. A few years later, his father got in a car wreck which messed him up pretty bad. When that happened, the two of us formed a really strong connection. It's so hard to deal with something like that when you're so young and still in school. Losing a parent is a lot to go through at that age, and we really bonded by talking about our experiences.

MATT: A lot of Jeff's friends were my friends. The people that I hung out with would come around the house, so Jeff got to hang out with an older crowd. It translated back with Shannon, who was like a little brother to Jeff.

JEFF: The gap between me and Shannon is the same as the one between Matt and myself. When I was a senior, he was a freshman. But I hung out with him more than I hung out with anybody else. I'd take him to parties—just like Matt did with me.

Matt took me to senior parties and all the girls would say, "He's so cute!" That was back in my Vanilla Ice period, so I would get up and dance, just totally turn it out. Even though I was a freshman, that really put me over. The same thing happened with me and Shannon—except he wasn't as good a dancer as I was.

MATT: Neither Jeff nor I was real big with the ladies back then. It's not that they didn't like us—because they did—it's that we had so many other interests.

JEFF: I was so shy when I was a teenager. The longest girlfriend I had through school lasted maybe a month. There would be girls I'd like so much and I couldn't even speak to them. Being a WWE Superstar has helped me so much, as far as being open and being able to talk to anybody about anything. Man, you go out there in front of that many people every night, you get pretty damn comfortable with yourself.

MATT: I think in a lot of ways, it had to do with our mom dying. After being so close to her, we were worried about getting close to anybody, especially females.

SHIRLEY

MATT: After our mom died, Daddy didn't date for a long time. But eventually he started seeing a woman named Shirley. It started at a party at one of our neighbors' houses. We saw that Dad and her were being real flirty with each other, and we thought, *She better not even think about going out with Daddy. It's the three of us guys and that's it!*

We didn't have any use for any other female being around. We didn't have a need for a replacement mom. Well, Shirley started coming around, and we didn't like her one bit. We definitely had heat with her. Not because she was a bad person—she turned out to be a great lady—but we didn't want anybody trying to take our mom's place.

One night our dad was going over to Gary Oliver's house, who was our friend and Shirley's nephew. The two of us got all dressed in black and got on our dirt bikes and rode over there. We got a hammer and some nails and started hammering them into her tires.

JEFF: Actually, I just looked out for cars and Matt did the nails.

MATT: We did one, but then we heard somebody coming out, so we got on our bikes and split. We started riding home when a car started coming over the hill toward us. "Uh-oh!" I said. "We'd better hide!"

We tossed our bikes into the ditch on the side of the road, then jumped in and landed right on top of each other. The guy driving the car saw all this and he pulled over. There we were, lying on top of each other: "Um . . . are you guys okay?"

"Yeah, we're just fine. Don't worry about us."

And we're lying there in this ditch, face-to-face, chest-to-chest. It was tremendous!

JEFF: Daddy and Shirley had no idea that we'd done anything. They just came out to a flat tire.

MATT: Jeff struck again on the day of *WrestleMania VI*. It was a big day, Ultimate Warrior vs. Hulk Hogan, and we were real excited. We were of course big Macho Man fans, so we turned against Hogan after the Mega-Powers broke up. We were definitely hoping for Warrior to beat his ass, which he did.

JEFF: The day of the Pay-Per-View, I came back over to our house with our friend Johnny Smith to get something. Daddy and Shirley were gone, but her car was there.

I don't know what came over me. I couldn't help myself. Shirley had one of those old Monte Carlos, with the gas tank in the back. I unscrewed the gas cap, grabbed a handful of dirt, and threw it in there. Then Johnny picked up two more handfuls and just threw it all over the car. I was like, "Dude, what are you doing?"

We screwed the cap back on and tried to clean it up a bit, but I was real nervous, so we just split.

MATT: When Shirley came out of the house she saw dirt and handprints all over the back of her car. She called Daddy, and said, "I think somebody put dirt in my gas tank."

JEFF: When we got home that night—we were all fired up because Ultimate Warrior won—Daddy asked me if I'd done anything I wanted to tell him about. "No, sir, I don't know what you're talking about."

Inside I was like, *Oh Lord, I'm in for it*. I made up some bullshit: "There were some kids driving around and one of them must've done it."

But it was pretty obvious that I did it and Daddy was pissed. The next morning, he woke me up at 4 A.M.—he used to go to work delivering the mail at five—and told me he was driving me to school. He dropped me off at 4:30 in the morning, three hours before school started! I'll never forget what he said to me, it was so powerful. He just looked at me and said, "Get out, boy, I ain't never gonna be able to trust you again."

It was cold as hell, and I had to sit out there until school started. That was my punishment.

MATT: Daddy wouldn't let him out of his sight. He made Jeff go everywhere with him. He thought Jeff was the devil. I think one of the reasons he was so upset was because he had to pay for Shirley's engine to be overhauled. He held that over Jeff's head for the longest time.

JEFF: As time went by, we grew to like Shirley. She was a real nice little country woman. Looking back, I understand why I did it. But I also understand how bad it was for Daddy, how lonely he must've been. He kept dating her for a while longer and then something happened that made him break it off.

MATT: We had started wrestling at the fairgrounds, and just down the way was the David Bibey Ministries, which was where Shirley went to church every Sunday. One Sunday, the preacher said in his sermon that wrestling is the work of the devil. It must've been driving him crazy seeing everybody around the wrestling ring and not down there putting money into his collection plate. Shirley told our dad what he said and they got in a big argument. He said, "You can go support a preacher who says wrestling is the work of the devil, but me, I'm gonna stick with the Hardy Boyz."

JEFF: Later on, when we started getting some TV time and became more and more popular, Daddy totally rode the wave. All these women around Cameron would come around to get autographs for their kids. It was tremendous. Every other night he was visiting some different lady.

COUNTY FAIR

MATT: I graduated high school in the spring of 1992, then went off to college at UNC-Charlotte. I decided to major in engineering, even though I knew that it wasn't what I really wanted to do. The only way I would be content with life was to wrestle.

Over the summer, fate intervened. Tracy Caddell used to drive a truck for Coca-Cola and he heard about a guy in Robbins, a local carnival promoter by the name of Kenneth Morgan.

JEFF: Kenneth was a weird dude—he looked like an old hermit. He was a pilot, and he owned a bunch of old gimmick biplanes, like the Red Baron used to fly.

MATT: Kenneth had been looking for us, these kids that wrestled in their backyard and made videos. "I've got this idea," he said. "For a long time I've been interested in doing wrestling at county fairs. I've got this trampoline that I converted into a wrestling ring. Maybe we should get some guys together and start trying to make a few bucks on the fair circuit."

We went and checked out his ring, which was just a total piece of shit, more trampoline than a wrestling ring. It was twenty by twenty feet, and the mat was two pieces of plywood board with a trampoline in the middle. We'd bump halfway on the wood, and halfway on the trampoline, which is just murder on your back!

JEFF: We got in there and started playing around. We would run up the ring post and jump onto the trampoline then spring into the corner. It was totally absurd!

MATT: We decided to line something up. Kenneth talked to the guy who ran the Moore County Fair, which was the local fair that we'd gone to every year since we were little.

JEFF: The Moore County Fair was the first big show of our careers. Man, it was unbelievable. We didn't even have wrestling boots in those days. We wore colored socks!

MATT: We went down there with Marty and Tracy and some of the other TWF Superstars. When we first got to where the ring was set up, there were only four or five guys there. Then, at show time, we looked out there and there were people everywhere. It was probably around three hundred people. We were really nervous, but really excited at the same time.

JEFF: Matt and I wrestled six times each that night! The first match was Wolverine vs. the Super Adaptoid. That was one of Matt's cooler gimmicks. He was like the Krulls, who were these Marvel Comics villains, green aliens that were able to absorb the superheroes' powers. The Super Adaptoid was a similar deal; he mimicked other people's finishing moves.

We went out there for that first match and it was so awesome. It was the first time we were ever in front of a real crowd and everybody was cheering and going crazy. It felt so good, like the feeling people get from being on drugs. Man, we were high. That night was our first taste of success. And we got two hundred and fifty dollars, which was damn good money!

WILLOW THE WHISP

MATT: Because we were working so many matches on the same cards, we came up with a ridiculous number of characters. I had names like White Cheetah (which was my tribute/rip-off of the "Macho Man"), Grim Reaper, Evil Knieval, Executioner, but mostly I was none other than High Voltage.

Jeff had a few characters—Galaxian, Gladiator, Mean Jimmy Jack, the Iceman—but he was usually one of two Superstars: Wolverine, where he wore face paint not unlike classic early-nineties Sting, and his most famous creation, the masked and mysterious superheel known as Willow the Whisp.

JEFF: The name Willow the Whisp came from the Marvel Comics bad guy Will O' The Wisp, which in turn came from an English folktale about a guy who was murdered, and then his body was dumped into a swamp. His ghost became known as the will-o'-the-wisp. It was a mischievous spirit that would appear as a bright light which led travelers off the roads into the marshes. A more scientific explanation would be that the light was just marsh gas, but that's the legend.

Willow was inspired by my love of Jushin "Thunder" Liger, the legendary Japanese wrestler. Liger's look and his style were such a huge influence on me. He looked like a real-life superhero. He combined great mat wrestling with awesome high flying—he really stood out in contrast with the WWE Heavyweights I grew up watching.

Willow the Whisp was supposed to be just pure evil. He was known as the Demon from Down Under—I used to be introduced as being from Broken Hill, Australia. Even though he was a heel, he was just insanely over. It was such an amazing-looking character, mostly thanks to Ted Hobgood, who made the masks. They were so intricate and whacked-out!

It blows my mind how to this day, people come up to me and want to talk about Willow.

THE TRAMPOLINE WRESTLING FEDERATION

MATT: After the fair we decided to do some more business with Kenneth. The Teenage Wrestling Federation became the Trampoline Wrestling Federation.

I'd come home from Charlotte every weekend to work on putting together shows. College was fun, but the truth is, I'm not exactly a big people person, and I didn't really have a lot in common with the other students. The things they wanted to do compared to what I wanted to do were completely different. I don't drink, I'm not a big partier.

I didn't live in the little dorms where all the other guys lived. The people I lived with were mostly juniors and seniors, and while they were cool guys, I never formed a close bond with them. If I'd see them around campus, I'd say, "What's up?" but we never really clicked.

All my energies were focused toward the TWF. College was almost an afterthought. I didn't care about it. I was only going because everybody said, "You need to go to college." But in my heart, all I wanted was to be a wrestler.

JEFF: In November 1992, we rented the armory in Southern Pines and booked another show—the *Thanksgiving Thrash*. Marty worked with Matt on setting up all the promotion and local advertising around the show. He was his usual self, getting a little carried away: "Man, there's going to be five thousand people there. We're going to have to turn them away."

Needless to say, there were maybe a hundred and fifty people there. We didn't charge very much for tickets, and by the time we paid for the armory and all the expenses, we were out of cash. We didn't lose money, but we didn't make any either.

ECW...F

MATT: After we did the *Thanksgiving Thrash*, Kenneth decided he wasn't as interested in being a wrestling promoter as he'd thought. It turned out that he was only looking for a quick buck. "I don't know, Matt," he said to me one night. "I don't think this rasslin' thing is going to make any money."

"Okay," I said. "How about we buy the ring from you?"

The only problem was, we didn't have any money. "Well, boys, I'll take what I laid out in expenses," Kenneth said. "Let's call it six hundred."

JEFF: All of us threw in what we could and we were able to buy the trampoline ring from Kenneth. We brought it to Tracy's backyard up in Vass, North Carolina, and used it for practice.

MATT: One afternoon Tracy was down in Hamlet, doing his Coke run, and he got into a conversation with a guy about wrestling. Tracy told him that he was a wrestler and the guy said, "Oh really? My name's Eddie Rainwater. I wrestle with the Italian Stallion."

Tracy knew the Stallion from NWA-TV. He also ran a local wrestling promotion, the PWF—the Professional Wrestling Federation. Right away, Tracy started pitching, telling Eddie about what we were doing with the TWF. "We're trying to do a new concept. Our gimmick is that our ring is part trampoline, part ring."

"Maybe I'll come check you guys out sometime," Eddie said.

JEFF: The first time Eddie Rainwater saw us wrestling on the trampoline, he couldn't believe it. He stood on like the solid part, putting his foot on the trampoline like it was freezing cold water. Like he was sticking his toe in the tub.

"I don't know, boys. That seems real dangerous. I wouldn't work in this thing. You boys need to get yourselves a real ring."

MATT: We realized that Eddie was right. We'd never be able to take our promotion any further without a hard ring, so we decided to rebuild.

We took the trampoline ring and we shortened it to sixteen by sixteen. We built a framework around it so it was like a real ring. Unfortunately, we did a piss-poor job with the engineering. We had no idea what we were doing. It took like eight hours to put it up and take it down. It was brutal.

JEFF: Once the trampoline was out of the picture, obviously we needed to change the name of our promotion. We named it the ECWF—the East Coast Wrestling Federation. This was before anyone had even heard of ECW, which was still known as Eastern Championship Wrestling at that point.

MATT: Since our first Southern Pines Armory show had gone down so well, we booked another night for the spring. We were so excited about it. Tracy and I worked so hard getting it all together. I traveled back and forth from UNC-Charlotte every weekend and he picked up the slack during the week.

JEFF: About a month before the show, Tracy got into a serious wreck and almost died. He had been up all night making posters for the armory show, and he fell asleep at the wheel. The truck was totally destroyed. It was an out-and-out miracle that he survived. They had to cut him out of the wreckage with the jaws of life. The paramedics figured he was dead for sure, but then they saw his arm moving and started trying to get to him. He heard them and said, "Hey guys, I'm TC Flexor and I wrestle. Have you heard about our show this weekend?"

Man, he loved wrestling.

MATT: They operated on Tracy's knee and took his spleen out, so he was on the shelf. It totally screwed things up, because he was doing the major- ity of the promoting. We decided that we'd put things on hold for a couple of months while he healed up.

WCW AMATEUR CHALLENGE

MATT: While we were waiting to kick off the ECWF, I entered a contest that WCW was holding for aspiring wrestlers, the WCW Amateur Challenge. I didn't win, but my entry tape featured a particularly electrifying promo, if I do say so myself:

> *The training has been finished. The preparation has been intense. But now the time has come for me to justify, every day, every hour, every minute, every second of my preparation. You see, it is time for a new dawning in the world of professional wrestling. And that ascending force goes by the title of High Voltage.*
>
> *Almost like a godsend, the WCW Amateur Challenge is issued and I accept what I feel is my destiny. And you ask me why I feel I would be successful in WCW. Because of the same reasons I will be successful wherever I choose to wrestle. Because right now, take a good look at an athlete, eighteen years of age, six-feet-one, 230 pounds of strength; 230 pounds of agility; 230 pounds of knowledge; 230 pounds of drive, determination, willpower, and desire. An athlete who takes his body to EXTREME physical limits. An athlete who has an everlasting burning inferno within his heart and soul to succeed.*

High Voltage knows what he must do to make his mark in the wrestling world. I must deal with the technicians. I must deal with the aerialists. I must deal with the giants. All that compose the WCW vanguard. It is time for me to utilize the time spent training in my self-built ring, the time spent in the gym, the hours poured into studying, reviewing, and learning the art of wrestling. You see, you ask me why would I be successful in WCW. Because take a good look at an athlete who possesses a work ethic second to none! An athlete who has the physical, who has the mental, who has the emotional attributes to get the job done and go all the way. You see, a long time ago a very wise friend of mine said, "Success is a journey, not a destination." And High Voltage has packed for a very, very long trip.

And to all those that doubt High Voltage, the stupid-stinkin'-sorry-snivelin'-silly-sassy-pitiful-pathetic-low-down-lousy-dirty-filthy-nasty-idiotic-foulmouthed-selfish-childish-punkish skeptics, watch me as I do what I do best. Prove people wrong, and wrestle. So maybe when I execute the Megahertz—jump up onto the middle of the top rope, spring back in a backflip, splash and pin my opponents—maybe then the disbelievers will realize why my fate is utter success. So whomever I may face in WCW, what are you gonna do, when ten thousand watts flow? Can you survive? I don't think so! Every tick of the clock, grows nearer your shock, countdown to your Armageddon!

WORLD TO BLACK

MATT: After my first year at UNC-Charlotte, I came home for the summer. I got very into building up my physical condition, getting ready for the upcoming ECWF show at the Southern Pines Armory.

I started working out at the Vass Fitness Center, where I struck up a friendship with this big guy named Jason Ahrndt. He was in a black hole of depression after breaking up with his girlfriend and was trying to get himself in shape. I thought he was a decent guy, a little on the strange side, not exactly Mr. Personality. He was at a real lonely time in his life and didn't really have many friends, so he started hanging out with the ECWF gang.

JEFF: In July we got a call from Eddie Rainwater, inviting us to a PWF show that the Italian Stallion was running in Kings Mountain. We went up there and met Stallion for the first time, and also Eddie's running buddy, John Adcock, who worked with NWA as John Savage. We brought our gear and told Stallion we were ready to try out for him, and he said, "Oh no, brother. We don't have any work for you. But if you want to come to my wrestling school, we can work out a payment plan."

We told him thanks but no thanks, and then he made us pay ten bucks to watch the show!

MATT: At the end of the summer, I was all set to go back up to UNC-Charlotte, when Daddy was diagnosed with a brain aneurysm. It wasn't an actual aneurysm, it was more like a blood clot. Luckily, they caught it before it burst.

JEFF: It was real scary. He woke up one morning acting all strange. They didn't know what was going on at first. The blood clot was putting pressure on his brain and he started saying the most flipped-out stuff. He was actually talking to his late sister, Joyce, about people who used to live here when he was young. The clot was jogging his memory.

MATT: Daddy's always been so tough and so proud. It was clear something was wrong, but he kept saying, "There's nothing the matter with me."

We said, "Maybe you should go check it out."

"Oh, there's nothing wrong with me. I'm not going anywhere."

JEFF: Finally this woman he worked with, Debbie, got him to go to the hospital. She was a lot younger than him, but he had been hanging out with her a lot. Anyway, she came out to the house and he was laid out face-down on the bed. She said, "Hey, what're you doing? I was thinking maybe we'd ride out for a little while. Have ourselves a little day."

Then she swerved him and took him to the hospital.

MATT: He had had perfect health up to that point. It was the first time he'd ever been in the hospital.

They said it was good that they caught it when they did, because if it had burst, that would have been it. He was in the hospital for two weeks and everything worked out fine. He had no more problems.

JEFF: That was when we got into Pearl Jam. For some reason, the local rock station—Rock 103 in Fayetteville—would always play "Black" late at night, and we got into a groove where we'd come home from visiting Daddy in the hospital, then stay up until we heard it. What's funny is that's when I got into my schedule of staying up until 4 A.M. and then sleeping till noon.

MATT: I really wasn't that interested in rock music, but Pearl Jam really touched something inside of me.

At that point in my life, I was primarily into very commercial rap music like DJ Jazzy Jeff and the Fresh Prince. Our neighbor David Oakley was a little older than me, and he turned me on to Public Enemy's *It Takes a Nation of Millions to Hold Us Back*. I thought it was tremendous stuff, really rebellious and tough. From there I started getting into harder rap, things like the Geto Boys and NWA. That's the music I listened to, until I got into Pearl Jam.

I thought "Jeremy" was a pretty cool song, but I just loved "Black." I thought that song was just so intense and moving, I loved how there were so many different ways you could interpret it. Most rap songs are pretty straightforward, they're pretty clear-cut about what's going on. But when I listened to Pearl Jam, I was amazed at how much I could relate Eddie Vedder's lyrics to what was going on in my life.

JEFF: I'm a huge Pearl Jam fan. *Vitalogy* is such an awesome record. It's got great rock songs like "Betterman" and "Tremor Christ," plus crazy shit like "Bugs" and "Heyfoxymophandlemama, That's Me." Those guys have been a major influence on my life and my music.

MATT: When Daddy got sick, I canceled my plans to go back to college. It was a scary time. Jeff was still in high school, and I thought, *What's going to happen?* What if our dad did die?

Somebody needed to be here to take care of things, so I put college on hold. Now, people might think that was a noble thing to do, but it wasn't that big of a sacrifice for me because I didn't care about going back.

Fortunately, everything ended up being fine. Daddy was fine, and I decided to go to Sandhills, which is the community college in Pinehurst. I figured I'd get my associate's degree, and then decide what I wanted to do from there.

Sandhills was good for me for a number of reasons. Mostly it allowed me to spend more time at home planning for a future in wrestling.

SUMMER SPECTACULAR

MATT: The good thing about having so much extra time between shows was that it enabled us to get more and more professional about things. We practiced constantly; we bought a bunch of beat-up old wrestling mats from our elementary school to use outside the ring.

In a real major leap into professionalism—I finally got myself a pair of real wrestling boots. I ordered them from Adrian Street, who was a famous wrestler back in the day. He was one of the first guys to be really flamboyant and over-the-top, with makeup and these garish robes. Then he started a company that sold wrestling wear down in Gulf Breeze, Florida.

The boots cost close to two hundred dollars. I had to haul a lot of pine straw to get them, so I was so excited for them to arrive.

JEFF: The day Matt got the package, I came home from school and he opened the door and jumped down the steps with the boots on. And, well, they looked kind of weird. They definitely weren't like the boots we saw on TV.

MATT: I opened the box and I was instantly disappointed, but I figured, *This sucks, but I'll just act like they're cool.* I knew Jeff would know the truth, though. He's always been ahead of the trends in terms of clothes. Jeff will wear some crazy shit and then a month later it'll be the height of fashion. But I jumped out with those boots on—"Am I cool, or what?"—and I saw how Jeff was looking at them.

"Yeah, I know," I said. "My boots are the shits."

JEFF: The Southern Pines Armory show—ECWF's *Summer Spectacular*—finally went down in September. We really put our hearts and souls into this show—the planning had gone on for eight months, after all.

Daddy had just gotten out of the hospital and he totally didn't get why we were working so hard. "What are you boys doing? This is crazy. Get yourselves a real job!"

That night was so crazy. Matt was really stressed out, because he was really doing the majority of the work.

MATT: I hadn't slept the night before, I was so busy getting everything ready. The day of the show I got to the armory at 9 A.M., and never had a second to spare to get something to eat. I was busting my ass, and just before show time, somebody brought me a sub.

JEFF: Finally it was show time. Just as I went out for my entrance, Matt puked that sub right up. I felt so bad for him!

I went out there and got into the ring, waiting for Matt to come out, and it was real dark in there. Matt came running out for his entrance and—*splat!*—he tripped on the big thick wrestling mat. Right on his face! I just stood there in the ring, shaking my head, trying not to crack up.

MATT: I came out in my ugly boots, turned one corner, and went down! But I got right up, acting all cool, like "I meant to do that." I grabbed a poster and ripped it up, going, "Yeaaaah! Aren't I sexy and cool?"

It ended up being a good little show, even though none of us really knew a damn thing. We were just a bunch of guys who did a good job copying moves that we saw on television. But all things considered, the ECWF made a pretty decent debut.

MEET THE STALLION

MATT: About a week after the *Summer Spectacular* show, I got a call from Eddie. "Hey Matt, if you want to come up to the show tomorrow, there's a couple of guys that aren't going to show, so Stallion said that you guys could wrestle."

The show was in Belmont, which is a little suburb outside of Charlotte. Unfortunately Jeff had football practice the next day, Marty was out of town, and Tracy was working. I decided that I'd go by myself. The next morning I went down to the gym and ran into Jason. We were talking and I told him what I was doing. "I'm kind of nervous," I said. "I'm wrestling for these guys and I have no idea what their deal is or what's going to happen."

"Man, I ain't doing anything tonight," Jason said. "I'll ride up there with you."

We started driving and we noticed that we actually had a lot in common. We really bonded that trip.

When we got to Belmont, Stallion said, "Okay, brother. I'm going to have you wrestle the Russian Assassin."

The Russian Assassin was a guy named Terry Austin. He was Stallion's right-hand man, and everybody called him Maverick. Terry and I got together and he asked me, "What do you do, kid?"

"Well, I do this flip and I do a moonsault . . ."

"Okay, kid. We'll just call most of it in the ring."

"No problem," I said, because I really wanted to do good. I walked out there with my High Voltage tights on, and not to pat myself on the back, but I was in the best physical condition of any of the other wrestlers. They were all fat, slobby, old men. So the crowd cheered for me and the Russian Assassin came out and we started wrestling. We locked up and he said, "Take an arm."

I twisted his right arm and he hit me in the head immediately. *Wham!* He said in my ear, "You're supposed to work the left."

I didn't know that the universal code in wrestling is to work left. Then he said, "Grab a headlock."

I grabbed him with my right arm and he said, "What're you, a mark?"

He put me in the corner and started chopping the shit out of me, just killing me. Eventually I got a little offense in; I slammed him then went up and did a springboard moonsault press. It was real pretty.

When we got to the back after the match, Stallion said, "Brother, you got beautiful moves. You bump and you sell, but you don't have any psychology. Who trained you?"

"Nobody trained me," I said.

He couldn't believe it. "Nobody's trained you?"

"No, I taught myself."

"If you start coming up to the training school, then maybe I could get you on TV one day," Stallion said. "We'll go up to WWE and you'll be a big star."

Meanwhile, Terry Austin is standing there and he's hot. "The kid's a mark," he kept saying. "He don't even know how to work."

When I left there, I was totally conflicted about the experience. It was fun to have gotten the chance to be in a real match, but at the same time I was disgusted. I told Jason, "Those guys could go to hell."

I did pick up some important tips, though. When I got home, I watched a few matches on TV and realized that they always worked from the left side.

Jason and I drove home that night. I was tired, but I had the wheel. At one point I fell asleep and swerved across four lanes of traffic. That was our first real on-the-road experience together. I told him that he should come out and train with us. "I'm just too shy," he said. "I wouldn't feel good out there."

As time passed, we became better friends and I kept on him about it. We would work out together and hang out on the weekends, and finally he decided to give wrestling a try.

HALLOWEEN HILARITY

JEFF: At the end of September, we went back to the Moore County Fair with the hard ring. They gave us three nights—Wednesday, Thursday, and Friday—and paid us three hundred dollars a night. The ring was structurally unsound, it would sag in the middle and was close to falling apart altogether, but we put on a good show and had a blast.

MATT: About a month after the County Fair, ECWF booked our first show at the Sanford Armory—*Halloween Hostility*.

We were really flying by the seat of our pants in those days. There wasn't much money, so quite often we simply had to make do. For instance, we didn't have a real canvas as our ring cover, we had one of those blue tarpaulins that you find in any hardware store.

The day of the Sanford show, we opened the tarp to put it on the ring and it was a mess. It had gone all rotten, with big moldy holes in it. It was Saturday afternoon and the show was just a few hours away, so we high-tailed it to Lowe's hardware to get another one. The problem was, they didn't have a blue one that was big enough to fit the ring. The only thing available was a gigantic brown tarp that was at least twice the size of the ring. We didn't have time to go search for another hardware store, so we bought it. It was horrible-looking, the exact color of baby shit. It immediately became known as "the Dookie Tarp."

JEFF: The Dookie Tarp was huge, man. It was way too big. It actually covered the ring, the apron, *and* the mat outside the ring.

The main event that night was Matt and me battling it out for the ECWF Championship. For the finish, I was out on the floor and Matt did a moonsault bodyblock off the top rope onto me. But he was so much heavier, so much bigger than I was back then, that when he hit me, I just *buckled*.

MATT: I went straight down and landed on my head. We had no padding out there and I smashed my head hard onto the concrete. I knocked myself out cold. When I came to, I was totally messed up, seeing three of every-thing. It was bad—my head was split open and I had a slight concussion. I lay out there for a minute or two, half unconscious, but I managed to get up and get back into the ring so that Jeff could pin me. That was my first-ever injury at a live wrestling event, the first of many.

After the show I was in the back getting ready to go to the hospital to get stitched up, when someone came to me and said that there was some-body from WCW there that wanted to speak to me.

I walked out and there was this overweight black lady. I introduced myself and she said, "Nice to meet you, Matt. I'm Karen. I really loved your match tonight. We're looking for some new talent in WCW, and I'd love to talk to you and your brother at some point."

I was thinking that she didn't look like somebody that worked for WCW, but then she explained that she was one of their talent scouts. She gave me her card, and it said: *Independent Business Scout.*

"I work out of my home," she explained, "but if you give me some videotapes and photos, I'll pass them along."

I couldn't put my finger on it, but there was definitely something fishy going on. But if she didn't have anything to do with WCW, why would she be there lying about it? What would be the point?

We exchanged a few phone calls and sent her some of our videos. A few days later, Karen called me and said, "They really love your tape and they want you to come down to the Power Plant and train a little bit. They also are interested in your brother, but they want him to gain some more weight, get in better shape."

She was saying all the right things, but something about her still felt slightly off. I called Tracy Caddell and said, "I don't want to call her a liar, but I'm a little suspicious of her. She wants me to drop off some more tapes at her house. Why don't you come with me?"

Tracy and I drove to Karen's place in Sanford, and it was this little house right smack in the 'hood. We went in and she had this huge WCW videotape collection. She had multiple copies of all of Sting's videos. "Steve gave me these," she said, dropping Sting's real name. "Steve's such a funny guy! I was out at the Power Plant with him one time and we were playing around in the ring. I was on the top rope and he tripped me. I fell and he just couldn't stop laughing at me."

It was a very weird situation. "Maybe there's somebody that I can talk to down at WCW," I asked.

"My boss is Ole Anderson," she explained. "He'll be giving you a call in a couple of days."

"Okay," I said. "Thanks for all your help."

When I got home, I decided to give WCW a ring. I asked for Ole Anderson, but they wouldn't put me through. "Um, can you tell me if you have an employee named Karen?" I asked.

They put me on hold and a few minutes later came back on the line. "No, sir. We don't have anyone named Karen here."

Now I was hot! I called Karen and left a message for her. "I just called down to WCW to talk to some people," I said. "I asked them if they knew you, but they weren't too familiar with who you were. Actually, they told me that they never heard of you. I was just wondering why that is."

When I got home later that night, there was a message on our answering machine. "Matt Hardy, this is Ole Anderson," the message said, in what was obviously a black woman's voice. "I'm calling you because I understand you've been questioning my assistant Karen. She works for me and you don't need to be calling around behind her back. Karen is the connection. Thank you."

That was it—I never heard from her again. I never could understand why someone would do something so crazy. What on earth would she have to gain from that? But if there's one thing I've learned over the years, it's that the wrestling business tends to attract some seriously weird people.

CURIOUS GEORGE

JEFF: During my sophomore year in high school, I was totally in love with this senior girl, Leslie. It didn't last more than month or two, but I was crazy about her! I was so nervous around her because I liked her so much. I would kiss her and I'd have to stop myself from saying "I love you."

Unfortunately, I had a rival for her attention, a friend of Matt's named Jay. He was really popular in school—he was great at tennis, and had a reputation as a serious partier.

Pretty soon, Leslie started acting weird; she was getting all distant. I didn't know what was going on. One night she told me she was going somewhere with her mom, and I didn't believe her, so I decided to see what was going on.

I was in my car with my friends Scott Matthews and Michael Clouse. We cruised toward Leslie's house, and there she was, driving around with this guy. "I'm going to follow them," I said.

I trailed them down this dirt road to her house. When they turned down her driveway and around the back of her house, I pulled off into a field, hiding out in the darkness.

I waited there for a while—they were probably fooling around. After a half hour or so, Scott and Michael got tired of sitting there—"C'mon, Jeff. Let's go, man"—but I was getting hot.

"No way," I said. "I've got to see what's going on."

We were off the road a good ways, staked out in this field, pretty much out in the woods. Finally I saw his headlights coming toward us. I expected him to turn right and go back up the dirt road the way we came. But instead, he turned left and chugged right toward us. *Oh shit,* I thought. *There's going to be a fight.*

They must've seen my car as they pulled out of the field. He cruised up next to me. I rolled down my window and looked directly at Leslie.

"What's going on?" I said. I was so angry right then.

She didn't say a word.

"We're not doing anything," Jay said. "What're *you* doing?"

"I'm just being curious," I said.

He looked right in my eyes. "Curious George, huh?"

"Yeah. That's me."

"Well, you can get in trouble for being curious."

I was ready to get out of the car and go at it with him. I didn't care what happened. He could've had a gun in his car, but I was getting crazy.

Meanwhile, Leslie is just sitting there, not saying a word. I hated her so much right then. After staring each other down for a minute or two, Jay said, "Forget this. We're out of here."

"Okay. Fine. Whatever."

I felt like such an asshole. I was sitting there in the middle of this field, totally busted for following them.

Later that week, Leslie wrote me a letter saying that I deserved better than her, blah blah blah. Not long after that, she ended up moving out of town.

What was important was that the whole Leslie experience really prompted me to start writing my poetry. I was so brokenhearted, I really needed a way to let those bad feelings out.

Then I heard the Stone Temple Pilots song "Still Remains." That song hit me so hard. "If you should die before me / ask if you could bring a friend"—that's just so powerful. It really knocked me out. I thought, *Man, I want to write something that moving and beautiful.*

Between that and my broken heart, I was totally inspired. Writing has always made me feel better. Especially after something happens in my life, I can go off and nail some pretty emotional stuff.

NEW FRONTIER

MATT: The next show we did was at the Southern Pines Armory in April 1994, the *Spring Fling*. That was the night we met Jens Luts. He owned a video store in town and claimed to be a heavy-duty businessman.

The truth is, he was a big goof. He told us he had an open room at his video store where we could put our ring. "Let me invest in you guys," he said. "I've got connections in TV."

JEFF: Our ECWF shows were really entertaining. We were drawing good crowds, and Jens thought he could jump on the bandwagon. He saw himself as this superb businessman. He was going to be our rocket to the moon.

MATT: We decided to take a shot and went into business with Jens. We moved our ring from Tracy's yard into the Showtime Video Rental building—which was great, because now we had a place to train that wasn't outside. With his investment, we changed the name of the promotion to the NFWA—the New Frontier Wrestling Alliance.

FIRST J.O.B.

MATT: Back in those days, *Raw* wasn't always a live broadcast. WWE would do three days of TV taping, including a month's worth of matches for all their shows, including *Raw, WWE Superstars, WWE Wrestling Challenge,* and *WWE Action Zone.* Now it's Superstar vs. Superstar all the time, but in those days they used to have squash matches where the Superstars would beat up on unknowns. Those nobodies were known as enhancement wrestlers, or the more common term, jobbers. The Stallion had a special booking arrangement where he would supply wrestlers from his promotion to serve as enhancement guys to do the job for the established wrestlers.

In May of '94, I got a phone call from Eddie Rainwater. "You mind if I give Stallion your number?"

"What for?"

"Well, he needs some extra guys to work WWE TV with him and he was wondering if you could go."

"Sure," I said, trying not to act excited. "Tell Stallion to give me a call."

Stallion called me the next day. "We're going up to WWE to work three days," he told me. "You get paid a hundred and fifty dollars a day. They might want to sign you to a contract. You might end up being a huge star."

He was throwing out all these great lines. "Just guarantee me you're going to be there. If you stand me up, I'll ruin you."

I was freaking out, but played it cool. "Yeah, man, I'll be there."

JEFF: When Matt told me he was going to WWE, I was so bummed that I wasn't going to do it, too. Then Stallion called back a day or two later: "Hey Matt, are there any other wrestlers around there that can go with us?"

"Well, there's my brother, Jeff," Matt said. "He's real good. And there are a couple other guys that would probably be all right."

"Bring them to my show on Saturday and we'll have a tryout," Stallion said. "If they do good, I'll take them with me."

The show was up in Elkin, which is about a three-hour drive from Sanford. I drove up there with Marty, Tracy, and the Devastator, Robert Nattie. Stallion wanted Matt to come, too, but he knew that Stallion didn't pay anybody.

MATT: I figured I'd already passed my tryout. After all, he called me.

JEFF: I wrestled Marty in the first match. We went out there, did a bunch of high spots. We didn't know anything about working the left side and all that. Then they put me in the ring against George South. I'd seen him on TV, doing jobs in Mid-Atlantic Wrestling, and that was enough to make me nervous. I introduced myself to him, and he said, "Just listen to me out there. We'll do a tackle drop down . . ."

"What's that?" I said. Because I seriously did not know.

MATT: That's like the most basic move in wrestling.

JEFF: He just looked at me. "You don't know what a tackle drop down is?" "Do you mean where I take you down like this?" I said, describing a drop toehold, which I knew from listening to commentary on TV.

George just stood there, shaking his head. "Look, I'll give you a tackle and you drop down, lay on your belly, and I'll run over you."

We did the match, and it didn't go too badly, all things considered. It was a great experience for me, just to get the feel of a real match.

MATT: They all passed their tryout, though I think there was no way to fail it. Stallion was just looking for bodies. All he wanted was to make sure you were alive, and that you wouldn't humiliate him in front of his WWE connections. When the time came to go up north, Devastator—who's a big guy, gets into fights all the time—ended up chickening out and not going. That first trip, it was me, Jeff, Marty, and Tracy. We drove to Charlotte and met Stallion at the Waffle House at around midnight.

JEFF: Stallion asked about my age, because WWE required you to be eighteen. I told him I was sixteen, and he said that as long as I had a letter from my parents, it'd be okay. When I gave him the letter from my dad, he just threw it away.

"Look, kid, when they ask how old you are, you have to lie about your age."

It's funny—Jim "J.R." Ross, currently the senior vice president of talent relations at WWE, didn't know that I was two years younger until we officially signed with the company.

MATT: Stallion would take fourteen guys up to where WWE was working, and he'd charge every one of us a booking fee. We had to go to his hotel room at the end of the night and give him a hundred dollars. We were getting paid one-fifty, and he'd take a hundred! If you didn't pay him, he'd leave you wherever you were and not bring you home.

He drove the church's bus, which he took for free, and then charged WWE. They paid him for the van, and then another thousand for booking all the guys.

JEFF: Man, that van was cramped. He packed guys on top of one another like sardines.

MATT: Our first WWE matches were on May 23, 1994, in Youngstown, Ohio. When we pulled up to the building, I saw the TV trucks and in my heart I couldn't help but think, *I really don't want to go in there. I'm not ready.*

I was just hoping they'd turn the van around and drive back home. We got out of the van and Stallion said, "Whatever you guys do, don't talk to anybody. Just be quiet and do what I tell you."

JEFF: I couldn't believe it was really happening. *We're not really going to be on WWE TV,* I thought.

MATT: We walked into the building and there's Razor Ramon (Scott Hall). He saw us and started laughing, "All right. It's the troopers."

Then Shawn Michaels walked in with his bags. He looked at Razor, he slapped his hand, and they hugged, "What's up, man?"

This was just a few months after their legendary *WrestleMania X* ladder match, and seeing them together was my official confirmation that wrestling was not real. *These guys are in a feud,* I thought, *and now they're best friends.*

JEFF: It was wild. Here were two guys who are supposed to hate each other, acting all buddy-buddy. Part of us still thought they were really fighting to get that Intercontinental belt.

MATT: Everywhere we turned we were seeing these guys that we idolized. The 1-2-3 Kid—also known as X-Pac or Sean Waltman—was standing there and Jeff whispered in my ear, "He's not that big."

A lot of the guys didn't look as big as they did on TV, but there were other guys, like Bam Bam Bigelow, that had me in awe. "Wow—he's huge!"

JEFF: We all stood there with no idea what the hell to do with ourselves. Wrestlers were walking around, talking to one another and picking up their airline tickets and schedules. I was thinking, *Man, how cool would it be to do this?*

Eventually, they put us in this little dressing room, like, "Hey, stick the geek crew in there."

MATT: It was this little room attached to the main locker room, and most of the guys didn't even acknowledge our existence. Bret Hart walked in and didn't say a word. Then Razor and Diesel (Kevin Nash) came in and broke our balls a bit, like "Look at these little guys." But it was cool. They may have been making light of us, but at least they were kind of talking to us.

JEFF: Before the show, all the guys started coming in to get dressed. Shawn Michaels was on the floor, lying on his back.

MATT: Scott Hall was supposed to wrestle one of Stallion's guys on the pretaped *Raw*—they taped the next week's episode before the live broadcast. They were setting up the match, and the guy—one of Stallion's fat, sloppy, has-been losers—told Hall that he couldn't handle his finishing move, the Razor's Edge. This was right before they were going out for the match. The next thing we knew, Gerry Briscoe, the WWE agent for the match, grabbed Jeff: "Okay, kid, it's you and Razor."

JEFF: Hall was hot: "Look, here's what we'll do. We'll go out there, fight back and forth a little bit, maybe a suplex, then Razor's Edge." He was still pissed off about the other guy chickening out.

MATT: Jeff was turning all pale, going "Okay, okay." It was breaking my heart.

JEFF: I was pretty nervous. Plus, earlier that day I was in the bathroom—it was a messed-up building with these military-type bathrooms that didn't have stalls or anything, just toilets. Well, you know how when you're in a public rest room taking a shit, you don't want to make loud obscene noises? I was sitting on the toilet and Hall came in, dropped his drawers, sat down right next to me, and just started doing his business. *Bloooshhhh!* Right beside me! God, it was horrible! And that was right before I found out I was going to be wrestling him.

MATT: Just before the match, Stallion went up to Razor and said, "These kids are great. Real highfliers, they do flips and moonsaults, all kinds of moves. You should put some of that stuff in the match."

"Hey, ten years from now this kid can do all the moves he wants," Razor said. "Right now he's mine."

JEFF: The match was brutal. I didn't understand the whole live-to-tape business. I thought I was on live TV. The mat was harder than any mat I'd ever worked on. Everything hurt so bad. Razor was still hot and he beat the shit out of me. His chops were so hard, they completely knocked the wind out of me. At one point, he picked me up, turned me upside down, and ran me into the turnbuckle. I hit my knee on the pole, and I hurt it a little bit.

MATT: Usually when wrestlers throw chops and punches and kicks at their buddies, they make sure to protect them and take care of them. But if they're just doing it to some job guy, they have no problem beating the living shit out of him. And that's what our job was. We were dummies for the Superstars to beat up.

JEFF: Back in the locker room after the match, Nash, Hall, and Kid were hanging out together and they started pointing at me. My hair was standing straight up, and I had some lines cut in the back, and Nash turned: "Look at him, he looks kind of like Vanilla Ice." And the 1-2-3 Kid started singing the riff from "Ice Ice Baby"—"Bump bump bump bump bump bump." From that day on, Scott Hall always called me Ice.

MATT: When Jeff came back, Eddie Rainwater came over to us and said, "Razor, Diesel, all these guys, they're talking a bunch of shit on Jeff, saying he's green, he ain't no good. They said that match will never make it onto TV. They already threw it in the trash. They're probably never going to let Jeff come back."

JEFF: I was already down. I thought, *Man, I just want to go home. I don't want to be here anymore.* Of course, they aired the match the next week.

MATT: After the tapings ended, I was up. I was booked on the live *Raw* against Nikolai Volkoff. He was a real WWE legend, a twenty-year veteran who had fought Bruno Sammartino and was a top heel—alongside the Iron Sheik—during the glory days of Hulkamania back in the eighties.

But by 1994, Nikolai was getting older, he had started to break down a little bit. Tony Garea, who was the agent for the match, came to me and said, "Kid, whatever you do tonight, you can't mess up. You're on live TV. Don't screw up." I stood there thinking, *I've only wrestled six matches in a hard ring. I've never been seriously trained, and now I'm going out in front of millions of people with a guy who barely speaks English! What have I gotten myself into?*

Tony brought me over to Nikolai and we started talking. "Ve'll go out dere, I'll shoot you into de ropes, maybe I'll bodyslam you, den you duck a couple, maybe I'll suplex you, and den I'll put Boston Crab on you," he said. Then he patted me hard on the shoulder. "Don't vorry about screwing up, keed, because I screw up in every match."

All I could think was, *Zoinks!*

Before my match, Stallion told Nikolai the same thing he'd told Razor: "This kid does flips—frontward, backward, sideways, whatever you want. Let him do something."

So at one point during our match, Nikolai shot me into the corner, I jumped up on the top and went for a cross body. He moved out of the way and I just splatted. Man, that ring was so hard. You had to be like King Kong Bundy to make that thing move. When you think about all the things that Shawn Michaels did in that hard ring, it just blows the mind. If he had been wrestling in our rings, I doubt that he would have had to retire early because of his back problems.

We were in Canton the next day. It was raining real hard when we pulled in. When Hall came in, he walked over to me: "Hey man. Where's your brother? Is his knee okay?"

I thought that was cool. He knew he had been a dick to Jeff. I ended up wrestling him that night, and he gave me a couple of things to do in the match, a bit more than he had given Jeff.

JEFF: I guess Hall felt kind of bad about beating the hell out of me and banging up my knee, because the first thing he did when he saw me was apologize.

I wrestled the 1-2-3 Kid that second night, which was much more along my lines. It was actually a great match. That was good for my soul, because after that first match, I didn't want to go back. It was not what I expected. It's funny, though, because to this day, Razor says that he saw something in us right from the start. He always says that that match proved to him what kind of worker I was, and how much potential I had. I know he's had his problems, but Scott Hall is a cool guy in my book.

MEANWHILE, IN THE HALLS OF HIGHER EDUCATION ...

JEFF: When I got to school the following week, I thought I was so cool. I told everybody, "Check it out, I'm going to be on TV next Monday night."

Nobody at Union Pines took what Matt and I were doing too seriously. We used to show our TWF tapes to the coaches, and they'd just laugh. The coach really got into breaking my balls: "Hey Hardy, we're starting an amateur wrestling team. Let's see what you can do on the mat."

I said, "Oh yeah? I'm up for it."

I'll be the first to admit, it was hardcore. Mat wrestling takes a lot out of you. But, man, it was so boring, especially compared to the professional vibe.

Then someone from the athletic department said to me, "Hardy, you have to make a decision. You're going to have to quit this professional wrestling business if you want to keep playing sports in high school."

Now, I could understand if I was in the NFL, I couldn't come back and play high-school football. I told them, "This is sports-entertainment," but they weren't having any of that. They told me I had to pick.

"Fine," I said. "I'm going to keep wrestling."

GETTING BY

MATT: We tried to make a go of it with New Frontier, but Jens just started coming up with the dumbest ideas. When you've never been in business with someone before, you don't really know what they're like until you experience it. And someone who wants part of the creative control is guaranteed to be more of a headache than it's worth.

JEFF: We worked with him for a few months, and pretty soon we just hated his guts. He was a total clown. He thought he could wrestle because he played football in high school, but he was fat and out of shape. He came out and trained with us but couldn't do anything.

At the end of the summer, we did the county-fair shows together, but by then we had had some serious heat between us. Jens decided he wanted out. That was fine by us, but he also wanted us to give back the little bit of money he'd invested.

MATT: Jens was such a jerk that he held our ring hostage. The only way we could get the ring out of his building was if we gave him eight hundred dollars.

"I'm a thousand dollars in the hole," he said.

"You were supposed to be the investor," I told him. "It's your deal to lose money."

In the end, we gave him six hundred dollars and we told him that was all the money we had. It was pretty brutal, because we were seriously broke at the time.

I was fully devoted to wrestling by this point in my life, and a real job would've gotten in the way. I made a few dollars hauling pine straw, but I definitely needed another way of putting money in my pocket.

In addition to doing our graphic-design work—posters, tickets, that kind of stuff—and working as our ring announcer, Ted Hobgood also made gear for all the wrestlers around here. As with everything he did, Ted did great work, but he was also ridiculously overpriced. I figured, why don't I get into that racket?

With that in mind, I sat down at Mom's old sewing machine and taught myself how to sew.

JEFF: That was an amazing natural talent that he had. I was always impressed because of the patience that's involved in that.

MATT: I got pretty good at it, too. I ended up making gear for most of the wrestlers in North Carolina. They were all in Matt Hardy Merchandise.

I also made money by going out and getting sponsors for our wrestling promotion. I would dress up nice and walk into local businesses with my little briefcase: "Hi, I'm Matt Hardy and I'm with the New Frontier Wrestling Federation . . ."

JEFF: You basically had to be a wrestling fan if you were going to sponsor us. Most people thought they'd be better off giving their money to walkathons and things like that.

MATT: I was rejected so many times, but I persevered. There were thirty-dollar sponsorships and fifty-dollar sponsorships. I'd say, "Well, if you're a thirty-dollar sponsor, it comes with ten free tickets and you could sell them at five dollars apiece."

I tried to come up with all these reasons for them to cough up a few dollars, telling them their business name would be featured in the programs and on the videos.

There ended up being a few regular sponsors in Southern Pines and Sanford—Pat's Café, Rent-A-Wreck, Vass Fitness Center, Davenport's Galaxy Supermarket, Perry Brothers Tires, Phillips' Self-Service Supermarket, That's Entertainment Video, U.S.1 Pizza & Subs, Miller's Family Restaurant, and Lakeside Garbage Services. They came to the shows and saw how hard we were working and gave us money every time.

The whole time we did our own promotion, I never lost money. I wasn't always able to pay a lot, but everybody always got paid. I had to pay two hundred dollars to book the armory and then I would set aside five hundred for the boys, but there were times where I took in over a thousand dollars in sponsorships, so I usually did okay.

Between promoting and sponsors and sewing and hauling pine straw, I was able to provide myself with a living. I lived at home, so my only expenses were car insurance and gas.

MATT: At the same time we were developing New Frontier, we started working shows for the Stallion at PWF. He basically told us that if we wanted to continue working WWE jobs, we'd have to work for him. Obviously, it was a no-brainer.

JEFF: Man, those PWF guys couldn't stand us. They were all big fat outcasts and losers who never made it. It was like the Island of Misfit Toys.

MATT: Stallion was engaged in questionable antics as a wrestling promoter. He would pass a jar around the crowd at PWF shows, saying that he was raising money for a homeless child. At the end of the night, he'd come back to the locker room and say to George South, "Pretty good night tonight, George. We got about twenty-five bucks." Which he then put into his pocket. We don't really know what happened to the money after that.

It was nasty business, but regardless of how nasty he was, Stallion got our foot in the door, so we'll always appreciate that.

JEFF: At the end of every show, Stallion liked to top things off with a big battle royal. We were in there one night working with another local wrestler named Scott Powers. He gave me a Tilt-A-Whirl, and as he grabbed my midsection, he cut this huge curvy gash across my stomach. There was blood everywhere!

I was bleeding all over the place. *What the hell?* I thought, and got myself eliminated so that I could get out of the ring. I couldn't figure out what happened. There was no reason for anyone to have a blade in there. I figured I must've gotten cut by some guy's fingernail. There was nobody there, maybe ten people in the crowd.

MATT: I know there are people out there who think that there's something fake going on when they see wrestlers bleed. The fact of the matter is, the easiest way to get a good Crimson Mask going is by "gigging"—cutting yourself and just letting the juice flow.

The first time I "gigged" was at one of the early New Frontier shows. I just wanted to try it, and I didn't do a very good job. To do it properly, you have to cut through the skin then open it up a little bit. You stick the blade in and turn it—that's the best way to get a nice flow of blood.

Gigging is pretty simple—you take your basic razor blade and cut off a small piece with scissors. The old-school wrestlers used to tape it to their finger, which is way too dangerous. The standard way is to tape it to your wrist, then cover it with three or four more wraps of tape. When it's time to gig, you just unwrap the tape and you're ready to go. You have to be careful, obviously. After you make the cut, the ref will usually get rid of the blade for you. You don't want it floating around the ring where someone can get sliced.

The best place to make the slice is on the forehead, up by the hairline. If you do it right you can get nice color going with minimal damage to your face. There are too many guys out there, especially indie workers, who are too careless or too casual with the blade. I hate to see a talented young wrestler—Steve Corino, for example—with a forehead covered with gig marks and scar tissue from blading night after night.

Anyway, back to the battle royal—I saw that Jeff was bleeding pretty badly, then someone pointed out that I was bleeding, too! Powers had cut me near my ear with one of his punches. It was a good three-quarter-inch slice.

JEFF: It seemed that Powers had his gigging blade in his wrist tape, and somehow it had become exposed. But it was the last match of the night, so there was no reason for him to have his blade. He might've gigged in his earlier match, but he should have gotten rid of it for the battle royal. By the end of the match, he had cut open four wrestlers!

MATT: After the battle royal, we went to the back and Stallion was mad as hell. He knew Jeff was underage, and if we wanted to make trouble, he'd have been screwed.

Stallion pulled Scott Powers aside and chewed him out: "What the hell were you thinking?"

He ran him out of the dressing room, which was probably a good thing, because Jason was really upset and ready to start a fight. Had Scott Powers stuck around, there would have been a serious altercation back there.

JEFF: We were more worried about what our dad was going to say! We were scared he was going to get hot and make us quit wrestling. I probably could've used a few stitches, but there was no way we were going to the hospital, so I just taped up the cut as much as possible.

MATT: Scott was actually a halfway-decent worker, but having a blade in your wrist when you weren't going to be gigging is completely idiotic. On that specific night, he was definitely a gigantic idiot. Years later, I ran into him at the Wal-Mart in Southern Pines. It took me a second to recognize him.

MATT: During the NFWA days we had developed a decent audience. Southern Pines and Sanford were our two major markets, and we also did shows in Wallace and Robbins and Pine Crest. But after we got rid of Jens, we took a couple of months off from doing our own shows because we were starting to get very busy working independents all around the Southeast. We were working every Friday and Saturday, doing a lot of bookings with ACW—American Championship Wrestling.

JEFF: ACW was run by a guy named Mitch Goude. He talked a big game, looked just like a cross between Fred Flintstone and Mr. Potato Head—with a Hitler mustache. They were officially based out of Laurinburg, North Carolina, but they ran shows in a lot of different towns.

MATT: He had a bunch of investors, so he was able to afford a film crew, with some nice TV equipment. They had a TV spot on a local cable station in Myrtle Beach and a couple of places around the Carolinas.

JEFF: ACW acted like they were the damn WWE. They'd done four or five shows and were already talking about doing a Pay-Per-View.

MATT: ACW's TV show wasn't bad. It was pretty professional and it had some decent TV exposure, and that's what we were looking for.

Mitch paid us forty dollars a show, which was pretty decent. Thomas Simpson, who was one of his partners, would hit us with another twenty or twenty-five on top of that, just to keep us happy.

JEFF: Thomas is a college professor, but he has some family money. He's always been a huge wrestling fan, and he felt it was worth it to spend money on what would be a good wrestling promotion. He'd rather drive a shitty car and spend his money on wrestling.

He was a big fan of our style. He loved the Japanese/Mexican stuff that we were doing, so he wanted to make sure we were happy and kept coming around.

GIGOLO

MATT: One of the other ACW investors was a woman who lived in South Carolina. I don't want to embarass her, so we'll call her "Sally Jones." We liked Sally a lot—she was a real sweetheart.

We met her the first time we met Mitch and Thomas. She was very interested in booking us for ACW, not because of our consummate skill in the ring but because we were "nice-looking guys."

She asked us to work the next couple of ACW shows, and to seal the deal, she invited us out to dinner. At the dinner, we met Sally's daughter, Jill (not her real name). She was a junior in high school. Jill was a big girl, and she was kind of shy and nervous around us.

Later that week, I got a phone call from Sally. "I know you're booked on our show this Saturday," she said, "but I was wondering if you were free the following Friday?"

I checked my calendar, assuming she wanted to book us for a wrestling gig, and we had no plans.

"Well, Matt," Sally said, "that's the night of my daughter Jill's junior prom. I was wondering how you'd feel about being her date."

I wasn't involved in a serious relationship at the time, though I was dating this one girl, Jason's ex-girlfriend's cousin. I wasn't interested in Jill, but I wanted to be diplomatic.

"I'm kind of seeing someone," I explained, "and I don't want to upset her. Thanks for asking, but I'm afraid I can't accept."

Sally was understanding, and that Saturday, we saw her at the ACW show. After our match, she came to me and said, "Hey Matt, can I talk to you for a second?

"If you would go to the prom with my daughter, I'll pay all your expenses *and* I'll give you a hundred fifty dollars."

"I'm sorry, Sally," I said, "but I can't. I wouldn't feel right about it."

"Okay; well, I just thought I'd ask."

I told Jeff what happened, when we got in the car to go home. We thought it was hilarious! "Can you believe it? She offered me a hundred and fifty dollars! For fifty more, I would've gone!"

On Wednesday night, my phone rang and it was Sally. "I know you said you didn't want to go," she said, "but will you go to the prom with Jill if I give you three hundred dollars?"

"Where do you want me to be," I said, "and what time do you want me to be there?" I didn't feel 100 percent right about it, but three hundred dollars was a lot of money for me back then!

Sally was so excited. "Oh, Matt, that's wonderful! I'll pay for all your expenses—your meals, your tuxedo rental, a limo, everything!"

Jason and I had plans to go to Myrtle Beach that weekend with his ex and her cousin. The beach wasn't too far from Sally's hometown, so Jason drove down there with me. While I was at the prom with Jill, he hung out with Sally's two sons, each of whom were about four hundred pounds. They were a big family, those Joneses. They all went out to eat at the local truck stop. Jason told me later that the two boys ate waffles with mustard on them.

When I got there, Sally gave me the three hundred dollars plus another hundred for dinner before the prom. "You guys go out and eat somewhere nice," she said.

We got in the car and I asked Jill where she wanted to go eat. "Anywhere is fine," she said, and mentioned a couple of places where her friends hung out.

We were driving and we passed a Western Sizzler. "How about that place?" I asked. "Do you want to go there?"

"Okay," she said. "I guess that would be fine."

We went in there and I spent maybe twenty dollars on the meal. I made three hundred and eighty dollars that night, which was much more than I'd been making as a wrestler!

We went to the prom, and it was a very uncomfortable scene. All the other kids in her school knew something wasn't right. First off, I was twenty years old. Plus, all I did was train back in those days, so I was in great shape. I simply didn't look like I could be Jill's boyfriend, and everybody at the prom must've been thinking, *Something here doesn't quite add up . . .*

I basically sat there all night, making excuses for not dancing with Jill. Finally, at the end of the prom, I agreed to dance with her to the last slow song of the night.

Then we left, the limo dropped us off back at her house, and Jason and I hopped in the car and drove to Myrtle Beach. We stayed with those two girls and had ourselves a classic wild weekend with the money I made from being Jill's gigolo.

I guess Jill had a wicked bad crush on me, and her mom was just trying to take care of her.

The next year came around, and I got the gig again. I took Jill to her senior prom, but this time my rate went up—I got three hundred and fifty dollars!

The funniest part of it is that neither Jeff nor I went to any of our own proms because we were busy working as wrestlers. The only proms I went to were as a gigolo!

KINGS OF THE RING

MATT: Stallion had us doing WWE jobs on a fairly regular basis, and every time we had to give him more than half of our pay. He had some racket going! Eventually, we realized that we had to get away from him. One weekend, Stallion got pissed off at us for some reason and didn't want to bring us to the TV tapings in Augusta, Georgia.

We decided that we would drive there ourselves and see what happened. Chief Jay Strongbow was working as an agent, and he kind of liked us, so we explained to him how Stallion was not being evenhanded. He told us that from that point on, we could deal directly with him.

After a while, we began getting some attention and appreciation from the top guys. It used to be that the Chief was the only person who knew us, and everybody else just referred to us as "those kids." But eventually people started to know our names. I remember J.R. saying, "Hey Matt, thank you for last night. That was real good, what you did out there tonight." So we knew that we were making progress.

JEFF: We worked the 1995 *King of the Ring* at the Spectrum in Philadelphia. We were so psyched, because not only was it the first WWE Pay-Per-View we ever went to, we were going to get paid for it!

When we got there we were told that our job was to be the two guys that opened the gates when the wrestlers came out. They gave us these spandex jester outfits to wear, which were waaaay too big for us. They were clearly made for two big jacked-up dudes, not skinny little guys like us.

MATT: The place was off the charts that night. I had the headset in my ear so they could buzz me and tell us when to open the doors. The crowd was so loud and it was hard to hear. I got so nervous. I didn't want to blow it. If we didn't open the door and they started playing the entrance music, everybody was going to laugh.

About two-thirds of the way through the show, when one match had just ended and the next one was about to start, Bruce Prichard, senior writer/producer for WWE, said to me, "Open the door now."

I signaled Jeff and as we reached for the door—*wham!* Somebody from the upper deck threw one of those twenty-four-ounce cups full of ice and soda and hit me right on the head.

JEFF: It knocked him silly. I had to try so hard to keep from laughing. I mean, I felt bad for Matt, but it was damn funny.

MATT: I could see it in his eyes. He was trying so hard to maintain his composure, but he was cracking up inside. Of course, there was no reason for the fans not to laugh and they totally busted up. Meanwhile, I'm soaked with soda, and for the whole rest of the night, I was completely sticky.

JEFF: That was the *King of the Ring* where Mabel—that's Viscera to you younger kids—won the tournament. The next night on *Raw*, we were the people that carried Mabel out. It was myself, Matt, Jason Ahrndt, and Marty Garner. It was torture. I could barely lift my feet. He weighed over four hundred pounds, and the chariot was a hundred and fifty pounds. It was just brutal. We got to the ring and set the one end of the thing on the apron and I stumbled a little. Mabel said, "Whoa! Easy, boys!"

Man, it would have been funny as hell if we had dropped that big bastard!

MATT: Being a jobber was a great learning experience, but it was also very disheartening. When we did matches, we wouldn't get our own entrance music. We would just go through the curtain behind the referee to the sound of the crowd laughing and jeering us. "You guys are going to get your asses beat!"

JEFF: We would stand by the curtain and they'd go, "Okay, you're up. Get rolling." Then they'd boot you in the ass and you'd go out there and the people would be totally vicious. "You suck, loser! Who's gonna beat your ass tonight? You fuckin' suck!" It's kind of an awkward situation.

MATT: I think there's a place for jobbers in the business. Job guys have always been an important part of building wrestlers. There are so many lower-card wrestlers in the WWE that aren't fully established with the audience. People don't know their moves or what their finishing maneuver is. They never get a chance to show off their characters.

If you put them on one of the weekend shows and let them have a match with some jobber, then they can get the audience familiarized with their characters and maybe look important for few minutes. That way, when it comes time for those guys to face a Hardy Boy or an Edge or whoever, they've got a little something behind them.

THE CLEANSINGS

MATT: On New Year's Eve 1996, the five members of our original wrestling clique—myself, Jeff, Marty Garner, Jason Ahrndt, and Shannon Moore—along with two of our buds, Scott "The Black Skull" Matthews and Aaron Decker, decided that we'd get together in the woods by Marty's house, build a campfire, and make resolutions for the New Year. We were all such close friends, plus we all had a common goal of making it in the wrestling business.

It was a perfect night, you could see every star in the sky. The seven of us sat around the fire and took turns talking about the year that was coming to a close, and then about our hopes and dreams for the year that was about to begin. Once we went around the whole circle, we each took a piece of wood and put it in the fire. It represented everything that was negative about the past year, clearing our slate for the New Year.

We weren't planning on being out too late, but once everybody started talking, we all got very into it. Before we knew it, it was two in the morning! It was such a moving and spiritual experience. We all genuinely felt that we'd cast away all our bad vibes, which is why we referred to it as "the Cleansing." It was one of those nights where we all knew something special had happened and that none of us would ever forget it.

SHANE AND MIKE

MATT: The usual way to get on an indie show was to go watch one show, then meet the guys: "We'd love to get booked. Here's our number."

In the spring of '96, we went to an ACW—a different ACW, Alternative Championship Wrestling—show in Goldston, North Carolina. That was the first time we saw Shane Helms and Mike Maverick. Shane was in Mike's corner, acting as his heel manager. He had real heat with the crowd. Somebody actually threw a rock and hit him in the head.

A month or so later, we went to a show promoted by a guy named Harold Bass. He thought he was the shit. He acted like a mafioso wannabe, and talked a big game. His promotion was called—believe it or not—ACCW, for Atlantic Coast Championship Wrestling. To this very day, I'm stunned at just how uncreative wrestling promoters can be!

JEFF: After the show, we went to Denny's with a bunch of the wrestlers. That was where we first hung out with Shane and Mike. Shane was wearing this Superman jacket and a little nerdy vest. "We hear you've got the little ring down there in Vass," he said. "Me and Mike would love to come down there sometime."

They were both pretty cool guys, so they came out to the ring and started working out with us. It was the beginning of a true friendship, and the start of what would soon become . . . OMEGA.

JYNX

MATT: During our run with ACW, I created a spin-off of Willow the Whisp so that Jeff and I could tag together. In Latin, will-o'-the-wisp is *ignis fatuus*—the "foolish fire." When I created my version of Willow, I took that as my name, Ignis Fatuus.

JEFF: The attitude back in those day was that if you did WWE jobs for too long, you'd never get a chance to be a legitimate Superstar. We decided to pitch Willow the Whisp and Ignis to Chief Jay Strongbow. We explained how we had created these characters that wear masks, so for all intents and purposes, they could say we hadn't been on TV doing jobs.

"If you could get us a dark match," we said, "we'd really appreciate it."

"Send me some photos," he said, "and I'll show them to the Emperor." The Emperor was, of course, Vince McMahon.

MATT: A week or two later we got the call. "I got you guys a shot," the Chief said. "Come on up and bring the masks. We'll have you work the gimmick at the next TV tapings."

We were so excited! We got there and they asked us what we called our tag team and we realized, *Wait a sec. We don't have a name!* Thinking fast—maybe too fast—we decided to call ourselves Jynx. It came from the fact that both Willow and Ignis represented a kind of bad luck. Turned out, we didn't realize just how bad that luck would be!

The format said we would be facing the Grimm Twins—Ron and Don Harris—in a regular TV job match. We went to the Chief and said, "Look, if we're just going to do the job, we'd rather be Matt and Jeff Hardy."

The Chief was not amused, to say the least. "I went to bat for you," he said. "I went to Vince on your behalf and got you the chance to wear your gimmicks, and now you don't want to do it? That's how you treat me?"

"Chief, it's not like that," I explained. "We were just hoping to work a dark match so that we could show what we can do and maybe get a job here."

"Fine. Thanks a lot, boys. I'll never go to bat for you again."

We clearly didn't have a lot of choice in the matter, so we agreed to do it.

"Just go out and have a good match," the Chief said. "You never know. Maybe it'll work out good for you."

JEFF: Well, it didn't work out so good. They needed to put our names on the screen, so we tried to keep it simple for them and said we were Willow and Ignis. They thought Willow was too Walt Disney, so they changed it to Wildo. Ignis they didn't have a problem with, but whoever was writing the names for TV screwed it up and it became Ingis. Wildo and Ingis. Unbelievable!

It was clearly a jinxed situation. We had the match and it was the only time we did those characters on WWE TV.

MATT: The first time we were officially called the Hardy Boyz on WWE TV was in May 1996. We worked a pair of tryout matches with another North Carolina tag team, called the Overlords. First we lost to them at a dark match in Fayetteville, then the next night we beat them in the opening dark match in Charleston, South Carolina.

Because we won the dark match, we got to wrestle again an hour later as part of the *Superstars* taping. We fought the New Rockers, which was Marty Jannetty and Al Snow. It's funny, because when we came out for that

match, the crowd was kind of behind us because we had just beaten the Overlords. It was like, "Hey, these guys must be okay, because they won that first match." When we lost, it was back to "Boo! You jobbers suck!"

Later on that same night we wrestled the Smokin' Gunns on *Superstars,* and when we came down, the crowd booed the hell out of us. We started out winning the dark match and becoming babyfaces against the New Rockers, then a couple of hours later we were heels against the Smokin' Gunns.

JEFF: I remember the first time J.R. referred to us as the Hardy Boyz. It was the *Raw* after Kane had made his big debut at the *In Your House: Badd Blood* Pay-Per-View. They came back from a commercial and J.R. said, "In the ring, we've got the Hardy Boyz getting ready for a match against the Truth Commission."

Then the lights went out: "Oh my God, what is this? It's Kane! *It's Kane!* These two youngsters better run for their lives!"

Kane came into the ring and beat the hell out of us. The match was declared a no-contest, but it was actually really good for us. It gave the Hardy Boyz an opportunity to come in contact with one of the company's top guys, and that's always a good thing when you're just coming up.

A CHOICE

MATT: We'd been doing a lot of work with ACW, but there came a point where we got fed up with the way Mitch treated us. They were trying to act like they were a big deal. We weren't really making any money and they were taking the fun out of it. We were working hard, trying to build for a future in the wrestling business, and they turned it into a total hassle.

JEFF: One night we were getting ready to work a show and Mitch said to us, "If you guys are going to be taken seriously here, I want you to stop doing jobs for WWE. You're going to have to make up your mind. Either you stop going there or you stop working here.

"You're going up there and getting destroyed," he told us. "You can't come back here and be the Hardy Boyz when you've been on TV getting destroyed by WWE Superstars."

MATT: "Well, let's see," I said. "When we work for you, we make forty dollars a night, and when we work for WWE, we make three hundred. Let me do the math. I think we'll just stick with WWE, thanks very much."

I also thought there was real opportunity for us in WWE. People were starting to take note of us up there. They knew that when we went up there, we would always bust our asses.

JEFF: The next week we were set to wrestle a match in Asheboro against Lodi, who ended up at WCW a few years later, and an indie worker named Toad. We showed up and Mitch gave us an ultimatum. He told us that if we wanted to wrestle as the Hardy Boyz in ACW, then we were going to have to put his people over.

"If you're gonna job up there at WWE," he said, "then you're gonna job here for my guys."

I hate that attitude, like they're going to make us lose to try to punish us. I'll never understand that shit, all the politics.

MATT: We were in the locker room and Chaz Rocco came in to talk to us. He was Mitch's enforcer, the company badass. He'd been around for years but he was the drizzlin' shits. Lots of attitude, but he was no good. He came in and said, "Okay, you guys are first."

We weren't even sure if we were going out there after what Mitch had just told us. The show started and we just sat there, not even bothering to get dressed. Lodi and Toad were flipping out, trying to talk to us, "What're we going to do out there?"

JEFF: Matt looked over at me and said, "Do you want to leave?"

Thomas Simpson, Mitch's partner, came over to us and was totally apologetic. "Please do this," he said. "I'm sorry about Mitch. I'll make things right."

"All right," Matt said, "but the only reason we're going to do this is because of you."

MATT: Lodi and Toad went out to the ring and we were still sitting there, putting our tights on. They started playing our music as we were lacing up our boots. Chaz Rocco started freaking out, "You guys are on right now! You guys are on!"

Lodi and Toad were out there for seven minutes before we finally came out. We got to the ring and just beat the shit out of them for a good ten minutes before we let them get the pin.

JEFF: After the match, we decided to sever our ties with ACW, and our buds agreed to stick by us. If ACW didn't want the Hardy Boyz, then Jason, Marty, and Shannon wouldn't work for them either. Thomas Simpson chose to take our side and he went and offered Mitch an ultimatum.

"If the Hardyz don't come back," he said, "I'm not coming back."

"Well, they ain't coming back," Mitch said.

"Then I'm not coming back."

MATT: Thomas came to me and said, "How about we get together and we do our own thing? You just tell me what you want me to do and I'll do it. If you need money, I'll give you money."

I was so excited that I couldn't sleep. My head was just full of ideas! I was laying in bed thinking, *What can we call this deal?*

I thought it was super-important to name the promotion something that didn't necessarily have the word *wrestling* in it. Maybe instead of *wrestling*, we could use *grappling*. But I also wanted people to know we were a new thing, that we were "modern." And it came to me, just like that. OMEGA: Organization of Modern Extreme Grappling Arts.

I called Thomas the next morning. "How about we call it OMEGA?"

"OMEGA what?" he said. "OMEGA Pro Wrestling?"

"No, just OMEGA."

"Let's do it," Thomas said, and we were under way.

SURGE

MATT: At the last New Frontier Wrestling Alliance show we did, I came out and said, "I want to thank you guys for your support, but tonight will be my last night as High Voltage. From now on I will be known as . . . Surge."

I changed it because there was a tag team in WCW calling themselves High Voltage. A couple of years later, Chris Kanyon told me that they blatantly stole my name from my *WCW Amateur Challenge* video.

Kanyon told me that my tape was sitting out on top of the VCR in WCW's training facility, the Power Plant, and that's where they lifted High Voltage.

"Your tape was watched several times," Kanyon told me, so that when we started OMEGA, I decided I should take on a new name. I chose Surge because it was related to electricity like High Voltage.

THE BIRTH OF OMEGA

MATT: OMEGA was driven by nine people who had the same goal in mind—to make a living as professional wrestlers. You had the original clique of myself, Jeff, Jason "Venom" Ahrndt, Marty "Cham-Pain" Garner, and Shannon "Kid Dynamo" Moore. With the addition of Shane Helms, Mike "Maverick" Howell, Joey Matthews, and Christian York, we made up the incredible OMEGA Powers.

JEFF: Matt was the main mind and heart of the whole deal. He put together every match and did the promoting. Thomas was the financial guy, and we were the talent.

MATT: Thomas really busted his ass for OMEGA. He wanted to make us look as professional as possible, so he kicked off our OMEGA partnership by getting us a new ring. Our old ring was basically worn-out at that point. All four sides were sinking in. It was a disaster.

He cut us a check for fifteen hundred dollars to buy a new ring from a guy in Georgia. It was eighteen by eighteen, professional quality. We did another five hundred dollars' worth of renovation on it and that became the official OMEGA ring.

Next, he got us some solid steel guardrails, just like the kind they used on TV. So by the time of the premiere OMEGA show at the Sanford Armory on Saturday, July 25, 1997, we were looking pretty good.

We'd learned a lot over the past few years, from working in WWE and doing countless indie shows. We didn't have a great idea of what we were doing, but we had a pretty good one.

JEFF: My first match of the night was Wolverine and Kid Dynamo against Black Skull and Foma. We had worked out this spot where we did all these dives and I was going to top it all off with a moonsault bodyblock onto the concrete floor.

I sprung off there and one of the guys that was supposed to be there wasn't there. He had totally forgotten the spot, so it was just Shannon and Black Skull waiting there to catch me. Quite frankly, they didn't do such a great job of it. My leg smashed into the steel railing and bent in the worst way. I totally thought I broke it.

MATT: It looked unbelievable. Just brutal. It was the kind of thing that would have ended another guy's career. We were all watching, because that was the first big match of the show. When Jeff hit that leg, everybody was going, "Oh my God! What are we going to do? He's in the main event!"

"Don't worry," I said. "He's cool. Jeff's tough."

JEFF: The main event was Willow vs. Surge. A lot of the people knew that Willow the Whisp was really me, and they were really freaked out that I came out for another match.

I couldn't dance like I usually could, but I still made a big dramatic entrance. In the match, Matt put me through a table and I smashed into the concrete, but I survived. I felt like Superman going back out there with that leg.

RAGIN' BULL

MATT: The night before our first OMEGA show, Mike and Shane were booked on a show in Greensboro, North Carolina, alongside Manny Fernandez, the Ragin' Bull.

Manny had been around for years, working for the National Wrestling Alliance and Southwest Championship Wrestling. He also had a reputation for bullying his way onto shows. I'd never met him before, but I had heard he was trouble, and rumor had it he may have even carried a weapon, that kind of thing.

After the show, all the wrestlers went to this strip club. "Where are you guys booked tomorrow?" Manny asked Shane and Mike.

"We're booked up in Sanford," they told him.

"Yeah, Stanford," he said. "That's where I'm booked, too. How do you get there again?"

"I don't know," they replied. "We don't really have directions."

The next day, it's our first OMEGA show and as if I didn't have enough on my plate, here comes Manny Fernandez and his buddy Frankie Murdock walking into the locker room. They plopped their gear down, and I'm thinking, *This isn't good.*

Shane came over to me: "Matt, I swear I don't know anything about this."

I could see Jason was getting hot, because he didn't trust Shane and Mike. "Those guys had something to do with this," he said. "I know it."

I realized that I had to take charge of the situation, so I went over to Manny. Jason and Marty Garner had my back, just in case things got out of control.

"Hey Manny," I said. "What's going on? Can I help you?"

"Just ready to work tonight," he said. "What time does the show start, and where do I set my gimmicks up?"

"I've got to tell you, man, I don't think you're booked for this show."

"Oh yeah, I'm booked," he said. "I've been booked here for three weeks."

"Sorry, man, but I'm the only person that did any booking for this show."

Manny looked me dead in the eyes. "This is where I'm supposed to be."

At this point, Jason and Marty were ready to go at it.

"I don't know what to tell you," I said. "There's no room on the card, and all the money I have is already paid out."

Manny got right in my face. "Oh yeah? Well, somebody better have my money, or somebody's gonna get their ass whooped. And it might be you."

"I hate that you feel that way, Manny, but there's no room for you to work here."

He was close to hitting me, but then he looked over my shoulder and realized how many guys were behind me—Jeff and Jason and Marty and Shane and Mike.

"Well, if I can't work, can I at least go sell my gimmicks?"

I told him that would be fine and he set up a table so he could sell autographed pictures.

A year or so later we ran into Manny out on the road. "Kid," he said, "I'm proud of the way you stood up for yourself when I tried to force my way on your show."

Then, after we were in WWE, we stayed at a La Quinta hotel down by the airport in Charlotte and there was Manny Fernandez, working as a janitor. Sad but true.

TOUGH ENOUGH OMEGA-STYLE

MATT: All the OMEGA Powers were dedicated as hell. We used to all go out to the ring out at Tracy's place and train as often as possible. We would try new moves and work on upcoming matches.

All of us were so competitive. One of us would go up and do a backflip from the top rope to a mattress on the ground, and then the other one would go up and do it. Then another one would go up and do it.

Pretty soon, the word traveled about what we were doing and people started popping up to check us out. The first few people to come by just watched us practicing, but we started hearing that they were telling their friends that wrestling is all fake: "Man, those guys aren't really fighting."

After that, when people would come out to watch, we wouldn't let them. We would stop what we were doing and just sit in the ring.

JEFF: There were definitely guys who looked at what we were doing as some kind of joke. Saying shit like, "There ain't no future in that wrestling." But I think no matter what you do there are always going to be people who take pleasure in putting you down.

MATT: It wasn't long before people began to ask us about training. We charged fifty dollars for a tryout, and if you still wanted to train after that, it'd be three hundred.

When we started out, we would just do real simple, easy stuff. Some of the trainees would come back, but the ones who didn't often left thinking, *This wrestling business is kind of easy. It didn't hurt at all.*

But then we heard that from a few people and decided that if people came out to train, they would damn sure leave with some respect for wrestling.

JEFF: Matt and Jason wanted to be sure that no one was going to leave there thinking that wrestling was anything close to fake, so they beat the living hell out of new trainees.

MATT: It was more than proving that wrestling is real, it was proving that it's dangerous and that it hurts and that you shouldn't make light of it. We knew how real it was, because we'd all been hurt. We also wanted to make sure that these guys were tough enough for what we were doing.

JEFF: I felt the same way, but I didn't have the heart to do some of the things Matt and Jason were doing.

MATT: This one guy came out, he was probably thirty-five years old, weighed about two-forty, in decent physical shape. He'd been having some problems with his wife. "I've been a fan of wrestling all my life," he said, "and I really want to give this a try."

We showed him a few basic moves, then we put Jason behind him and I shoved him over. *Wham!*

We did that a few times, then Jason picked him up over his head and dropped him. *Wham!* He did it once, then picked him up to do it again. "Wait, wait," the guy said. "Put me down! Put me down! I'm man enough to admit when I can't do something. Thank you for taking time with me, but I can't do this!"

He had probably been there for a grand total of fifteen minutes.

JEFF: Shane Helms also used to help train with us, and he was a lot like Jason in that he also had a mean streak in him.

A friend of Shannon Moore's named Michael Teague kept coming around. He looked like Herbie the Dentist in *Rudolph the Red-Nosed Reindeer.*

"Dude, if you want to hang out here, you've got to try out."

"I don't have any money."

"Fine, but if you want to come around anymore, you're going to have to train."

MATT: Mike started working out with us, and man, we beat the shit out of him. To his credit, he came back every Sunday. And every Sunday, we beat the shit out of him. Finally he said "I'm out of here."

"Yeah, get out of here, wimp," Shane said. He picked up a lawn chair and beat that kid all the way to his car.

Whack!

"Get the hell out of here, wimp!"

Whack!

Shane must've hit him twenty times on the way to the car!

From that day on, Mike became our best student. He worked a few OMEGA shows as Will Powers. He still wrestles as an independent, under the name William Wealth.

JEFF: The thing is, after someone got through a few of those practices, we knew they were cool. It's a lot like the way the boys in the WWE locker room mess with new guys, though we didn't know that yet. They break you down and make you a man.

MATT: Another time this skinny little black kid, maybe seventeen years old, showed up with his daddy. "We saw you all wrestle in Southern Pines," Mr. Coleman, the daddy, said. "You all put on a good show. My boy Caprice would really love to do this."

"Call me Ice," the kid said, getting ahead of himself.

We explained that a tryout cost fifty dollars.

"I don't have that," the kid said, "but if I come back next week, can I try out?"

The following Sunday he came back with the training fee. His parents were with him, so we couldn't be too mean to him.

We were teaching him to cross his arms and take a back bump. When you do that, the idea is to fall flat on your back, but every time Caprice tried it, he'd land on his ass.

We made him get up and do it again. *Boom!* He'd land on his ass. We made him do it a hundred times, but he couldn't get it right. He kept landing on his ass.

Finally he started giving up: "I just can't do it."

His daddy came over to the ring and said, "You can do it, son. Come on. You're Ice."

Caprice tried again and again, but he just couldn't do it.

"Come on, son," Mr. Coleman said. "I'll do it with you."

He got in the ring next to him, took two ice cubes out of the soda he was drinking, and put one in each of Caprice's hands.

"Remember, son," he said. "You're Ice."

They both crossed their arms and Caprice still didn't get it. His daddy, on the other hand, did it perfectly.

Eventually, though, Caprice caught on. He started coming around on his own and managed to get through the training. We roughed him up a bit, but he made it. We started using him as a referee at OMEGA shows and one night he asked us, "Would it be cool if I came out to this music?"

"Dude, referees don't use music," I explained.

But he was determined to showboat, so he would come to the ring in his ref shirt and do a front flip over the top rope.

We reprimanded him about that, explaining that the ref's job is to be the ref.

JEFF: I thought it was cool, a referee doing flips into the ring.

MATT: I'm sure Caprice was thinking, *Matt and Jason won't let me do anything!*

"You'll get to be a wrestler when we say you're ready," I told him.

He stuck it out and ended up becoming a good worker. He's doing real well for himself now over at NWA Wildside. He calls himself Ice, and everything!

JEFF: Matt and Jason were pretty much in charge of the training. I would usually help with dropkicks or highspots. When it came to the technical stuff, I left it to those guys. I was too scared that we were going to get sued.

MATT: We weren't putting anybody in a position where they could break anything.

JEFF: They were in all kinds of positions where they could have broken something! That's what they kept telling people: "Don't worry! You won't break anything!"

MATT: This stupid redneck kid showed up late one afternoon, just as it was getting dark. As usual, he didn't have the fifty dollars, but Jason and I were in a mood, so we said, "Okay. How about you come into the ring and take a couple of bumps?"

From the second he got in there, we started beating the holy hell out of him.

"Here's a basic move you need to know," I said. "Duck one clothesline and take a clothesline."

He ducked the first clothesline, and as he came back, I just about took his head off with the second one. *Boom!* To make matters worse, he tripped and turned his ankle as I hit him. He went down, grabbing his ankle, screaming in pain: "Aaaaaahhhhh!"

"What's the matter, boy?" I said. "Does your foot hurt?"

"Aaaaaaaaahhhh! My ankle!"

"Dude, it's just sprained," I said. "It's fine."

"Get up, you pussy," Jason said to him. "Come on!"

Meanwhile the kid won't stop screaming: "Aaaaaaaaah! I can't move it!"

We helped the kid into Tracy's house. "Don't worry," I told him. "It's not that bad. We'll put a little ice on it and it'll be fine."

JEFF: I got down on one knee and helped him take his boot off. He was actually wearing calf-high Asic Gel boots. I unlaced it and took it off and saw his bone sticking out.

"Oh," I said, looking at Matt. "Okay. Um, you just need to put some ice on it."

Tracy brought him a little plastic bag with maybe four ice cubes in it. "Here," he said, "just put this on it."

"All right, man," I told him. "We better get you home."

Jason carried him out to his car and put him in there. As he drove off, he actually said, "Thanks a lot, guys. I'll try and make it back next week."

Needless to say, we never saw him again. We were lucky he didn't sue us!

MATT: No matter how you slice it, a pretty impressive roster of wrestlers worked out in our little ring in the woods. Shane Helms, Shannon Moore, Lita, Joey Matthews and Christian York, Mike Maverick, Ice, Will Powers. It's pretty amazing when you think of it like that.

THE HARDY BOYZ

INDIE HELL

MATT: In addition to all our OMEGA shows, we continued to drive up and down the East Coast in order to work as many other indie shows as we possibly could. Part of it was about gaining valuable in-ring experience, and part of it was simply that we needed to earn a living.

The problem was that these indie promoters would try to rip us off all the time. It's just one of the facts of life in the business. They'd say, "We'll pay fifty dollars," and then come back and give you five: "Sorry, guys, but I didn't make that much money tonight."

JEFF: Some of the guys who run independent promotions are such assholes. I used to get so sick of hearing how if you don't do what the promoters tell you, they were going to fire you. I'd think, *Shit, you're barely paying me! How can you fire me?*

NCW was one of the promotions we did a lot of work with. We pretty much built that house. We would do shows on the first Thursday of every month. We started with thirteen people there, which grew to packing in over three hundred.

MATT: We also used to do regular shows for SCW, this promotion around Raleigh. The promoter was named Count Grog. He had a whole Dracula gimmick going, with a cape and a little mustache. They did shows at this bar, the Berkeley Café, which would fill up with drunk college kids.

JEFF: We had to get dressed outside, then walk down into the bar. There were nights when we'd do shows in the middle of winter and we'd freeze our asses off just making our way to the ring.

The ceiling in that place was only nine feet high. It was too low to even jump off the top ropes. One time I jumped off the top, grabbed the pillars on the ceiling, and altered my flip in midair. Joey Matthews and Steve Corino did a ladder match there, and during the match, one of the lights got knocked out by the ladder. Sparks started flying everywhere and the place lit on fire. It was incredible! Just total chaos!

MATT: It wasn't always so low-rent. Sometimes we got to work with some pretty tough and well-known opponents. In February 1998, we worked against Rob Van Dam and Sabu at Eastern Carolina University in Greenville, North Carolina. It was for Greg Price's All-Star Wrestling. We were originally supposed to work with one of the regular ASW teams. The main event was originally RVD—Van Dam—against Tommy Dreamer, but Tommy couldn't make it, so Greg asked us if we'd work with RVD and Sabu.

"Sure thing," I said, but inside I was thinking, *Jeez, I hope they don't knock our teeth out.*

Jeff had worked his WWE match with Rob, but otherwise we didn't know anything about those guys other than what we'd seen on TV—and on TV, those guys looked dangerous!

JEFF: We didn't have much interaction other than the match, but Sabu wasn't nearly as crazy as I'd expected.

The two of us were fighting out in the crowd and we got to an area where there was broken glass on the floor. I thought, *Uh-oh! This psycho is going to want to cut me!*

But Sabu saw the glass and said, "Let's get out of here, man. There's glass over here!"

It was a tremendous match, very competitive, and more important, totally safe.

MATT: We really busted our asses over those years, logging countless miles on the odometer and taking just as many bumps. Sometimes it was brutal, sometimes it was a million laughs. There's no question that we picked up experience that would serve us later on. The wrestling business has always been one in which you have to pay serious dues if you want to make something of yourself, and we definitely paid our dues in full.

OMEGA 4 LIFE

MATT: For the next year or two, we devoted ourselves to building the OMEGA promotion into something extraordinary. We tried to put on the most exciting, most creative shows on the indie circuit. We worked ridiculously hard, but it was so worth it.

JEFF: The shows we did back then, I always worked twice, as Willow and as Wolverine. At that point I didn't care about money. I was having too much fun.

MATT: The OMEGA Powers formed an unbreakable bond, and that's one of the things that made it so special for me.

One of our traditions, from the New Frontier days through to OMEGA, was that everybody would go out to eat together after a show. We would drop the ring off at Tracy's, then we would all go to Kelly's Truck Stop or the

Huddle House in Southern Pines. Then, when we were done eating, we would all go back to Tracy's and watch a tape of that night's show. It didn't matter what time it was. We wouldn't get home until 8 A.M. We'd be thoroughly exhausted, but in the best possible way.

When we did our New Frontiers shows, when we did our OMEGA shows, we might not have always had a clue as to what we were doing. What we did have were twenty guys who all came together for one mutual goal. We all worked hard and we all had fun.

After Jeff and I signed our WWE contracts in 1998, we showed up at an OMEGA show wearing WWE ATTITUDE T-shirts. We got in the ring and told the fans—many of whom would travel around the Carolinas to see every one of our shows—that we'd be "WWE for the next three years." Then we ripped off the shirts to reveal OMEGA T-shirts: "But we're OMEGA for life!"

PART 2
TOP O' THE WORLD

DEAL

JEFF: In the spring of 1998, OMEGA did a show in Wallace, North Carolina, and I was in a match—Willow vs. Kid Dynamo. I knew not to do anything too crazy, because we had WWE shows the next week, so I was trying to be safer than usual. I went for a cross body and just landed wrong, hitting the floor right on the back of my head and neck. Man, I couldn't feel anything. I remember looking at my foot—it was jacked up on the rail—and trying to wiggle it. After about three or four seconds—it felt like forever—I was able to move it. God, I was so relieved. Then I got back in the ring and finished the match.

I was pretty freaked by the experience. When the match ended, I took a walk out in this field behind the armory and cried my heart out.

MATT: We were all looking for him: "Man, where's Jeff?"

I was scared because I knew he was in bad shape, and I didn't know where he was. We were slated to work a match against the Serial Thrillaz—Shane Helms and Mike Maverick—but since Jeff was hurt, I ended up teaming with Venom, an angle that ended up being paralleled in real life.

JEFF: The fact that I couldn't move my legs, even for just a couple of moments, scared me so bad. I've always been very emotional and I didn't want to be around anybody. I just wanted to get the hell out of there. I just didn't want to lose it front of the guys.

The next week, I was still hurting, both physically and emotionally. We went to WWE and that was the trip where they decided to offer us a deal.

MATT: We were supposed to wrestle Too Much. They told us not to think like job guys, that they didn't want a one-sided match.

The problem was that Jeff was still hurt.

JEFF: I had to tell them I could not wrestle. That was hard. There was a part of me that just wanted to do it, but my neck was still hurting, so I told J.R. that I was sorry, but I just couldn't do it.

MATT: They decided to put Jason in there with me to wrestle the match, which ended up being pretty great—Jason and I knew how to tag together and we looked damn good.

After the match, J.R.—in his role as Jim Ross, head of talent relations—asked us to come to the next day's show so that he could talk to Jeff and me. Unfortunately, one of the guys traveling with us—I think it was

Marty—had to get back home to work. J.R. was cool. He said, "Just come tomorrow. I'll pay all of you."

So everybody got two hundred and fifty dollars just for going to the show. When we got there, J.R. called Jeff and me over and said, "We want to talk to you boys."

JEFF: Bruce Prichard and J.R. sat us down and said, "We think you guys have a great future here, and we'd like to put you under a developmental contract. Would you be interested in that?"

MATT: "Yeah," we said. "That's something we could do."

It was unquestionably the greatest day of my life up to that point. My heart was beating so fast, I thought I was going to explode! I was totally, completely pumped! My dream of being a WWE wrestler had finally come true!

Jeff and I walked back out to the ring and Marty and Jason were just hanging out by the barricade. "What'd they say to you?"

"Well," I said, "they offered us a contract."

They were so excited for us, but I knew inside they were thinking, *Damn! I want a deal here, too!*

JEFF: We officially signed our deal with WWE in April 1998. We were so excited to get our contracts back, because they didn't become official until they were signed by both parties—us and J.R. When they didn't come in the mail immediately we started getting paranoid, like maybe J.R. had changed his mind. The contracts finally came back in May, and with them was our first WWE check, which was for three hundred dollars. That was the standard developmental deal at that time—three hundred dollars a week. I actually made a copy of that paycheck and had it framed.

MATT: Not long after we got signed, they offered a deal to Jason. They had a gimmick in mind for him where he would be a wrecker driver, which is what he did in real life. They were going to make like he was related to Jack and Gerry Brisco and worked at the world-famous Brisco Brothers Body Shop. Jason was getting ready to go to development at Memphis Wrestling when he got called up to WWE to be Joey Abs in the Mean Street Posse.

Unfortunately, Jason and I had a serious falling-out over a personal issue and our friendship came to an end. Then, to make matters worse, his ego got the best of him, and he was released from WWE.

We rarely speak these days, which I hate, because we had such a special bond. It's sad, but that's how life is.

"ARE YOU A PROFESSIONAL?"

MATT: When we first signed with WWE, Bruce Prichard—known to "old-school" WWE fans as the one and only Brother Love—said, "You guys should work all the indie shows you can, to continue to get experience."

That was cool. We worked house shows if they were local, or if they needed guys. But mostly, our weekends were free. "If you can get a decent payday," Bruce said, "take it. You've got my permission."

JEFF: In May, just after we signed our WWE contracts, we worked a wrestling show at the Harley-Davidson convention in Selma, North Carolina.

It was our last deal with ACCW and Harold Bass. We'd worked this angle with these two fat dudes called the Ringbusters. They'd beaten us a couple of times and we were supposed to go over in the blow-off match.

MATT: We got there and Harold starts giving us this whole rocket-to-the-moon spiel: "I'm going to film TV shows at all these Harley-Davidson events and I need you to sign a contract saying that your image is exclusive to me."

"Forget about it," we told him. "We just signed with WWE. If you don't want us to wrestle, that's fine. But we're not signing anything."

JEFF: One of the Ringbusters didn't show up, so there was a replacement fat guy named Slash Walker that was filling in. He wasn't a bad guy. Steve Corino trained him. But the main Ringbuster was Dave Renegade, and he was Harold Bass's enforcer.

"Why are you guys being hard to deal with?" Renegade started in with us. "You think you're big stars now because you signed with WWE?"

"No," Matt said, "but they told us not to sign anything with any other promotion, and that's all there is to it."

MATT: The finish of the match was supposed to be that we beat the Ringbusters, but now Dave Renegade says, "Forget that. You guys aren't going over tonight."

Fine. Whatever. This was our last hurrah with ACCW, so we didn't fight it.

JEFF: The match got under way and Dave Renegade and I had set up a spot where I did a front-flip Swanton off the top rope onto him outside the ring. "I'll catch you, brother," he told me. "I know how to spot people. Don't worry."

I jumped and he stepped out of the way so I smashed right onto the ground. There were no mats—it was just clay and grass, and it was pretty hard. I got right up and kicked him in the ribs as hard as I could. *Bam!*

I got back in the ring, going "Come on!"

Renegade was turning red, he was so hot. There was fire in his eyes. "You wanna go for real, you skinny little shit? You wanna go for real?"

"Are you a professional?," I said. "ARE YOU A PROFESSIONAL? Come on, let's go!"

I was about to lose it. I didn't want to fight anymore. So I tagged Matt.

MATT: Jeff tagged me in and Renegade is steaming. "Let's go! You want to be big shots?"

"Man, just chill out," I said. "Calm down. Don't be ridiculous."

Slash Walker was standing in the corner, just shaking his head.

Renegade went to knee me in the nuts, but I backed out of the way. He started swinging at me, so I hit that fat bastard in the face as hard as I could. *Wham!*

I tried to grab him from behind to stop him from taking any more punches, but he was so huge, I could barely get my arms around him. Then Jeff came in and dropkicked him right in the face. That did it. He went down!

JEFF: The referee was, of all people, Renegade's wife! She was crying, "I'll kill you! I'll kill you!"

Harold Bass was freaking out: "Stop! Stop!"

Renegade got up, screaming "I'm gonna kill you!" He tagged in Slash and stormed off toward the campers, looking for a weapon.

Shane and Joey had come out there with us. They weren't wrestling, they were just there watching the show. I could see them out in their seats, getting ready in case it turned even uglier.

We actually tried to wrestle with Slash, but there wasn't much point in going for the finish. We hit him with a chair, got DQed and just left.

We went back to these campers which were serving as the locker-room area, and it was just chaos. People were coming up to us: "Dave's going to get a gun. You all better get out of here now."

Renegade was over by the bed of a truck. He saw me and started yelling: "That little bastard knocked my tooth out! He knocked my tooth out."

He grabbed a tire iron and was heading toward me when Shane jumped in front of him with the ring bell in his hands. He was ready to go! Shane's such a little shooter—he loves a good fight.

Renegade's wife was pulling at him, trying to get him to stop. But before they could go at it, the promoter got in the middle. "Look, here's your money," he said. "You all get out of here. I don't want a mess. Just take your money and go."

So that's what we did. We took our hundred bucks and hightailed it out of there.

THE FUNKIN' DOJO

MATT: Finally, at the end of July, we got a call from Bruce Prichard, telling us we would be attending Dory Funk Jr.'s Funkin' Dojo, up in Stamford, Connecticut.

JEFF: The Dojo was run by Dory Funk Jr. and Bruce Prichard's brother, Dr. Tom Prichard. Dory, of course, was a wrestling icon, the son of Dory Funk, the brother of Terry Funk, and a legendary NWA and Mid-Atlantic World Champion.

Dory and Tom pretty much split the training between them. Once in a while Dory would take a bump, but Tom did the majority of the physical training.

MATT: Besides being an intensive training session, the Dojo serves as a test to see how much actual talent and how much wrestling knowledge you have. Now, while we had been wrestling for years at this point, we had never technically been to wrestling school, so we were more than a little nervous.

JEFF: Oh my God. The first day at the Dojo was rough and I hated it, but it was something that I knew I had to do. We didn't know what to expect. We just wanted to do good.

MATT: The roster at our first Dojo was Jeff and myself, Kurt Angle, Jay "Christian" Reso, Shawn Stasiak, Matt "Albert" Bloom, Andrew "Test" Martin, Glenn Kulka, and Teddy Hart, who was Bret and Owen Hart's nephew.

I had heard of Kurt Angle, because I knew they'd worked a deal out with the former Olympian. But most of the guys I had no idea who they were. Giant silva, from the Oddities, was also there. WWE had him living in Stamford and he came to all the Dojos because they were determined to train him. Every one of us really dreaded having to work with that guy because he was crazy. He was a nice guy, but unpredictable. WWE essentially found a guy who was seven feet five inches and said, "Let's try to make a wrestler out of this guy." Unfortunately, he lacked the necessary skills and had a tendency to be a bit reckless.

JEFF: Both Matt and I are very much loners. We were two of the last guys to arrive in Stamford. When we got to the hotel where we were all staying, we saw Christian, Test, and Glenn Kulka, all hanging out in the bar. They all knew one another from working and training together in Canada.

MATT: I thought, *Look at these guys, I bet they're going to be punks.* I'm sure they were thinking the same of us.

In the end, of course, all of us bonded in the biggest way, because the Dojo is such a tough experience. We would get up at 7 A.M. and go to Titan Towers to train in the gym—lifting weights, working out. Next, we would go eat lunch. Then we'd work out in the ring for six hours.

JEFF: We had a good opportunity with WWE and didn't want to be exposed because we had never been trained. A lot of the other guys had been trained, they knew the little ins and outs, the little technical things, and we didn't. As it turned out, we had nothing to worry about.

MATT: Christian was probably the most experienced person there. He had been working indies since 1993, and had been trained in a professional wrestling school up in Toronto. He was really solid as far as mat work and technical wrestling, which impressed the hell out of me.

JEFF: Dory and Tom just wanted to see what we could do. The first day they had us bumping flat, which was easy—we could do that all day long, with our eyes closed. Then it was arm drags, hip tosses, bodyslams.

MATT: Dory would call out a chain sequence, and we would do that. He had several different drills that he would play, like "Bull in the Ring." That was where one guy would be in the middle of the ring, surrounded by all the members of the Dojo. Dory would point to somebody, and that person would have to feed in and the person in the middle would just have to do some move to them. And then as soon as the first guy started coming in, Dory would point to somebody else, so as soon as you blast one guy, somebody else is charging at you and you have to do a different move on him.

This teaches you the ability to be spontaneous, to do things on the fly and still be safe.

JEFF: Dory would put a combination of different moves together, and we would all get in the ring and perform that chain. He would come up with a different sequence each day, teaching us technical wrestling. He had some weird drills, too. There was a code word that he would call out, and whenever he called it out, everybody was supposed to start fighting, no matter where they were. If you were standing on the apron, if you were getting a drink of water, Dory would call the word out and you had to go to somebody and start fighting. It was a way to see if everybody was paying attention.

MATT: Every day Dory would go over some new highspots, or new moves. He'd say, "We're going to do Whip into the Turnbuckle today," and then critique everybody on it. Then two of us would go in and work a spot, one person would leave, and somebody else would come in and work another spot. The drills were designed to test your overall wrestling ability.

Dory was a really good guy, really soft-spoken. He genuinely wanted to help out the young guys. I really admired that because someday I hope to pass on all the knowledge I've learned over the years to somebody who's young and hungry.

JEFF: Dory would say, "Okay, Jeff, you're wrestling Kurt. Matt, you're wrestling Jay. Andrew, you're wrestling Glenn. Take five minutes, get together about your match, and then we'll do interviews."

We would do promos, have our matches, and then everybody would get together and critique them. Each day, Dory would put together different combinations so you learned how to work with different styles of both interviews and wrestling.

The best thing about the Dojo was picking up all the technical things that we'd never learned. Wrestling came very naturally to us, but there was plenty that we needed to know before being able to hold our own in WWE.

Dory and Tom put us through some difficult routines. There were so many occasions when I was certain that I would mess up. I would be so scared, thinking, *Oh Lord, it's going to get complicated!*

Every evening we would have matches that they would film. One night we were having a match, Matt and myself against Christian and Shawn Stasiak. We had been training the whole day, I'd already bumped my ass off, and I was just wiped out. I missed a Reverse 450 Splash—which is a jump from the top turnbuckle, with a complete flip and a quarter in midair—and completely knocked myself out. It's such a fast move, and I was completely drained. I opened my eyes and everybody was looking down at me. When I stood up, I was seeing colors. It totally messed my head up.

MATT: One afternoon, we had a tag match against Test and Christian. We set Test up in the middle of the ring for our finisher, the Event Omega—Jeff and I would go up on opposite turnbuckles and hit him with a leg drop and a splash at the same time—and just as we were starting to come off, he took his hands and left them out by his sides. He didn't pull them in and set them on his thighs like he was supposed to. He left his hands out by his sides. So as Jeff came off the splash, his knee went directly into Test's hand and broke his finger. It was bad, too. His finger was turned perpendicular from his hand. He ended up having to have surgery on it. They had to put a couple of pins in there.

But Test didn't leave the Dojo. He was there every day, doing drills where he didn't have to bump.

Even though one or two guys ended up being disappointments, that Dojo turned out an amazing group of wrestlers. It was obvious right from the start that Kurt was a world-class athlete, but he was completely innocent when it came to professional wrestling. I was in the ring with him one afternoon, he was in the corner, and I chopped him and he was just shocked. He looked at me like, "What was that all about?"

The thing about chops is they really really hurt. When you chop somebody, you just slap them in the chest, as hard as you can. That's all there is to it. The better contact you get, the better noise you make, and the better the chop looks. It just hurts, period.

So I think Kurt wasn't ready for real pain. He was like, "Hey, do you want to fight?" I thought he was going to take me down and stretch me.

Once we realized Kurt wasn't a big fan of chops, we all started ribbing him a little bit with chops. His chest started showing the effects—the blood started to rise up and you could see handprints on it. What's funny is that Kurt does chops all the time now and they're nothing to him. It's just one of those things about pro wrestling, and once he accepted it, it was no big deal.

I wondered what kind of character Angle would portray. I never would have guessed that he would have become such a natural heel. But he had great charisma; his promos were hilarious. His mannerisms and facials were really great. In a lot of ways, that's what made him catch on so fast, even more than his awesome physicality.

JEFF: The Dojo is such a bonding experience. In most group environments, I tend to stay off to the side. I definitely was part of the group, but I also try not to get in the way. It's my nature to keep to myself. But it's hard not to develop relationships in a situation like that. We became buddies with Christian in the Dojo. He was definitely the guy we hung out with the most.

In addition to all the things you learn there, everybody gets close, almost like you would in boot camp. That's the best way to describe it. You had to be up at a certain time, you had to go to the gym, you had to do the wrestling exercises that Dory and Tom gave you to do. It all happens very fast, and it's a very intense experience, both physically and emotionally. But when you get through it and you're a WWE Superstar, you realize that not only was it all worth it, you actually needed the experience and training in order to survive.

The first camp was ten days. We did a couple of independent shows at the end of the week. At the end, they told us they'd be in touch, either to tell us that we were going to the next Dojo, or that we were going to TV. The developmental deal was, if you weren't on TV, you were assigned to the next camp.

MATT: We were really hoping we didn't have to go through another one of those camps, not because we didn't think we had more to learn, but when you know how to take bumps, there's no use in going out and taking a thousand bumps a day. All that does is shorten your career. You only have so many bumps on your bump card, and we didn't want to take 5 percent of our bumps off doing things that weren't on TV.

They called us a couple of weeks later and said we were going to the next camp, which started at the end of September. A lot of the same people were there—Christian, Test, Albert. Tom Howard, and Barry Houston were also at the second camp.

JEFF: The first week, J.R. came down to talk to us. He said, "We think this is possibly the most talented Dojo we've ever had up here. We really expect a lot out of this group."

Of course, that's the same bullshit that your high-school football coach tells you every year: "This is the greatest football team, blah, blah, blah." Whatever! But it was pretty cool. It gave us a little light at the end of the tunnel, like maybe they did think we had a future in WWE.

JIMMY LEGS

MATT: My legs are a little crazy. Most people's hip sockets are further in, toward the center of their legs, while mine are positioned a little further out. As a result, they don't rotate in as far as everybody else's, and like whenever I squat down, instead of my legs going straight up and down, they go out to the sides.

It's just something that I was born with, and because of my funny hip sockets, I'm limited in some things I can do. For instance, I can't squat down and stay flat on my feet—I have to come up on my toes. If I stay flat-footed, then my legs spread out wide.

Sometimes when I'm taking bumps in the ring, my legs stick out in weird positions. When we were in the Dojo, Christian thought they were the funniest thing he'd ever seen. "Your legs are crazy," he'd say. "Look at them! They're all sideways! They're Jimmy Legs!"

The Jimmy Legs are excellent for my leg drop. In fact, I think the way my legs spread out makes the impact a lot easier on me.

It's cool to have unique features that nobody else has. I could be a circus freak. When I'm good and loose, I can take my Jimmy Leg and cuff myself on the head with the side of my foot.

After Christian named my Jimmy Legs, we started calling anything that was screwed up a "jimmy." For example, Christian would do that second rope jump and when he'd mess it up, I'd say, "That's a Jimmy Jump."

It was a terminology we created, and now a bunch of guys in the locker room use it all that time: "Did you and so-and-so blow that spot? Oh man, it was jimmied!" Or "That guy is jimmy!"

ONTO THE ROSTER

MATT: In addition to our training at the Dojo, they also had us working indie shows, mostly around the New England area. One Thursday night Jeff and I wrestled Test and Scott "Scotty 2 Hotty" Taylor. Scotty was already on TV, so they brought him in as a draw. Pat Paterson—the legendary WWE wrestler, former Mr. McMahon stooge, and member of the WWE talent relations department—was there that night and he raved about what a good match we had.

"These guys are a great tag team," he said about us. "Look at these flashy moves they're doing! They remind me of an updated version of the Rockers!"

The next day, Bruce Prichard pulled myself, Jeff, and Christian off to the side. He asked if we had our passports with us. Christian had his, since he had to come down from Canada, but ours were back home in Cameron.

"Well, you'd better get them," Bruce said, "because we're sending you to TV tomorrow."

JEFF: It was the *In Your House: Breakdown* Pay-Per-View, which was at the Copps Colliseum up in Hamilton, Ontario. Matt called our dad and had him get our passports to Jason. Then Jason brought them to FedEx and had them sent overnight so we could pick them up at the airport on our way to Canada.

We flew into Hamilton, got our rental car, and drove to the airport in Toronto to pick up Christian. Then we went out to his family's house, which was real cool. It was great that the three of us were together for that whole experience.

MATT: The night of the Pay-Per-View, we were on *Sunday Night Heat*, against Kaientai—Sho Funaki and Mens Teoh. We walked out during the commercial break with the referee, Mike Chioda, and there were a lot of people that knew us from doing jobs on TV: "Hey, pussies! Who's going to beat you tonight?"

Chioda was cool. "Make them eat their words, boys."

We got in the ring to this generic entrance music: "Introducing, from Cameron, North Carolina, the Hardy Boyz!"

Then Kaientai came down and the match started. Shane McMahon was doing commentary back then, and he totally put us over. "These Hardy Boyz have been around for a while," he said, "and they've got some real potential."

It was a good match, which ended with us doing the Event Omega leg-drop splash on Sho Funaki. *Wham!* 1-2-3!

We started celebrating like we had just won the $26 million lottery. "This has to be considered a major upset," Shane said.

It was so cool. We had imagined winning a match on TV for so long. And the crowd was totally surprised. They all thought we were coming to do a job as usual.

JEFF: The next day we went down to Detroit, and we taped a thing for *Shotgun Saturday Night.* Too Much defeated a couple of job guys, and after the match, they were beating them up. Jeff and I ran in and made the save. We ran Too Much out of the ring, setting up a match for the next week's *Shotgun,* which they also taped that night.

At the end of the match, we hit the Event Omega on Scotty—1-2-*No!* Brian Christopher came in and nailed the ref, knocking him out, so we won it with a DQ. Two matches, two wins—not bad for a start.

MATT: We taped the following week's *Heat* on Tuesday, and I wrestled Funaki in a singles match. Gerry Brisco was the agent.

"As a tag team, you guys are good," he told us, "and you're kind of a threat in that department. As singles, your weaknesses are exposed, so Funaki will be able to get one on you and get back his loss from the other night. But that's okay, because people are going to start to know you as a tag team."

We actually had a good little match there. I was willing to take a whole lot of bumps off my bump card every night at that time.

JEFF: From that point on, we probably lost about thirty matches straight.

AMY

MATT: In January 1999 we all went down to Union Pines to check out an NWA Mid-Atlantic show. That was the first time I laid eyes on Amy Dumas. She had a match against a girl named Strawberry Fields and it was brutal, just a complete train wreck. But it was obvious to me that this girl was trying hard—she was athletic and daring, jumping off the ropes, doing things that you didn't typically see girls do. She was also really attractive, with this strange and powerful charisma that just shined through.

Amy had been dating this guy Beau Beau, who was in a punk band called Avail, out of Richmond, Virginia. They had a very on-and-off relationship, with him going on tour all the time. The next time I saw her was a few weeks later at another NWA Mid-Atlantic show, this time in Rutherfordton, North Carolina. NWA Mid-Atlantic was a shady little operation, run by this guy Slim, who owned a bunch of strip clubs and was a part owner of this club in Charlotte, Club 2000.

Some people ended up going back there, and Amy and I hung out awhile. The next thing I knew we were sitting in my Cougar, making out. We went back to Slim's house and hung out in his Jacuzzi. We actually dared each other to get naked, but that was all we did at first.

We did end up spending the night together, and that morning she talked about how she had this boyfriend that she was getting ready to leave. "I don't typically do stuff like this," she said. She was feeling very awkward about it, but I told her it was totally cool, it was a fun night, no problem.

I gave her my number and told her to call me and I'd help her out with her wrestling career.

After that she said, "I'd love to train with you guys, if you don't mind." She was living in Richmond, Virginia, but would drive down to Cameron every weekend. We'd go over to a friend's trailer and fool around, but neither of us saw it as anything serious.

What was important was that Amy had truly fallen in love with wrestling. It was obvious that she'd finally found the thing she wanted to do with her life.

OMEGA RULEZ

MATT: We wrapped up our OMEGA career in January 1999 with a match that has come to be regarded as a true classic. In fact, one Web site called it the best indie match of the nineties, and I have to be honest—they may be right.

It was in the gym at Shane Helms's elementary school in Wendell, North Carolina—the Serial Thrillaz vs. the OMEGA Tag Team Champions, the Hardy Boyz. What made it different was that we worked as heels, while the Thrillaz—who were amazing heels—were the hometown babyfaces.

JEFF: Matt and I came to the ring and totally went for the cheap heat, talking about how we were big-time WWE Superstars: "If Vince McMahon were here, he'd be embarrassed! Now that we're making big money with WWE, we can finally get the hell out of North Carolina!"

We said we were going to make examples of these two pitiful local boys. It was great, because we had so much heat. The crowd was just enraged!

MATT: I was crazy busy that day, getting the show together, so we threw the match together right before we went out. That happened to me a lot—because I was so busy doing other things, it was my match that would suffer.

We hit the ring and Shane and I faced off. "Well, this is it," I said.

"What are we doing?" he asked. "I don't remember. Did we talk about the beginning of the match?"

We're in each other's face, jawing back and forth, acting all aggressive.

"Yeah, we talked about the beginning of the match," I said. "But you know what? I don't know what we're doing at the end. What are we doing for the finish?"

"I don't know the beginning," Shane said. "You don't know the finish. What the hell are we doing out here?"

Eventually we got our act together, and it was me and Shane in there. I nailed him, then turned around to jaw with the crowd for a little while. Shane ran at me, gave me an unbelievable Lou Thesz Press, and started beating the shit out of me. Then Jeff came in and tried to intervene, but Mike ran across and speared him. *Wham!* It was cool, because the spear wasn't a big move yet.

JEFF: The way I take the spear is a big part of what made it look so good. It doesn't always look right, but I try to really fold up when they hit me. So much of selling a spear involves the head. What you do with your head

EXIST 2 INSPIRE

87

makes everything look good. Wherever your head goes, your body follows.

MATT: That match was great because we got to do all kinds of cool heel tactics which we never get to do. At one point, we got some heat on the Thrillaz and Jeff ran over and kissed me full on the mouth. It was hilarious!

JEFF: We really did heel it up that night. At one point, I stood on Mike's back, just acting like a total asshole, and he stood up, flipping me into the air and onto my head!

MATT: Finally we did a ref bump finish. The ref got knocked cold, Jeff and I hit the Event Omega on Shane, then a new ref—our pal Aaron Decker—slid in to make the count. 1-2-*No!* Shane kicked out! My God, the place went apeshit! I swear, if we'd have won, it was going to turn into a full-blown riot.

We were so pissed! I powerbombed Aaron and grabbed hold of Shane as Jeff went for a chair.

"Don't worry! I'll get him, Matt!"

He came swinging the chair at Shane, but at the last second, Shane ducked and *Wham!* He hit me with it, knocking me silly. Then Mike came running back in and threw Jeff out of the ring, where he landed with a hellacious bump!

JEFF: I was outside, lying on my back. Shane and Mike went for their big finish, the Falling Star Bomb—Mike would get on the top turnbuckle and Shane would climb up on his shoulders and do the Shooting Star Press off of him.

They hit the bomb on Matt, who was still selling the chair shot, and like a miracle, the original ref woke up in time to make the count: 1-2-3!

The Serial Thrillaz were the new OMEGA Tag Team Champions and the crowd was pumped! Damn, that crowd was as fired up as any I've ever seen! They just about booed our asses out of the building.

MATT: I'm so damn proud of OMEGA. It was really something extraordinary. Looking back, it's incredible how similar to ECW our shows were, especially considering that we really had no idea what we were doing! If I knew then what I know now, OMEGA could've definitely developed the same kind of cult following the ECW had.

JEFF: The impact of OMEGA never ceases to amaze me. The circulation of OMEGA tapes is a true phenomenon. All over the world people come up to me and want to talk about OMEGA. Considering that we were just this small indie promotion in North Carolina, that makes me so proud, like we were doing something truly special.

MATT: To this day, we still see the occasional OMEGA RULES sign out in the crowd. One of the coolest signs I ever saw said, WWE FEARS OMEGA. Damn right!

WELCOME TO WORLD WRESTLING ENTERTAINMENT

MATT: There's a tradition in the wrestling business of pulling practical jokes—also known as "ribs"—on new guys. Even though we had been around the locker room for a few years, once we became full-fledged WWE Superstars, we knew it was just a matter of time before we got ribbed.

JEFF: Undertaker was, and is, the locker-room leader, due to his experience and the amount of respect he's earned over the years. The Acolytes are his enforcers, in charge of breaking in the new wrestlers, making sure no one gets out of line. If somebody is screwing up, or if the boys aren't really sure if they're going to fit in, Bradshaw's the one who keeps a watchful eye on them.

MATT: Our first rib came after a house show in Greensboro. We were getting ready to drive home and Bradshaw came over to us. "You guys don't live too far from here, right?"

"No," I said, "it's just like an hour away."

"All right, then," Bradshaw said. "I'm going to give you boys a little assignment. I want you to buy two six-packs of beer. On the drive home, I want you to drink them then throw the bottles at road signs."

"Okay," I said, even though I was pretty sure we weren't going to do it. The next day we were in Charlotte. Bradshaw pulled me aside and said, "Hizardy. Your mission was fairly simple. Were you successful?"

"What's that?"

"Did you get the beers and throw them at road signs?"

"No, man, we didn't," I said. "We don't drink."

JEFF: All we had to do was lie.

MATT: We should have lied. It would have been a lot easier. Bradshaw was pissed off in the worst way. For the next few weeks, we'd say hello to him and he'd just say, "Go to hell."

JEFF: We'd go to shake his hand and he would look at us, not extending his hand. "Go to hell."

MATT: About a month later, we were in San Antonio. We got dressed in the locker room with a few of the other guys and then we went to do a little meet-and-greet with some contest winners. When we got back to the locker room, everybody's bags were gone except ours. Right away I knew we were in trouble. Bradshaw must have come in and said, "All you guys get out. Just leave the Hardy Boyz in there all by themselves."

Our match was next, so we went to the ring and wrestled, and when we came back, our bags had disappeared. Our clothes, our money, our credit cards, everything. The room was completely empty. Then Bradshaw came walking in and said, "What's wrong, guys?"

"Well, our bags seem to have disappeared," I said. "Somebody must have taken them."

"That's terrible," Bradshaw said with a completely straight face. "Maybe if you two guys weren't such prima donnas and dressed in the dressing room with the rest of us, the other wrestlers would probably watch your bags and make sure nobody messed with your stuff."

JEFF: We were cool about it. Because once a rib begins, you have to go with it. We walked out of there and Road Dogg came over to us. "I don't want to get any heat with them," he whispered, "but your bags are out in the Dumpster. Don't say I told you, okay?"

So we went outside and our things were sitting on top of the Dumpster. They were actually cool about it. Our bags were zipped up, so nothing had fallen out. They could've really screwed with us and dumped all our stuff in the trash.

As time went on, we started to win Bradshaw over. We were in New Haven, and he came to us and said, "Hizardys. I got a little something for you to do. You guys know the Monkey Boy, right?"

That's what everybody called one of the wrestlers. He's not in WWE anymore.

"As you know, not too many people are too fond of him," Bradshaw said, "so if you pull off this mission, I would imagine you would probably be accepted into the ranks. And Taker would be very very proud of you. What I'd like you two guys to do is just scan this whole building and find out where the Monkey Boy is dressing. It's a little bit tricky because he doesn't dress in the locker room with the other guys."

MATT: Jeff and I started snooping around the building, checking out the closets and these little workrooms. We checked every nook and cranny of the building, but we couldn't find him anywhere. Then we looked out in the parking lot and saw him putting his bags in the trunk of his car. It was an SUV, like a Blazer or something.

JEFF: The Monkey Boy was so despised in the locker room, he had been forced to change in his car.

MATT: We went back in and found Bradshaw and Faarooq and told them, "He's not dressing in the building, he's dressing in his car."

Bradshaw almost came out of his gimmick for a second when I told him. "See, Faarooq, I told you that sumbitch . . ." he said, then got back into character. "Good job, Hizardy. Very good work. Now let me think about your next assignment. Give me a second to get back to you."

JEFF: So we were sitting in catering when Bradshaw came in. X-Pac was there and he said, "Hey John, tell them to do the old toothpick rib."

Bradshaw came over to us and gave me a box of toothpicks. "Let's just suppose you happened to take some of those toothpicks out of the box and let's just suppose maybe you went over to the Monkey Boy's rental car," he said. "Then let's suppose you happened to take those toothpicks and stuck them in the keyholes and they just happened to break off. He would probably have a pretty hard time getting into his car, don't you think? If that were to happen, I'm sure Taker would be a very happy man."

"Consider it done," Matt said.

"Make sure to only do it to the four doors," Bradshaw said as we started getting up. "Don't do it to the trunk. I want him to have to crawl through the car to get to the driver's seat."

We went back out to the parking lot. I was the lookout, just like when we were kids putting nails into Shirley's tires.

MATT: As usual, I did the dirty work. I felt bad about doing it, but at the same time I wanted to get us out of hot water. I went and did what I had to do. Then we got out of there before the Monkey Boy discovered what had happened. It worked, too. After that, we were totally cool with Bradshaw and Taker. We were officially accepted as part of the locker room.

SHOTGUN SUPERSTARS

JEFF: We lost match after match, mostly on *Shotgun Saturday Night* and *Sunday Night Heat*. But in a way we became the kings of *Shotgun*, which is a dubious achievement, but it's a stepping-stone in every WWE Superstar's career. If they're lucky.

The agents kept telling us, "You guys are doing great. Hang in there and we'll find something for you."

MATT: The New Age Outlaws and Owen Hart and Jeff Jarrett were the dominant tag teams at the time. We worked a match with Owen and Jeff on *Heat,* and afterward, Owen said, "I love working with you guys."

They actually suggested that we wrestle them on *Raw* and score a fluke win for the titles. I thought that was so cool of them. They were just looking for new guys to work with. But it was not to be. They were told, "Well, we're not really ready to do that with those guys just yet."

JEFF: Owen Hart was the best worker I've ever been in the ring with. I'm so glad I got the chance to wrestle him. He was so smooth! The first time I wrestled him was just a little job match, but he gave me so many spots. It was back in December 1995. The match ended with Yokozuna—who was Owen's tag partner at the time—doing the Banzai Drop on me! It was awesome.

When we would drive up to do jobs, everybody always wanted to wrestle Owen. He was so cool with the job guys. Owen would give us the opportunity to show what we could do.

I was real torn up when Owen died. Matt and I have met a lot of people in this business, some good, some bad. Owen was one of the best—he was a sweet, funny dude who treated people right. We both still miss him to this day.

MATT: In February, Ed Ferrara—who was head writer Vince Russo's assistant in the WWE Creative Department—came to us and said, "Okay, we have an idea for you guys. We want you to try and pledge your way into D-Generation X, like you're trying to pledge your way into a fraternity. When you go to the ring, give the DX symbol, and the commentator will talk about how you're trying to impress DX."

JEFF: Every time we came out, we'd get on the top turnbuckles and throw the crossed-arm DX sign. For six weeks or so, we kept doing it. There was even an article in the *WWE Magazine,* saying how we were influenced by people like Shawn Michaels, who started DX: "Will the Hardyz end up in DX or will it be the worst mistake of their careers?" But nothing ever happened. Somewhere along the line, whatever plans they had for us and DX were shut down.

THOSE '70S BOYZ

MATT: Being WWE Superstars has given us a number of opportunities to do cool extracurricular activities. In January 1999, we were asked if we'd like to make a guest appearance on *That '70s Show.* Well, yeah!

JEFF: We got the gig because they didn't want to risk using someone important, just in case anybody got hurt. Plus they knew we would go in there and bump.

The Rock played his own dad on the episode—he even wore an afro wig so that he'd look like Rocky Johnson. He wrestled Ken Shamrock, while Jeff and I were just background players. If you want to get technical about it, I played "Wrestler #2" and Matt was "Wrestler #3."

MATT: We were in the background in the locker room, and then we have a little match during the scene that takes place in the arena. We did a handful of moves, which they shot three or four times to get them from all the different angles. In the finished episode, they cut to us in the ring for about five seconds of thrilling wrestling action!

We both had seventies-rock-star hairdos, short in the front and long in the back. Jeff's hair was brown, all big and bushy and pulled back on the sides. There were two outfits—one was a singlet and the other one was briefs. The costume person said, "You guys have a choice between these two," and I grabbed the singlet as quick as I could!

JEFF: We didn't have any dialogue, but we hung out some with the cast. They were all really cool. I think we were all pretty much the same age, so it was easy to talk to them.

ENTER MICHAEL HAYES

JEFF: A couple of weeks after the DX bit faded away, we were told they had a new idea for us. Michael "P.S." Hayes was our agent in the back. A wrestling legend from the eighties, Michael was part of the Freebirds, one of the greatest tag teams of all time.

One day Michael came to us and said, "This is what they're going to do now. I'm going to be doing an interview with the Brood, and they're going to give me the Blood Bath. Next week, when they come to the ring, the lights are going to go dark, and they're going to be covered in blood. Then, when the lights come back on, you're going to be up on the ramp with me. We're going to form a group, like a new Freebirds."

And that's exactly what happened.

MATT: Being paired with Michael helped us a lot. He taught us so much about tag-team wrestling. But at the same time, he was a total old-timer and we were the epitome of the new school.

The typical old-school mentality was, you would work your match, go out and party all night, sleep two or three hours, wake up, train your ass off, drive four hundred miles, and do it all over again. I don't know how anybody could do that. I would be dead if I lived that lifestyle. But that way of life changed when the business became more mainstream and they demanded more professional behavior in the younger wrestlers.

JEFF: The three of us became a team, both on TV and off. Michael said, "Since we're going to be together, we travel together."

"Yes, sir," we said. Because when you're with someone's that ahead of you in the pecking order, you do what they say. It's a time-honored tradition.

MATT: I was the night driver, because I'm programmed to stay up until three or four o'clock in the morning, then sleep until noon. That's just the way I am. Michael would drive during the day. And Jeff slept in the back. Day *and* night.

JEFF: Michael's gimmick was classic old school. We'd leave the building and all Michael wanted to do was get something to drink for the road trip. Matt and I would sit down and eat something, and Michael was just appalled with that.

"I don't understand this sitting-down-and-eating shit," he would say. "You get a little food to go, then drive to the next town and drink!"

MATT: We would stop at some restaurant, and Michael would ask, "Is there a bar there?"

"No," I'd say.

"Then we can't stop there. There's an Applebees across the street. We can go there as long as they have a bar."

Every night we would go somewhere to eat, and as long as there was Jägermeister available, he was cool. We would order food and Michael would drink. He'd order something and let it just sit there while he drank.

And every night, he would

bum a cigarette off somebody. That was his gimmick: "Hey buddy. Let me get a cigarette."

When we were through eating, Michael would get his food put in a box. He'd order a fifteen-dollar meal and never eat it.

JEFF: There were times when traveling with Michael was totally aggravating, but there were other times when we had a blast. It was great for us to have that kind of exposure to a veteran.

BECOMING

JEFF: When we first joined up with Michael, that's when Vince started talking to us. He'd see us in the back and say, "You guys are doing great. Keep up with the hard work."

MATT: The time we spent with Michael as our manager was an important step in our evolution. From our wrestling gear to our in-ring work, a number of the elements that make up our gimmick began to come together.

JEFF: One great thing about it was that we were told to go out and get some new outfits. I had already been wearing the Kikwear pants in real life and we decided to give them a try. Once we started wearing them, people began referring to them as "Hardy Boy pants."

MATT: When we first put on the Kikwear pants and T-shirts, I hated it. It felt wrong, because we were so used to wearing tights.

Vince also said he wanted us to always wear bright colors. That was something I wasn't very thrilled about. I'm definitely more of a dark guy; I prefer black shirts and black pants to just about anything else. But Michael said, "Well, hello, he's the boss! And whatever the boss says, we've got to do."

JEFF: In addition to our gear, we began putting together all of the daredevil moves that really helped to define our characters.

MATT: Our original finishing maneuver was the Event Omega, which in reality was a terrible finisher because you can't go into it quickly and that takes away all the drama of a false finish or a surprise finish out of nowhere.

The Dudley Boyz' 3D is probably the best-ever tag-team finishing move, because it can be hit in an instant. All the best finishers are like that—the Stone Cold Stunner, Sweet Chin Music, the Twist of Fate.

JEFF: My Swanton Bomb was inspired by the Japanese wrestler, the Great Sasuke. I was so impressed with the gracefulness of his Senton Somersault. I'd wonder, *What makes it look so pretty?* I started watching the tapes in slo-mo and I saw how he would arch his back and hold his head up as he jumped off the top. I started practicing it on the trampoline and that's where it came from.

I remember when I told Kevin Kelly about changing the name from Senton to Swanton. "I just want to put a little twist on it," I told him.

"I don't know," he said. "That sounds kind of weak."

Now everybody calls it the Swanton. The word has fully entered into wrestling terminology.

MATT: I created the Twist of Fate in a brainstorming session with Michael. We were trying to come up with a finisher for me to use and Michael suggested that I do something similar to Diamond Dallas Page's Diamond Cutter. Basically, I hook a guy in a left-arm front face lock, throw the guns—"Ahhhhhhh!"—then swing my right arm underneath his chin, connecting with my left arm. Then I jump out, effectively putting his head in a vise and pulling him down with me. The idea being that I take him down, choking him as I drive his face into the mat, thus knocking him out of his mind and into oblivion.

We were trying to come up with a name for it and Michael suggested I should call it the JLT—Just Like That. Because it's the kind of move that I can do in an instant, before the other guy knows what hit him.

As it started getting more and more of a reaction, I decided it needed a name that better reflected my character. *Let's see,* I said to myself. *I'm a big believer in destiny, that what goes around comes around. It's kind of a twisting move. Hey! How about the "Twist of Fate"?*

JEFF: It pumps me up how people catch on to a move. Like when Matt does the Twist of Fate, and the whole crowd yells *"Ahhhhhh!"* That's so cool.

MATT: My other big move is the Side Effect, which is similar to a Reverse Bulldog. I hook underneath their chin and around the back of their head, and as I lean forward, I jump back, driving them back and up. Then as we come down, I drive the back of their head into the mat. Both the Side Effect and the Twist of Fate are centered around my opponent's neck, which is my whole basic in-ring strategy. It's very old school, but I always try to make my matches revolve around my doing damage to the other guy's neck.

JEFF: The Poetry in Motion is a classic double-team move. We get our opponent into a corner, then Matt will drop down on all fours and be a base for me. I run and jump off his back into a sidekick that catches the other guy around his chest, throat, and face. *Wham!*

MATT: Michael Cole actually was the first person to refer to that move as "Poetry in Motion." Up until then, we just called it Kick off the Back. Which isn't as good.

When Jeff heard Michael say "Poetry in Motion" in his commentary, he got so excited—"That is so cool, man. Let's call it that!"—but again, we were told it sounded too effeminate.

"Look, it might appear that way at first," I said, "but it really connects with Jeff. He's very abstract and very poetic. Trust me, it's perfect."

They went for it, and just like the Swanton Bomb, that move is now universally known as Poetry in Motion.

JEFF: It's funny, but the names of our moves trip people up for some reason. When Tazz first started doing color, he couldn't get our moves right. "Oh my God," he'd say, "Matt Hardy just hit Edge with the Twist of *Faith!*"

One thing is certain, though—everybody admires our creativity. To this day, the boys will come up to us and say, "Can you name our finisher?" That means we're doing something right.

CHAMPIONS!

MATT: We were backstage at a TV taping and Michael said, "Matt, Jeff, I need to talk to you guys."

He was looking around to see if anybody was there, so we walked into the arena and pulled up a couple of ringside seats.

"This is what we've got going on," he said. "We're going to go to *King of the Ring,* and that night you're going to wrestle the Brood on *Heat.* The Acolytes are going to do a run in and beat you all up. Then the four of you will get a Number One Contenders Match on the Pay-Per-View."

We were psyched! That would be our first Pay-Per-View match!

"Hold on a second," Michael said. "There's more. You guys are going to go over, and then either Monday night or Tuesday night, you're going win the tag-team titles."

It was unbelievable. I felt just like when they told us they wanted to sign us to a deal. It felt like the Fourth of July—I was exploding inside. I wanted to jump up and down and scream and yell. But I was totally professional. "Okay, that sounds cool."

"Don't say anything to anybody," Michael said, "because nobody else knows right now."

Oh well, I thought. *It's never going to happen.* They're going to tell Bradshaw and Faarooq and they're totally going to ixnay it.

"After that, we'll work with the Acolytes and from there, who knows," Michael said.

That meant they would appease the Acolytes by telling them they were going to win the titles back during the next Pay-Per-View. But still! We were going to win the belts!

JEFF: We were so nervous that night. The Pay-Per-View was in Greensboro, which is pretty close to home, and that always adds a little excitement for us.

First we had a short little match with Edge and Christian on the live *Sunday Night Heat* broadcast that preceded *King of the Ring*. That went to a no-contest when the Acolytes interfered, setting up a Number One Contenders Match on the actual Pay-Per-View.

MATT: Right before we went out, they chopped our match down to just a few minutes—we had been scheduled for twelve minutes, but they cut it to six. That kind of sucked, because we had been working on the road against the Brood, and we'd been stealing every house show. Every night we were the opening match and we were just on fire. We were having awesome matches, because we were all good friends. We all had such a similar style and we all trusted one another.

When we got out there, we had to go home real quick, but the match went really well. We didn't get to do a version of the house-show matches that we'd been doing, but still, everybody was very happy with it.

JEFF: On Monday, we did TV in Charlotte, and we did an in-ring interview for *Shotgun*. Michael did the majority of the talking as usual, but Matt and I got to say a few things. "When we came to WWE, we were green and we knew it," I said, "and no one would give us an opportunity but Michael Hayes."

It was the first time we did an in-ring promo. They gave us both a couple of paragraphs and we tried our hardest to memorize it, but it didn't go so well.

Oh well, I thought, *I'm sure they hated how that came off. Now we're not going to win the titles.*

MATT: The next night we were taping the following week's TV in Fayetteville, which is about as close as it gets to our hometown. First we had a match against Kane and X-Pac that would air on *Heat* the night before *Raw*. They beat us, then the Acolytes came down to jump us, but Kane ended up giving Bradshaw a Tombstone Piledriver on the steel stairs. That set him up to sell an injury for our title match on *Raw*.

So far, so good, I thought as the *Raw* taping started. *They haven't changed the finish. Hopefully neither of us will get crippled in this match and it will really happen.*

The Acolytes were very professional, but you could also tell they weren't thrilled about having to put us over. They were one of the main tag teams on the scene, they were two big badasses, and we were these skinny little rookies. But it went down really smooth—everything that we said we were going do in the back, we did in the ring. When I go back and watch it now, I think it's actually a pretty good match.

JEFF: Before the match, Matt and I were talking about who was going to do what. One of us was going to hit Bradshaw with Michael's cane and the other one would do the DDT and pinfall. I said, "I know how much this means to you, man. You can pin him."

MATT: We started out the match with a little back and forth. Michael and Faarooq started going at it at on the apron, then Jeff hit Bradshaw over the head with the cane. I quickly hit the Tornado DDT on Bradshaw—1-2-3!

I didn't truly believe it was going to happen until I was holding the belt in my hand. The crowd were genuinely surprised when we won it. It was such a tremendous feeling to win the belts in Fayetteville. That's where I saw my first-ever wrestling match! To go there and win the WWE Tag Team Championships, that was a dream I'd had since I was a kid. For it to become reality was overwhelming.

JEFF: Winning the WWE Tag Team Championships was one of the best experiences of my life. After we won, I actually wore the belt wherever I went. I went into restaurants with it on. I took it to Myrtle Beach and wore it all over the place.

Now the belt—any belt—doesn't mean as much to me. Hell, sometimes I forget to take it to the airport. It kind of sickens me how much people get into wanting one belt or another. I want my character to be the kind of guy who doesn't care about that sort of thing. I want him to be about entertainment, and making people happy.

BETH

JEFF: I met my girlfriend, Beth, just after we won the Tag Team Championships. It was at Dockside, this club in Southern Pines where we used to hang out. The guys that ran the club had told us that if we ever won the belts they were going to put up a big banner: CONGRATULATIONS TO THE HARDY BOYZ—THE WWE TAG TEAM CHAMPIONS.

We went down there, and sure enough, there was the banner. It was so exciting, feeling like a big hero in my hometown club.

I'd seen Beth there a few times, but I never really got up the nerve to talk to her. So we were hanging out, dancing, and Beth came over to me, just to say congratulations. We danced a little bit, and I was really attracted to her. The next day, Matt and I had plans to go to Myrtle Beach with a few friends and I asked her to come with us. That kind of freaked her out. "I just met you," she said.

She didn't go to the beach, but we exchanged numbers. I called her that Monday after we got back from the beach. It was so strange, but I just knew she was the girl for me. I couldn't explain it, but there was an incredibly strong connection between us, right from the start. I wanted to see her so bad, but she was going to UNC at the time, and would come home every other weekend.

We talked on the phone night after night, and eventually she came down and we got to spend time together. Neither of us had our own house, so we used to hang out at Johnny Yow's place. It was such a great time in my life. Things were going great in my wrestling career and I'd met this amazing fun girl.

It's a pretty intense relationship. We have some serious arguments, but we really love each other a lot. There are things about me that make her crazy. I'm not the kind of guy who remembers things like anniversaries, and that totally freaks her out. But that's just the way I am.

We'll probably get married one day, but that's not that big of a deal to me. Our relationship is what's important to me. She probably has a fantasy of a big traditional wedding, but she also knows that that's something I want nothing to do with.

It's hard to describe, but Beth reminds me of my mother, even though they're completely, totally different. She doesn't take care of me—hell, she aggravates me. But she also makes me so crazy happy. It's like she fills a void in me.

WRESTLER'S COURT

JEFF: The day after we won the belts on *Raw*, we had a house show up in White Plains, New York. After the show, we drove to the airport and Michael was still real excited about us having the tag-team titles.

MATT: Michael thought we deserved to upgrade to first class. There were two free seats and one standby seat. Everybody that should have been sitting in first class was up there, except for Kane. We took our seats, but we knew it wasn't such a good idea. I said, "Michael, man, we shouldn't sit here."

"Sit down," he said. "You're the champs. You should celebrate."

"Look man, really, we'll sit in the back."

"Relax," Michael said. "The guys are cool. They don't mind you sitting up here."

Just as the plane gets ready to take off, we see D'Lo Brown come running on board, followed by Kane. Turns out he had been holding D'Lo's ticket and had been waiting for him at security. The standby seat we had taken was his. Kane looked at us sitting there, and said, "What's going on? I don't have a first-class seat now. Well, at least the Hardy Boyz do."

I started getting up. "Hey man, take the seat."

"No, it's cool," Kane said. "You stay there. You're already situated."

"Seriously, man. Take my seat."

Then Jeff got up. "Really, man, you could have my seat."

JEFF: I would have tackled somebody just to get back to coach. I knew we were in trouble.

MATT: They were getting ready for takeoff as this was going on and the flight attendant started getting pissed. "Gentlemen, you've got to take your seats." So Kane, who's a super-nice guy, went back to coach and we flew first class.

We got to the next house show and Bradshaw told us, "You guys have been sentenced to Wrestler's Court. Your trial is set for next week at *Raw*."

Wrestler's Court is exactly what is sounds like. All the wrestlers gather in the locker room, and they hold a mock trial. Taker is the judge and Bradshaw is the prosecuting attorney. It's pretty scary, because once you get up there on the stand, everybody's against you.

JEFF: Before we went into court, Taker grabbed me and said, "I know Michael put you in those seats, and I know you guys didn't want to sit there. Don't worry, we'll let you off easy. But we're going to make Michael's life miserable."

MATT: We went in there and Taker called the court into order. He explained the charges, and then Bradshaw got up. "Gentleman of the WWE, here we have the Hardy Boyz, who have only been wrestling in WWE for less than a year.

"Then, my friends, we have Kane, a former WWE Champion who, out of the kindness of his heart, was waiting for his friend D'Lo Brown. He happened to have D'Lo's ticket and was going to stand there and give it to him, even if it meant sacrificing his first-class seat.

"It seems the Hardyz believe that being our current Tag Team Champions entitles them to sit in first class, no matter whose seat they occupy. I guess if it had been Undertaker and he'd been waiting to give a ticket to his friend, they would have taken his seat. Or maybe even Stone Cold Steve Austin, our current WWE Champion.

"Or, my friends, it could be each and every one of your seats . . ."

JEFF: Then he called Kane to the stand. "I knew it was an important show in White Plains, but D'Lo Brown is a great friend and a great human being and I didn't mind waiting for him," he said. "But I would have thought that after I went through the trouble of waiting for D'Lo and getting on the plane late, the Hardy Boyz would have at least given me my seat. Worse, when I came on the plane, they wouldn't move. In fact, they laughed at me. I didn't mind, though, because the most important thing to me was that D'Lo Brown got on that plane and that we made the show in White Plains, and that it was a success, and that WWE is doing good business."

"Thank you, Mr. Kane," said Bradshaw. He called a couple of other people up and finally Bradshaw really laid it on Michael.

"It's my belief that the Hardy Boyz are relatively innocent in this affair and the person that should truly take responsibility is"—Bradshaw stuck out his finger and pointed to—"Michael Hayes."

MATT: It's all very real. Taker's sitting there with a gavel, taking notes. We could have had somebody represent us, but that's more trouble than it's worth. Once you get called to court, there's no winning. Whenever we tried to say anything, Bradshaw would say, "You're lying. I could hold you in contempt of court, son."

In the end, Undertaker said, "We'll let you two off easy, but we're going to have some fun with Michael."

The final verdict was that Michael had to carry Kane's bags for the whole week. All we had to do was buy Kane dinner.

JEFF: I think the way to deal with court is to just go with the flow. If you do go in there, there's usually a good reason for it. You know you've screwed up somehow when you're in there, and you need to make sure to correct it. Because if there's a second and third strike, it's going to be bad. It's a way for a problem to be dealt with in a way that lets the boys be boys, and still have a few laughs.

MATT: In the wrestling business, it's just as important to get along with the locker room as it is with the office. If you don't get along with the boys, they'll drive you out of there.

FULLY LOADED

DATE: July 25, 1999
LOCATION: Buffalo, New York
ARENA: Marine Midland Arena

JEFF: We did a promo in the back with Michael Hayes, and they asked him, "What's it feel like to have your boys become Tag Team Champions?"

"Don't ask me," he said. "Ask them."

Vince watched us doing the interview and he kept telling us to relax. "Be natural," he said. "Just be natural."

MATT: We were supposed to be heels, but the only team we had any heel heat against was Edge & Christian, because they were starting to get over. With everybody else, we got babyface pops. Even though we tried to act like heels against the Acolytes, we came off as babyfaces because they wouldn't really sell for us.

JEFF: After we won the titles, we worked house shows with the Acolytes, and they beat the living daylights out of us every night. It was like torture. Let me tell you, after a couple of weeks of that, I was ready to give the belts back.

It's already in the record books, I thought. *You can have them back now. We'll just wait until you guys retire and go after them again.*

MATT: It wasn't that they didn't like us. They were simply proving a point. The Acolytes were cool with us, and they did business the whole while, but it was clear that they didn't want two smaller guys like us beating them on a regular basis. We'd occasionally squeak out a win or a DQ at

the house shows, but we would always get the shit beaten out of us. After a couple of weeks of that, I was more than ready to drop the belts and move on. But during the course of that month, we definitely earned the Acolytes' respect and even started to become friends.

JEFF: The fact that we were getting some serious push and didn't act like we were getting big heads is when we became officially down with everybody in the locker room.

MATT: The plan for *Fully Loaded* was a handicap match for the titles—the Acolytes vs. us and Michael Hayes. The week before the Pay-Per-View, Michael had a singles match on *Shotgun* against Tracy Smothers, just to show that he could still go in the ring.

The plan was that Michael would score the pinfall, then we would run in and beat Tracy down a bit. I was supposed to hit him with the Twist of Fate, then Jeff would do a Swanton on him through a table. Then the Acolytes would come down and run us off.

The match ended and we came running down and started beating on Tracy. As soon as we started pulling out the table, we got nailed from behind. It was the Acolytes! They started beating the shit out of us, then *they* set up the table and powerbombed Jeff through it.

When we got in the back, they said, "Sorry. Bruce Prichard sent us down early." I don't know for sure, but to this day I think that was a rib on us.

On one hand, it continued our feud, but I've always thought that if it had gone down as it was planned, we might have gotten the table gimmick before the Dudley Boyz ever came to WWE.

JEFF: When the *Fully Loaded* handicap match was booked, Bradshaw told us, "You boys don't have anything to worry about. Just make to tag in Michael when we tell you to." I guess they had some heat with Michael from back in the day, and this was their chance for payback.

It turned out to be a decent match. I took a crazy bump where I got tossed outside and landed on my head!

When Michael got in there, Bradshaw was definitely stiffing him. He snapmared him over and kicked him in the back, and Michael just looked at me like, "Please help me!" The Acolytes' attitude was "How do you like that, you old SOB?"

In the end, we got thrown to the outside and the Acolytes hit Michael with a double powerbomb for the pin. And that was the end of our first WWE title reign.

"WHEN THE HARDYZ TURN ON MICHAEL HAYES, THEY WILL KILL HIM"

JEFF: We were in Philadelphia and they came to us with a prototype of our first T-shirt. It was awesome—it said 2 EXTREME on the front, and had these little tribal gimmicks on the back with our name.

Michael Hayes sneaked up behind us and said, "What is that?"

"It's our first shirt, man," I said. "Isn't it cool?"

He looked at it a second and said, "Wait a minute—where the fuck's my name?!"

"I don't know," Matt said. "Maybe you should take it up with the merchandising people."

"Well, I think I will. We're a team, aren't we?"

MATT: Bradshaw saw how Michael was acting with us and said to me, "Oh brother, I feel sorry for you guys."

He used to go around the back, saying, "When the Hardyz turn on Michael Hayes, they will kill him." He would say it all the time. It was hilarious. He was right, too: when the time came for us to turn on him, we roughed him up pretty good.

JEFF: We were doing TV in Chicago. Matt and I were sleeping in our hotel room and we heard somebody knocking on our door, yelling, "Get up! Get up! Get up!"

It must've been 7:30 in the morning, and Michael came in, all out of breath, a cup of coffee in his hand: "They're going to split us up!"

MATT: Part of me was thrilled, but a little part of me was worried that we were going to take a couple of steps back. For Michael, he knew that no matter what happened, it wasn't good for his career. "We've got to take a stand," he said. "We've got to tell Vince that we really need to be together."

I just looked at him and said, "Sorry, man, but we're not really in a position to say anything. You're the one that taught us that what the boss says goes."

JEFF: It was sad, because Michael's old Freebird partner, Buddy Roberts, was coming to the show that night, and he was so excited. Then he finds out that this was the night we were going to turn on him.

That night at the arena, Michael was pacing back and forth in front of Vince's office. You can always tell, like, if somebody's got a problem when you see them hovering around Vince's door. Finally, he talked to Vince and Vince wouldn't change his mind.

MATT: Later that night, Vince came over to Jeff and me. "We've done all we can do with you and Michael," he said. "In order for the Hardy Boyz to grow and move on, we've got to take him away from you."

JEFF: The Brood had already broken up. Edge & Christian were turning babyface, and that night in Chicago there was a match between Gangrel and Christian. Matt and I ran down and distracted Christian, then Gangrel spit the blood in his face and pinned him, 1-2-3. Then the three of us started beating the shit out of Christian. Edge came running down, and we start beating on him.

Michael ran in as we're all kicking Edge, and started pulling us off, like, "What are you guys doing?!"

"What do you mean, what are we doing?! We're beating their asses!"

"Well, that's enough," Michael said. "Come on, we're leaving."

Michael turned his back and *wham!* Matt and I jumped him. I gave him a Twist of Fate, and just about ripped his head off. I didn't mean to give

it to him that way, but I caught him funny and it was pretty rough. Then I did a Swanton on him, and Gangrel came over and we all started putting the boots on Michael.

When the three of us finally left the ring, we walked separate from Gangrel so that our relationship remained a question. And that's how we became the awesome and revolutionary New Brood.

MATT: The following Sunday night we did a backstage interview on *Heat*.

"Is this how you pay back Michael Hayes for bringing you to the top?" Terry Taylor asked us. "First Gangrel broke up with Edge & Christian, and now the Hardy Boyz have split up with Michael Hayes. What does all this mean?"

"This isn't about Michael Hayes," Jeff said. "This is about us getting stronger."

I pulled the mike over to me. "We're hungry," I said. "We have a thirst that cannot be quenched."

Then Gangrel said, in his most sinister voice, "This is the New Brood."

THE NEW BROOD

MATT: There's no doubt that Michael Hayes had been a huge factor in our moving up the WWE ladder. He had been doing tag-team matches for a long time, he was incredibly fluent in the way tag matches were supposed to go, and his involvement in our work really helped bring us to the next level.

When we first split up, I was a little worried. There was a little bit of doubt in my mind, like our matches wouldn't be quite as good if he wasn't helping us put them together. I thought, *We've learned so much in the couple of months we've been with Michael. I hope we can still carry this off.*

JEFF: The best part of being the New Brood was coming up in the elevator through the ring of fire—that was awesome.

MATT: Just after we began the New Brood gimmick, I went up to Russo and said, "Since we're demonic now, don't you think we need to wear black?"

"You're right," he said. "Don't wear that bright stuff anymore."

I was like, "Yes!"

JEFF: We began going for a goth look. I started painting my fingernails, trying to make myself look different. We had already been wearing the stockings on our arms, which is a gimmick that I stole from Trent Reznor. I saw that and thought, *Damn, that looks cool.* When we became the New Brood, I started cutting holes in them and they looked even cooler. Matt asked me to cut his because he thought it looked great.

"Come on, man," I said. "You don't want me to do the Twist of Fate. This is something I want to keep for myself."

Besides, it's hard enough for me to get myself ready every night.

MATT: The Hardyz Finger Symbol—the Guns—was born during our New Brood phase. We went through so many gimmicks. Gangrel would get on the top of the steps, we would get underneath and bow our heads in prayer, and he would spit his blood. We were trying to do things along the spiritual/satanic lines. One time, I did a leg drop and did the praying hands afterward. When I got to the back, Undertaker came over to me and said, "That thing you just did? Don't ever do that again."

It was like stepping into his territory. I guess he had the religious angle all tied up.

THE HARDY BOYZ

110

NO MERCY

DATE: *October 17, 1999*
LOCATION: *Cleveland, Ohio*
ARENA: *Gund Arena*

MATT: *Summerslam* was a Tag Team Turmoil, with the winners getting a Number One Contendership. The first two teams were us and Edge & Christian, and they gave us ten minutes, more time than any of the other teams in the tournament.

We had a kick-ass match, with Edge & Christian going over on us. They ended up getting a title shot against the New Age Outlaws at *Unforgiven*, where we came down and screwed them, keeping our feud alive for one more go-around at *No Mercy*.

JEFF: Edge, Christian, Matt, and I all came up with the idea of doing a ladder match at the next Pay-Per-View. The four of us were obviously all big Shawn Michaels fans, and one day we were talking about his classic ladder matches and then one of us—I can't remember who it was, because it was everybody's idea really—said, "Hey, what if we do a ladder match?"

MATT: We presented the idea to Vince and Russo and they were into it. Then they came up with the Best-of-Five Tournament. We were like, "Yeah!" We were all fully confident we could do something special. Our initial thought was to do a different gimmick match each time, but they felt that that was a bit much.

JEFF: Then Russo came to us with the idea of the Terri Invitational Tournament—whoever wins the best of-five will get $100,000 and Terri as their manager. That really bummed us out. We were ready to strike out on our own. The whole thing with Gangrel was kind of awkward, because he wasn't exactly our manager, and the three of us seemed to be not much more than a cookie-cutter version of the first Brood.

MATT: The original plan for the Terri Invitational Tournament was for us to go down to the final match at *No Mercy*—the ladder match—and Edge & Christian would win and Terri was going to become their manager. Then they were supposed to do a bit where they went to the bank to deposit the $100,000 but got attacked by the Mean Street Posse, who had been with Terri in the weeks before that. That would set up a program between Edge & Christian and the Mean Street Posse.

JEFF: We were even after the first four matches of the tournament and got to *No Mercy* thinking Edge & Christian were going to win. But that day Vince called us all together and said, "The Hardyz are going to get the win. They need it more than Edge & Christian."

Edge was real disappointed when he found out they weren't going to win that day—I think he knew the match was going to be a big deal.

MATT: Giving us the win was a good decision, because we definitely needed it. Edge & Christian were already over as babyfaces, and we knew that a ladder match was a perfect chance to truly make us. Of course, as it turned out, the match made everybody.

JEFF: Matt and I had done ladder matches over the years, but Edge & Christian had never been near a ladder. I don't think they'd ever even climbed a ladder to paint a house.

The Friday before the Pay-Per-View we went up to Stamford to work some stuff out. But Edge got trapped by a blizzard and couldn't get there. So it was largely just Matt, Christian, and myself putting it all together.

The day of the match, we all gathered together one last time to discuss the match, and Edge contributed some important ideas. We also needed to tweak a few things, especially since we were now going to win.

MATT: A lot of guys told us to be careful that night. Steve Austin came over to us and said, "Hey Hardyz, you guys be careful out there tonight."

"We'll be as careful as we can be," I said.

"I know what you mean," Steve replied.

JEFF: Shane McMahon said, "Remember the two S's: Safe and Spectacular." Well, I don't know if you could say it was safe, but it was definitely spectacular.

MATT: People don't realize just how unstable those ladders are. When you're up on top, the ring is moving underneath you, and it feels pretty damn shaky.

JEFF: The top of the ladder is a lot higher than you think when you look at it from the mat. When you get up there and add the actual eight feet of ladder with the height of your body, you look down and realize, *Wow, that's a long ways down.*

I love the camera shot from above the ladder, because it shows just how far and how long it is until you hit the canvas.

MATT: At one point in the match, Edge & Christian wanted to do the stackplex—Christian would go on Edge's shoulders and give one of us a

superplex off the top—which was a finishing move I used to do in OMEGA when I was tag-teaming with Venom as V Force. They had seen it on a video and asked me if it was cool that they used it.

JEFF: The stackplex set up the seesaw spot I had come up with. Two ladders were laid out in the corner—one was folded, sitting on top of another open one. I was up on the top rope; Christian got on Edge's shoulders to try to hit me with the stackplex, but Matt came across and blasted Christian. As they were punching each other over the ladder, I jumped off and landed ass first on the ladder, sending it seesawing into their faces. It was one of those spots that should have been impossible to pull off, but it went down perfectly.

MATT: I still can't believe that Jeff didn't break his tailbone doing that. When you look back at the whole match, man, so many things went right when so many things could have gone wrong.

JEFF: Nothing really went wrong. One of the funniest moments was when Edge & Christian were jamming me with the ladder, and Christian was saying, "We've got to get another ladder. This one's broke."

"It's okay," I said. "I can fix it."

And I did, too! If you watch the match carefully, you can see me bending the hinge back into shape.

MATT: We did a good job of taking a number of very well-planned calculated risks that looked completely spontaneous. J.R. and Jerry "the King" Lawler really did an amazing job selling the fact that were doing spots that no one had ever seen before.

"Have you ever?" Lawler exclaimed at one point during the match.

"I have never!" J.R. replied.

JEFF: The crowd was a huge part of the match's success. The first really big pop was when Christian rammed a ladder into my ribs, pinning me in the corner. Then he ran up the ladder and dropkicked me in the face.

It wasn't like a high-pitched *Wooooooo!* It wasn't a low *Ooooooooh!* It was very respectful, like, *Wow, yeah! That's amazing!* Those amazed pops kept getting bigger and bigger as the match went on. By the last few minutes, the whole arena was standing there, twenty thousand people clapping and shouting their appreciation.

By the end of the match, there was no way around it—we were babyfaces. We tried wrestling as heels, but the people were cheering for everything.

MATT: By the finish, we were all sort of disoriented. The four of us climbed up the two ladders, then Edge pie-faced me off into the ropes. I hit the ladder that Christian and Jeff were fighting on, and as it fell over, Jeff stepped over onto the ladder where I had been fighting with Edge.

JEFF: The day of the match when they told us we were going to win, Matt said, "I want you to get the moneybag because you let me get the pinfall when we won the tag-team titles."

After I stepped onto the other ladder, I shoved Edge off and went for the sack of money. But it wouldn't come loose! I decided to sacrifice my body by grabbing the bag and falling to the mat. It totally knocked the wind out of me, but what better way to get the bag than just putting all my weight on it?

MATT: J.R. was so excited at the end that he called it wrong, yelling "Matt Hardy's got the money!"

Both J.R. and "the King" really put the match over. "What an amazing display," J.R. said after the finish. "What an amazing effort. This is absolutely beyond verbal description."

We got to the back and everybody was waiting for us—it was the proverbial curtain sellout. It was the first time I'd ever seen that happen, where the whole locker room was there at the monitor. Everybody was ecstatic: "Oh my God. That was amazing!" Then Edge & Christian came back—they had gone through the crowd—and we didn't even say a word to one another, we just hugged. We knew we had done something special. We held one another a good minute or two, and when we stopped, everyone just started clapping. It was tremendous.

JEFF: It's been said a million times since, but that night I remember Matt said to me, "Well, we just went from being WWE wrestlers to WWE Superstars."

MATT: The four of us were all banged up afterward. At one point in the match, Edge had hit me with a ladder and almost cut my ear off. Not only did it knock me silly, but my ear went completely numb. I remember reaching up to feel it, like, "Is it still there?"

People wonder how we can take all that punishment and not get really hurt, and the answer is, we don't. It hurts a lot!

But first and foremost, we all know how to take falls. Typically we take shorter bumps and don't have to fall as far, but this time we took bigger bumps and fell much further. The fact is, we're all going to pay for those ladder matches and TLC matches years down the road.

JEFF: We were very fortunate that nobody landed on their head or broke anything. Basically, we just beat each other up real bad. The worst thing is definitely taking the big bumps. That's what's so rough on your body.

MATT: The four of us got to the dressing room and I said, "Hey, let's drink a beer."

"Well, if there was ever a night to drink one," Edge said, "I guess this is the night."

"Hallelujah," I said.

I just felt that a beer is something people drink to celebrate, and we were going to drink one that night. It was such a magical night, and despite what my mother had taught us about drinking, I knew that if you're a good person, you're a good person. If you drink a beer, you're not a bad person. It's no big deal. There were some cold ones in the back—I think

they were Steve's—and the four of us had a toast. That was my very first beer. At the ripe old age of twenty-five. It didn't do a thing for me. I guess I just don't have a taste for the stuff.

JEFF: The day after *No Mercy*, we had *Raw* in Columbus, which is about a three-hour drive. The next morning, we were all feeling pretty beat-up, so they essentially gave us the night off.

MATT: We limped out to the ring and did a little interview with Michael Cole. "I just want to set the record straight," I said. "We're the Hardyz. We're *Matt*, we're *Jeff*, we're *the Hardyz!*"

Edge & Christian came out and for a second it looked like there might be a fight. "The best-of-five series could have gone either way," Edge said, "but last night, twenty thousand people gave the four of us a standing ovation."

"You're damn right!" someone in the crowd yelled out.

"Now, guys—I'm shooting here—we came out here tonight out of respect," Edge continued. "Guys, it was an honor."

We all shook hands and the place just erupted, with everyone getting out of their seats and giving us another standing O.

That's one of my favorite moments of my career, because that standing ovation was just as big as the one we received the night before. It was one of those things that sends chills up and down your spine.

JEFF: I don't think anybody expected another standing ovation. Everyone was shocked by that. It was very touching, to say the least. I felt it in my soul that night. Those are the kind of moments that make you appreciate all the damage that you've done to your body and all the hours you spent on the road driving, every bad bump you've ever taken and every cut you've had. It makes it all worthwhile because that's a feeling that very few people ever get to have in life.

MATT: As the crowd was applauding us, Terri came walking down the ramp arm in arm with Gangrel. "I'm glad you guys had such a great match last night," he said, "but while you were in your hotel rooms, licking your wounds, I'm the one that scored!"

We looked at Edge & Christian, looked back at Gangrel, turned to Edge & Christian, and then we all beat the hell out of him. Then Terri left with us, and they went out through the crowd. It was a weird segment, but the thinking was, "Okay, now we've got to get the Hardyz away from Gangrel, so what are we going to do?"

JEFF: After the ladder match it was obvious we were becoming babyfaces. Guys our size are so much better in a babyface role, especially at that point in our career, when we weren't fully established and the thing we were known for was our flashy and spectacular style. Unless you've developed characters for people to hate, our style of wrestling is always going to draw cheers.

SUPERSTARS

MATT: After the success of the ladder match, we had the idea to form a unit with Edge & Christian and go up against DX. The four of us were working house shows together, and we were just incredibly over. I thought we could do some serious business as a team. I even had a great name for our faction—Version 1.

The V.1 concept was that the four of us represented the future of our business. The combination of our athletic skill and our ability to entertain the crowd set a new standard for a modern wrestler.

But it was not to be. *Survivor Series* was the next month. The four of us took on the Hollys and Too Cool. And we lost. After that, we were fighting one another all over again.

But that couldn't kill the Version 1 clique. It became a backstage in-joke which grew to include all of our buds—Lita, Chris Jericho, Shane Helms. I even came up with a hand symbol, the V sign and the pinkie up, with the thumb holding down the ring finger—V.1 baby!

One thing I knew for certain—I was going to get Version 1 onto TV someday.

JEFF: The four of us were all babyfaces but we couldn't get along, like, "We're the best young team around here!"

"No, *we're* the best young team around here!"

The whole thing was basically just a setup for a return ladder match at *WrestleMania*.

MATT: In the weeks leading up to the next Pay-Per-View, *Armageddon,* we went to a little TV program with the New Age Outlaws. That was very good for us because they were the definitive tag team at that time.

JEFF: We'd have the Outlaws beat every time, but that damn X-Pac kept screwing us.

MATT: The four of us had a cage match on the Thanksgiving *SmackDown!* which is actually one of my favorite matches. There was a great spot where I was getting ready to climb out of the cage, but they were beating up Jeff, so I did a moonsault off the top of the cage onto Jeff, Road Dogg, and the referee.

Eventually Jeff pulled himself out over the cage and hit the floor, but of course, the ref was still knocked out. X-Pac ran down and put Jeff back in the cage. As I was getting ready to get out of the cage, X-Pac kicked me in the head and knocked me back in as Billy went out the other side. Screwed again!

JEFF: The following week we wrestled in a six-man match, the Hardyz and Big Show against X-Pac and the New Age Outlaws. It was the main event of *SmackDown!* which was the first time we headlined a TV show. Matt pinned X-Pac clean that time, and that was pretty much the blow-off on our little deal against DX. Getting a clean pinfall against those guys was a big deal for us, because DX was one of the hottest things in the company.

MATT: At *Armageddon,* we were in a tag-team battle royal to determine the Number One Contenders to face the Outlaws at the *Royal Rumble*. It came down to us and the Acolytes and they beat us, which was a big disappointment for me at the time. I really wanted to win the belts from the Outlaws, because that would have been a true passing of the torch. It would have really established our position as *the* top tag team.

THE HARDY BOYZ

FLYING HIGH

MATT: We were all on the red-eye, heading home from doing TV in San Francisco. Everybody was drinking a little bit so that we could maybe get some sleep on the plane. Of course once we all got our buzz on, we did the exact opposite—we started having fun. We were all in the back of the plane—me, Jeff, Edge, Christian, and Test.

Eventually things calmed down. Christian was the first one to start nodding off. Somebody pulled out a Sharpie and started drawing on his arms. Once it was clear that he'd fallen fast asleep, we got more ambitious. We drew a checkerboard on one side of his face, then we drew a People's Eyebrow on him. He just sat there snoring away. It was hilarious!

Pretty soon, the rest of us started drifting off. We were all pretty exhausted. I woke up and looked at Christian sitting next to me and burst out laughing—he looked like a Picasso! The stewardess came by our seats, took a look at Christian, and said, "Looks like you guys had a good time tonight."

"Oh, it's just a little makeup," I said. "Would you be interested in getting some?"

"No thanks," she said, grinning. "But I see that you've gotten some yourself."

Whaaat!

I sprinted into the bathroom, and sure enough, they'd drawn these big dimples on my cheeks. Plus, right there, smack in the middle of my forehead, was one word: DICKFACE.

I was hot, but it was funny. I washed it off as best I could, and when I came out of the bathroom, everybody was cracking up, including the flight attendants!

JEFF: That kind of behavior used to happen all the time, but not so much anymore. When it does, nothing's ever done to be mean. It's all in fun.

If you're cool with everybody, then people don't rib you. That's pretty much the theory. Matt and I don't mess with anybody, so nobody messes with us. Of course, there are guys who are constantly stirring up trouble, and they get it right back.

There aren't any great pranksters these days. It's sad, but the two greatest practical jokers are both gone now—Owen Hart and Davey Boy Smith. Those guys loved to play with people's heads, but in a lighthearted funny way.

MATT: I think WWE is much more of a sober working environment now. Make no mistake, we still have plenty of fun. To me, the best times are when a bunch of us get together after a show, have some food, maybe a girlie drink or two, and just hang out. The one thing that's consistent is that when we get together there's always a lot of laughter.

FAN MAIL

JEFF: After the ladder match we were definitely among the most popular WWE Superstars. All of a sudden we started getting bags and bags of fan mail, which was such a rush. It let us know that we were genuinely connecting with the people out there in TV land.

We still get upward of five hundred letters a week at our PO box in Cameron, and that doesn't even include all the fan mail that goes to WWE headquarters in Stamford.

There are die-hard Matt fans and die-hard Jeff fans. I definitely attract the darker, more goth type of fans. I've gotten letters written in blood, which is just so scary and uncool.

MATT: It's funny how a great deal of our fan mail has one sentence in common: "I'm not a psycho or anything." As in, "I'm a huge fan, I'm just writing to tell you that I love you so much, I want you to come stay with me, but *I'm not a psycho or anything.*" Now, they probably really aren't crazy stalkers, they just feel kind of awkward writing to us.

While maybe 50 percent of the letters are of the "I'm not a psycho or anything" variety, the rest are from people saying that we've inspired them in some way, that our words and actions have motivated them to follow their dreams just like we have. I find that so flattering and very moving.

JEFF: I love it when people write to me and say, "You have inspired me. Your words have motivated me. I feel like a better person because of your influence." That makes me very proud and happy.

MATT: We also receive a lot of mail asking us to donate money—they're trying to redo the interior of their church, they've got this animal shelter, things like that. There are also letters saying "My child is sick, can you come see him?"

Those letters definitely pull at my heartstrings, but I'm only one person. My schedule is already out of control. I'm on the road five days a week, which doesn't give me enough personal time as it is.

JEFF: Matt and I are also among the most requested celebrities from the Make-A-Wish Foundation. When we visit with sick kids, it's always very emotional for me. You see those kids' faces light up and you know that you've done something to ease their pain, even if it's only for a short while. Meeting us makes them feel special, and to be honest, it makes us feel special to be able to affect someone's life in that way.

MATT: It's pretty amazing what kinds of gifts people will send. The best thing I ever got from a fan was a DVD player, which is now sitting in my living room. What's funny is that the day that I got it, I had just gone out and bought one. Usually when fans send gifts, they include a return address, and I'll send back a little letter or a signed photo to say thank you. But the DVD player just came with a brief note which said, "I appreciate everything you do to entertain me."

That was it. No name, no return address. It was very strange, but very cool. There was somebody out there who just wanted to show how much they liked my work and didn't want anything in return.

The day it arrived, I came home and said, "This is incredible! Another DVD player!" I took the one I'd just bought and gave it to Amy. "Here you go, I bought you a present!"

But then I told her the truth. I'm like George Washington—I cannot tell a lie.

JEFF: There's one girl who sends me cookies every week—we've never eaten them, obviously. We get lots of paintings and pictures, lots of clothes.

We've also had bras and panties sent to us in the mail. It's not something I would want to encourage people to send to me, but it's pretty flattering. It's so completely sexual, that these girls want to share their undergarments with you.

MATT: I used to fantasize about walking down the street and everybody knowing me from TV. It pisses me off when guys get so aggravated with it, because we all wished for it. Sure, there are times where it gets a little ridiculous. People can be strangely inappropriate, asking to shake your hand when you're standing at a urinal or sitting down to eat in a restaurant.

When a fan comes up to me as I'm sitting there eating my dinner, I think about when I was a little kid and what I'd have done if I'd seen Ultimate Warrior or "Macho Man" sitting in a restaurant. I would have gone over and said, "Can I shake your hand? Can I get your autograph?" I'd have been so excited to see someone that I looked up to and idolized so much. It's such a freak chance that it overtakes your common sense and you go do it.

But there are lot of wrestlers that get offended and upset when people come over and talk to them while they're eating. I just say, "Hey, nice to meet you. If you want to socialize, can you just wait till I get through eating?" I always try to be kind because I understand that they're feeling overwhelmed, because I've been there.

It's all part of the gig. I don't mind signing autographs for people. I'm sure that if it stopped happening, and nobody ever recognized me anymore, I'd miss it.

JEFF: What's important is that we don't see ourselves as being anything special. We're just regular people who go to work and do our job. It just so happens that we have the coolest jobs in the world, and people can see us doing it on TV.

ROYAL RUMBLE

DATE: *January 23, 2000*
LOCATION: *New York, New York*
ARENA: *Madison Square Garden*

JEFF: Even though he had stopped managing us on TV, Michael Hayes was still a very big part of our career, serving as our agent in the back. Two weeks before *Royal Rumble*, Michael came to us and asked, "Is there any kind of gimmick match we can do with you and the Dudley Boyz?"

"Maybe we can do something with tables," Matt suggested. "The rule could be that you have to put both members of the opposing team through a table to win the match. It would be the first-ever WWE Tag Team Table Match."

"That sounds pretty cool," Michael said. "Let me talk to Vince about it." Well, needless to say, Vince loved the idea. He loves doing anything that's never been done before.

MATT: The Dudleyz had come into WWE just before *No Mercy*. We had heat with them right from the start due to something that had happened early in our WWE career.

We had been starting to get wins on *Shotgun* when Michael Hayes came to us with an idea for a new finishing move. "You guys double-shoot the other guy in, and as he comes back, Jeff picks him up on his shoulder and you hook him with the JLT and drop with him."

"Um, it's kind of like the 3D move the Dudleyz do," I said.

"Who the hell are the Dudleyz?"

"They're an ECW tag team."

"I've never heard of them. Just try it tonight, because I think Vince will think highly of it."

Michael was our coach, so we agreed to do it. Turns out one of the ECW crew was watching *Shotgun* that night and saw it. He immediately called Bubba: "Hey man, the Hardy Boyz just did the 3D on WWE TV!"

Well, this was back when Amy was working up at ECW. All those guys knew that she and I were kind of seeing each other—our official terminology was "We hang out once in a while."

At the next ECW show, Bubba grabbed Amy. He pulled her aside and said, "You date Matt Hardy, right?"

"Well, I'm friends with him," Amy said.

"You just tell Matt Hardy that next time I see him, he's dead," Bubba said.

So when the Dudleyz came into WWE, they were totally planning to kick our asses. But apparently someone told D-Von, "Don't mess with the Hardyz, they're Undertaker's boys."

Which was weird, because while we were definitely cool with Taker, we weren't his boys by any stretch. When we finally met the Dudleyz, Bubba and D-Von came up to us and said, "Hey guys, nice to meet you."

JEFF: The first time I met Bubba Ray Dudley was just after I had seen their last ECW promo, where they talked about how they were the best tag team in the world and that they were going to tear shit up in WWE. It was hilarious and powerful at the same time. I knew we would be able to do great business together.

MATT: When they came to WWE, the Dudleyz were immediately put in a program with the Acolytes. There was a bit where they were supposed to jump the Acolytes and hit them with two-by-fours. Faarooq looked at Bubba and said, "You do know how to work that thing, don't you?"

"Uh, yeah," Bubba said.

"Well, I hope you know what you're doing," Faarooq said, "or you're going to be in serious trouble."

That was the Dudleyz' welcome into WWE. These were two guys who had been doing all kinds of violent shit in ECW, and now there were real limitations on what they could do.

JEFF: Vince gave us the go-ahead to have a table match with the Dudleyz, and Bubba and I got together to discuss it. He was totally into it, because he'd been wanting to start working tables into their gimmick.

MATT: The week before the Pay-Per-View, we did *Raw* in New Haven. I had a singles match against Bubba, which ended up with Bubba superbombing me through a table—with Jeff on it!

JEFF: *SmackDown!* was in Providence, Rhode Island. Matt got a DQ against D-Von in a singles match after Bubba interfered. We fought up the ramp and brawled for a bit on the stage. Just as Bubba was set to power-bomb Matt off the stage through some tables that were set up on top of all this electrical equipment—cables and wires and such—I made the save. I smashed Bubba over the head with a chair and he bumped backward off the stage through the table. It was awesome—a good ten-foot drop!

Then I hit D-Von and he rolled down the ramp. I ran down, set him up on another table, then Matt did the "*Ahhhhhhhhhh!*" and leg-dropped off the stage, putting D-Von through the table. It was great—they were both real good pieces of business, and an excellent setup for our match at the *Royal Rumble*.

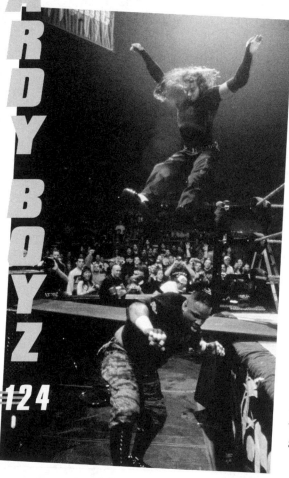

MATT: The *Royal Rumble* is always one of the bigger Pay-Per-Views, and the fact that this one was being held at Madison Square Garden made it even more special. Now, some of the guys really love wrestling in Madison Square Garden. It is the Mecca of our sport, after all. I remember before we were wrestling professionally, we thought it'd be so cool to wrestle in Madison Square Garden, because that means you're somebody. But after you've worked there a few times, you realize that it's more trouble than it's worth.

JEFF: A lot of the boys don't like working the Garden because they hate dealing with the troubles of New York City. You can't find a hotel room, it's hard to get around, and it costs forty dollars just to park. And that's across the street from the arena, because there's nowhere to

park inside the building! Guys like The Rock get dropped off inside, but most of the wrestlers just walk in the door on Eighth Avenue. They've got an underground entrance you can use, but most times you just have to run across the street. We sign a few things, take a few pictures, but it really is kind of a headache.

MATT: We started the match by immediately pulling out a table. The first person to be eliminated was Bubba—we did the Event Omega on him, with Jeff coming off the top turnbuckle and me coming off a ladder. That's pretty rough, all that weight coming down on you, then the table breaking and you're smashing onto the floor. Bubba was actually knocked cold for a few seconds.

JEFF: The tables we use aren't gimmicked in any way, because they don't need to be. Put any kind of weight on them and those things just snap. I would much rather take a superbomb through a table than straight onto the ground, because it actually breaks part of your fall.

MATT: We went back in and started working on D-Von. I propped up one table from the barricade to the apron, then I hit D-Von with a chair to set him up on there. D-Von got on the table and I blasted him again. *Wham!*

I went for a leg drop, but D-Von moved out of the way and I crashed and burned through the table. But the rule for that match was that if you try and put somebody through a table and they move, you're not eliminated. You have to go through on an offensive maneuver. That was the only table match where they stuck to that rule—from there on in, they kept it simple and said if you go through the table, you're eliminated.

JEFF: Eventually I got D-Von on another table and tried to put him though with a Swanton Bomb, but he moved again and I crashed and burned. Bubba came back out and they started going to work on us. They pulled Matt into the ring, brought both the steel stairs in there, put a table on them, and superbombed him through the whole deal.

MATT: It was real crazy, because the stairs were set up so that the steps were turned inward, so there was a very small margin of error between them. I had no idea, but my body landed perfectly in between them. That was one of those times where we were very lucky somebody didn't die.

JEFF: Matt was lying in the ring selling, and the Dudleyz grabbed me and we started brawling. Bubba and I fought up through the crowd, very ECW-ish, all the way to the balcony. D-Von was down below us, setting up a couple of tables.

Bubba was getting ready to hit me with a powerbomb, but I managed to get out of it and nailed him with a nut shot. I followed that with a vicious blast to the head with a chair, sending Bubba flying off the balcony into two tables that D-Von had stacked up on top of each other.

By this time, Matt had recuperated, so he came up behind D-Von and whaled on him with a chair, then set him up on another table down below where I had been fighting with Bubba. I pulled my shirt off, gave the guns, and *wham!* I hit the Swanton Bomb off the balcony and put D-Von through the table, giving us the win!

MATT: Jeff's Swanton off the balcony was very cool, a definite part of any Hardy Boyz highlight reel. That was the craziest thing Vince would give us permission to do, though.

The one thing Vince specifically wanted out of that match—besides nobody getting hurt—was for Jeff and me to get in the ring in the end and raise up our hands. Jeff was dead-selling after flying off the balcony, and I'm going, "C'mon! We've got to get in the ring!" I knew our time had run out, and when you're not the main-event guys, you stick to your time. Jeff was still dragging, so I shoved him over the barricade and he fell backward on his head on the floor outside the ring. Then I picked him up and threw him in the ring. I got in there and held up his hand, with his arm around me.

JEFF: There were a lot of opportunities for that match to be a complete disaster, but it turned out great, even though we hardly sold anything at all. Basically we just broke tables right and left. It was a very non-WWE-style match—it was more like ECW in terms of the logic.

MATT: The Tag Team Table Match was an instant classic, to the extent that highlights from it were featured during the Super Bowl on *Halftime Heat*. They interviewed all four of us and showed different clips from the match.

I definitely think the fact that we won bothered the Dudleyz. They felt like they should have gone over because the table gimmick was theirs. Plus, it was in the Garden, which is a big deal for Bubba, because he's from New York.

JEFF: The next night, *Raw* was in Philadelphia and we got a title shot against the Outlaws, who had retained against the Acolytes at the *Rumble*. Matt and I were selling that we were injured from the night before—Matt's ribs were all taped up—but the McMahon-Helmsley Era was in control and they said that we had to wrestle the Outlaws that night or we wouldn't get another shot.

We did a pretape where we were in the back and everybody was congratulating us on our great match. The Dudleyz walked in and got in our faces, and for a second, it looked like we were going to go at it. But instead Bubba said, "Where we come from, we know what it's like to be hardcore and you guys are definitely hardcore."

We shook hands and they pulled us tight and told us that they had our backs. "And remember," Bubba said, "if you guys win the titles tonight, we get first shot."

MATT: Later, as we wrestled the Outlaws, the Dudleyz came down to ringside and set up a table. Then they sat down on it and watched the match. We ended up getting screwed when the Dudleyz came in and 3Ded both of us. But rather than putting us through the table, they put Terri through it. That was the start of their whole putting-women-through-tables gimmick.

THE BLIZZARD OF THE MILLENNIUM

DATE: *January 25, 2000*
LOCATION: *Baltimore, Maryland*

JEFF: We were supposed to tape *SmackDown!* in Baltimore the next night, but as we were doing *Raw*, a massive snowstorm—some called it the Blizzard of the Millennium—swept over the entire East Coast, and they had to reschedule the Tuesday show for Wednesday night.

MATT: After the *SmackDown!* taping, the entire Version 1 posse got together in our room at the Baltimore Microtel out by BWI Airport. It was me, Jeff, Amy, and Joey Abs, plus Joey Matthews and Christian York, who had come to check out the show. None of us were too happy about being stuck on the road because of the snowstorm, so we decided to make the best of it. We went down to the local liquor store and got a few bottles of the Version 1 wine of choice—white zinfandel, a.k.a. "the White Z."

Edge, Christian, and Chris Jericho were staying at the Marriott across the street, but they dropped by for the party. They'd apparently been in their hotel bar before they came up, so we were all pleasantly wasted.

Things got a little rambunctious as the night went on. We were spearing one another and wrestling around in the hall and room, when Christian opened the window to let some cool air in. We were all talking about how beautiful the snow looked from our second-story room. Jeff was being his usual weird self, wondering about what it would be like to jump out the window.

JEFF: Edge looked at me and said, "Will you jump out the window if I do it?"

"You know I will," I replied.

"Okay," Edge said. "Watch this." That crazy bastard jumped out into the snow! We looked down and it was like when Bugs Bunny runs through a wall—all there was was a silhouette shaped like Edge in the middle of this three-foot snowdrift.

MATT: Next thing I know, there goes Jeff, flying out the window wearing only his boxer shorts.

Then Y2J took the plunge: "Woooooo!"

"Watch out below, slapnuts!" Christian yelled, then dove out.

What the hell! I jumped right behind him, dressed only in my socks and my boxers!

It was tremendous! It was twenty degrees out and there's the five of us, drunk on sweet white girlie wine, up to our waists in snow wearing only our underwear. Of course, none of us had a key, so we had to walk back into the hotel through the front door, all of us laughing and high-fiving.

JEFF: The hotel clerk looked at us like we were nuts, and rightly so! He probably just chalked it up to the fact that all wrestlers are completely crazy—which isn't that far from the truth.

OUTSIDE

MATT: Jeff has got this weird creative spark inside him that even he hasn't figured out yet. That's why he's constantly building things, making music and painting and writing on his arms. I don't think he knows what his artistic gift is yet. His gift might be for wrestling, but he's trying everything.

I was definitely responsible for getting us here, but then once we got here, Jeff is what got us noticed. He's got such a weird charisma. There are some guys that you just can't help but notice. It's a God-given talent, and it's completely natural. It's something that you can't manufacture. It's something that you can't create. It's just something you have or you don't. Some guys stand out because of their heart and drive. That's me. But Jeff, he is truly one of a kind.

In the locker room, Jeff feels like an outsider. Everybody likes him, but they know he's different. He's different from anybody I've ever met.

JEFF: Everybody—and I do mean everybody—thinks I'm weird. And that's me, man. If you ask any wrestler about me, they'll tell you, "That Jeff Hardy, he's a strange one."

The more people say that I'm "unique," the more pride I feel. J.R. and "the King" are always talking about my "individuality," and how I'm so different. It's like they think I'm from another planet.

It amazes me, and kind of freaks me out, that people in the wrestling business can be that close-minded. To me, coloring my hair or painting my nails is no big deal, but to them, it's completely mind-blowing.

I love walking into the building wearing something strange or just acting a little bit weird, just to see how everybody is going to react. Lawler has been busting on my hair for years. I've dyed it every color under the sun. It actually freaks people out when I *don't* color it and let the blond grow out.

A lot of it has to do with the environment I'm in. A lot of the wrestlers are old jocks who think poetry and pierced ears are for sissies. They don't really get alternative culture. It's funny, but wrestlers can be pretty dull. If I was in the music business, nobody would refer to me as being oddball. Bands like Green Day have been dyeing their hair different colors for years.

I am who I am. I can't help it if other people aren't as comfortable in their own skin.

INK

JEFF: My buddy Cary did all my ink work. He works out of Bill Claydon's Tattoo World in Fayetteville. He was a wrestler for a while, he did some WWE jobs. He's a great tattoo artist, and a great musician.

I got my first tattoo back in 1999. It's on my left calf, a dragon that I saw in one of Cary's books. He changed it up a little for me, making the face and the claws a little more dramatic. My plan was to eventually get it colored, but I've decided not to.

Next I got a couple of Chinese symbols on my right forearm. There are two characters—one for "Peace" and one for "Health." Both of those are things that will always be important to me, throughout my whole life.

I got the tiger done in 2000. After that I added some fire and a wave— all very elemental and powerful. The tiger's almost hidden on the inside of my arm, with the claws coming around the outside. It all flows with my muscles and I think the effect is bad as hell.

That one took an extra-long time to heal because the next night I decided to spray-paint my studio. I wore a bandage all day, but then I took it off and the fumes from the spray paint got into my skin and it got all infected. It actually caused the colors to fade, which looks pretty cool.

I've been thinking a lot about my next tattoo. I'm considering something like an octopus on my upper arm. Ultimately, I want to get my whole arm done, but, like, it just takes so much time. My main thing about tattoos is they're with you forever. I guess there's a way to take them off now, but I think you're a punk if you try.

I'm always trying to push the boundaries of my image. Once I realized that people were used to my colored hair, I wanted to come up with something new that would make me stand out. That's when I started drawing on my arms with Magic Marker. I wanted people to think it was a tattoo and that it was changing from week to week. I wanted them to *react*, like "What's going on here?"

At first I was using good old-fashioned Marks-A-Lot permanent markers, and everyone in the back looked at me like I was crazy. Crazier than usual. Bubba Ray Dudley stood there watching me like I was from another planet. "Is that a permanent marker?" he said.

"Hey man," I replied, "they just put that on the label to scare you. Besides, they mean permanent on paper, not skin."

I've actually moved on to washable Crayola markers. Not because it washes off, though—it's because there are a lot more colors to choose from!

I'm just following my artistic impulses, expressing myself through my tattoos and my fashion choices. I'm not concerned with trends or what's cool. People are so worried about what's in and what's out, but I never think about that stuff. I just wear whatever I feel.

People look at my clothes and say, "Only he could get away with that." The truth of the matter is that our wrestling gear—the Kikwear pants, the T-shirts—has been a big influence on the business. You don't see as many guys wearing spandex tights as you used to. Now most wrestlers wear some variation on street clothes. It used to be that the only time guys wore that kind of stuff was in a Street Fight, where they'd be wearing blue jeans as part of the gimmick.

It's crazy to me how people judge you for the way you're dressed or the color of your hair. It's sad that people will judge you on the basis of your appearance.

One of my favorite things is walking onto a plane and sitting in first class, looking the way I do. The looks that I get from those old business people are too funny! It's another example of how people will judge you based on your appearance. They see me and they can't figure out how I can be sitting up there with them, like I'm not respectable enough!

THE ROAD TO WRESTLEMANIA

JEFF: It had become obvious that we'd outgrown having Terri as our manager, and Bubba putting her through the table on *Raw* took her out of the picture for a while. We had a Number One Contenders Match with Edge & Christian at the next Pay-Per-View, *No Way Out,* and Terri showed up with the

Acolytes, who she had hired as protection. She caused us to lose the match, then Faarooq and Bradshaw beat the hell out of us for good measure.

MATT: We were back at the Garden for *Raw* the next night, and we did a vignette where we trashed the Acolytes' office. "We want payback for last night!" we told them.

Of course that was followed by a little match. Jeff made a sweet blind tag while doing a backflip over Bradshaw, then I got the pin after a Twist of Fate, just out of the blue—1-2-3! That was a pretty big deal, beating the Acolytes clean in the Garden, because people take that building very seriously.

JEFF: I think the working plan was to put Terri with Christian, with him turning on Edge at *WrestleMania*. But they both ixnayed that, which was probably the first time they put their foot down and said no to an angle. As it turned out, Vince fell in love with their shtick and decided to push them as heels.

The plan at that point was still us vs. Edge & Christian at *WrestleMania*. We were pushing to do a Hell in a Cell, but they wanted another ladder match. Then we were told that Vince wanted to put the Dudley Boyz in there, making it the first-ever Tag Team Title Triangle Ladder Match.

MATT: The Dudleyz had taken the titles off of the New Age Outlaws at *No Way Out,* so they were coming into *WrestleMania* as the tag champs. We were supposed to win the belts at *WrestleMania,* and Edge & Christian were going to split up. Two days before the Pay-Per-View we were told that Vince really liked Edge & Christian's promos and thought they would be great as heels. With that in mind, he decided they would win the titles at *WrestleMania*.

JEFF: Needless to say, we were a little disappointed. *WrestleMania* is such a huge moment in our business and we were psyched that we were going to come out of it as the champs.

MATT: I was a little brokenhearted about not going over at *WrestleMania,* but then Michael Hayes laid out Vince's long-term plans.

"I don't know if you guys know this," he explained, "but *SummerSlam*'s going to be in Raleigh. We want to build up to a huge match between you and Edge & Christian, and that's when we'll put the titles on you. That way it will really mean something."

"That's cool," I said. "I don't mind that at all."

ENTER LITA

MATT: Amy came up to WWE in February 2000, after a year working in Philadelphia with ECW. Of course, she wasn't Lita back then—when she worked in the indies, she was known as Angelica. Eventually she became Miss Congeniality, valet to Danny Doring and Roadkill.

Tommy Dreamer and some of the other ECW wrestlers kept telling Paul Heyman, the owner of ECW, that she was a talented athlete and that he should start to let her do more things, but he wasn't interested in females wrestling. He was more concerned with catfights and spankings and so forth.

While she was working in ECW, she was also paying her own way through Dory Funk's Funkin' Conservatory—this was after they'd severed their relationship with WWE—and was the star pupil of her class.

Dory and his wife had sent one of Amy's tapes up to Stamford, and one night Bruce Prichard and J.R. came to me with a question. "You know this Amy Dumas, right?" Bruce asked. "Is she your girlfriend?"

What! "No," I said, "but I do know her. We hang out some."

It's funny how gossip travels, all the way to top of the food chain. Vince wanted to know, "Is this one of your girlfriends? What kind of person is she?"

"She's real cool," I told him. "She's got a great attitude. In fact, she's almost got the personality of a guy, so she'd fit in here real well."

Russo had also watched Amy's tape and he hated her. "She's got nothing going on," he said. "And look at that terrible tattoo! There's nothing we can do with her."

On the other hand, Terry Taylor really liked what Amy was doing, and he pushed real hard for her to get signed. Amy became a part of the WWE just as Russo left for WCW.

When Amy first came to WWE, we weren't really a couple, we were still in hanging-out mode. It was probably being together so much that caused us to grow closer and closer. It was good because it was a gradual thing.

I really didn't want a girlfriend at that time because I was really enjoying being a WWE Superstar. It was fun to be on the road, it was fun to be free. It was a new experience and I was definitely living for the moment. But Amy was totally understanding. I told her what I was feeling and she didn't take offense at it. The punch line, of course, is that it turned out to be even more fun being on the road with her, having somebody to hang with every night.

WWE came up with the character of Lita and paired Amy with Essa Rios, a talented *lucha libre* wrestler who was pretty much relegated to the bottom of the card.

From day one, I was sure that Amy was going to break a lot of barriers, because she does things that no woman's ever done before, especially in America. I knew she would like to be idolized by the girls, but I didn't know how the guys would react to her.

There's never been a woman like her in WWE. Traditionally women in wrestling are either blonde-bimbo sexpots or scary bruisers. Amy is more like a real person, in a way that people in the audience feel like she's some-body that they could hang out with.

She is so different from the other Divas, and her physicality creates so many more options for Lita as a character. They spend hours getting made up to be sexy, but Amy is sexier than any of them, just by being herself. I think that's the reason why so many guys dig her—because she's real.

WRESTLEMANIA 2000

DATE: *April 2, 2000*
LOCATION: *Anaheim, California*
ARENA: *Arrowhead Pond*

JEFF: *WrestleMania 2000* was the first time any of us had the chance to compete at a *WrestleMania*. We were the semimain event, the second-most-advertised match on the card, right underneath the Fatal Four Way between Mankind, The Rock, Triple H, and Big Show. To be such an important part of what turned out to be one of the biggest *WrestleManias* ever was quite a feeling.

MATT: Right before we went out, we asked Bruce Prichard how much time we had. In a match like that, where there's so many intricate spots, you definitely have to have a timetable in your head. "You're slated for twenty-three minutes," he said, "but take whatever you need. Just get it done."

We came down to the ring and walked in under the ladder, which some would think was asking for bad luck, right off the bat. Superstition doesn't do too much for me. I think if you're going to have bad luck, it's not going to be because of a silly urban legend, it's going to be because you do something stupid. I'll walk under a ladder backward, forward, sideways, and on my hands.

JEFF: Having three teams made for a very different dynamic from the original ladder match, so we had to take another approach. We needed to make sure to tie people up so that they would be out of the picture for a little while, like with a big bomb or something that they could sell.

MATT: There were so many "holy shit!" spots during that match—Jeff running the rail and Bubba throwing the ladder right into his face, Bubba powerbombing me off the Spanish announcers' table through a table, and

of course, Jeff's insane Swanton off the twenty-foot ladder, putting Bubba through a table.

After all six of us fell off the three ladders, the plan was for everybody to stay down until the crowd came up big and started applauding. We all bumped down—D-Von's lying over on one side of the ring, Edge's lying there, I'm somewhere on the apron. We're all lying there and the crowd's starting to applaud, you could feel them starting to come, and all of a sudden we hear *boom, boom, boom, boom.* It was Bubba walking up the stairs! We're like, "What are you doing?!"

"Forget it," he said. "I'm not selling anymore. I'm getting up."
It was hilarious!

We had a hard time coming up with a finish. We had a few ideas, like handcuffing one of us on the ladder, but Vince shot that down because he thought it was too dangerous, that somebody was going to break their arm.

In the end we went with the spot where the Dudleyz set up the table on top of the ladders like a scaffold.

JEFF: The Dudleyz had everybody destroyed. They decided to set up a table on top of two ladders, making a platform that they could walk out onto and grab the belts. Unfortunately, they've got this fetish about putting people through tables, and they didn't go for the belts when they had the shot.

MATT: Christian and I raced up both sides of the ladder to get to the platform. What I didn't realize was that Edge had sneaked up behind me—the timing was just perfect. As soon as I put my fingers on the belt to grab it, he shoved me in the ass, I flipped onto a table, and it just disintegrated under me!

One thing about that bump—I didn't hit flat, but it didn't hurt at all. It was probably adrenaline, because those ladders were eight feet tall. I was worried about my aim, because the table was a long ways away, but I hit it right on the money.

It was such a huge bomb, I should have been selling dead. But that platform was really unstable, especially with Edge & Christian standing on it. If that thing had fallen, I could've been seriously hurt, so I just jumped out of the ring.

JEFF: We ended up going twenty-seven minutes. When we got to the back it was just like after the first ladder match—we got a standing ovation from everyone. There was a very cool moment—it actually turned up on our video, and I didn't even know they shot it—where all six of us were hugging.

HARDCORE!

DATE: April 24, 2000
LOCATION: Raleigh, North Carolina
ARENA: Raleigh Entertainment & Sports Arena

MATT: A couple of weeks after *WrestleMania*, we were in Raleigh for *Raw* and we had a tag match against the Hollys. "The Hollys are going to beat you," Michael Hayes told us, "but then one of you is going to win the hardcore title off of Crash. It doesn't make a difference which of you it is—it's up to you guys."

So Jeff and I flipped a coin, and I won. It was cool, because that was the first singles title for either one of us.

JEFF: It went down after our match with Hollys. They beat us, then as Bob Holly was going up the ramp, we remembered that the 24–7 rule was in effect. A Hardcore Championship match was on! Tazz and Perry Saturn came running out, and as everybody brawled, I gave Crash a Swanton. But Matt beat me to the cover—1-2-3!

MATT: The next night in Charlotte, Jeff and I had a hardcore title match against each other. It was short but sweet—we were beating on each other and a bunch of guys tried to interfere—Tazz, Saturn, Bob Holly. In the end, Crash got the pinfall on me and he ran off with the belt. That set up a six-man hardcore title match at *Backlash,* which Crash ultimately won.

JEFF: I dig working hardcore matches. We used to watch ECW late at night on the Sunshine Network. It used to be on at two or three in the morning, so it was hard for me to stay awake, because that was back when I was landscaping.

ECW was definitely exciting and innovative, especially considering what was going on in the mainstream at that point. I really loved seeing all the *luchadors,* like Psicosis and Rey Mysterio. I thought their whole look and wrestling style was so exciting.

I know that there are plenty of people that hate Paul Heyman's guts, but there's no getting around the fact that he loves wrestling with all his heart. He wants to put on the most entertaining show imaginable.

MATT: I thought ECW was good, but it was so over-the-top. I tuned in to see what was going on, but for me, WWE had such a larger-than-life quality that was very attractive.

Of course, Vince eventually took the best parts of ECW and integrated them into the strongest parts of his machine and came out with a truly awesome product—WWE Attitude.

Hardcore wrestling has its place, but it's just like anything else. You do anything in excess and it stops being interesting. Some of the stuff is just so outrageous. It stops meaning anything after you do so much of that nonsense.

That said, when it's done right, it's great. Like the Street Fight between Triple H and Cactus Jack at the *2000 Royal Rumble*—that was awesome. What made it work was that they only used a couple of gimmicks—the barbed-wire bat and the thumbtacks—and they were both used in the context of the match. It's when you use too many gimmicks, then you don't get those defining memorable moments that make a match a classic.

Hardcore does enable you to come up with new and original concepts, which is so hard to do now. The more tools you have to play with, the more creative you can be. But it has to be positioned in the right place and at the right time.

JEFF: People think that all the stuff in a hardcore match is gimmicked, but believe me, it isn't!

A garbage can is soft aluminum, you get hit over the head and it bends in and gives. A stop sign is heavier but still pretty lightweight. The worst is definitely chairs. They're solid steel and they hurt you. They're so heavy and so thick.

The fact is, things hurt. That's the way it is. This is wrestling and you get hurt. You just have to know that coming in. In some way, we all have some kind of love for real physicality or we wouldn't do it. This isn't ballet. You get hit and you get hit hard.

THE KINGS

JEFF: It was around that time that we appeared in the first-ever WWE music video. It was for a Run-DMC track that was on the *WWE Aggression* CD, which featured all kinds of cool hip-hop artists, like Method Man, Snoop Dogg, and Ice-T, doing rap versions of various wrestlers' entrance themes.

The Run-DMC song was called "The Kings," and it was a version of the D-Generation X theme. All the DX guys were in the video—Triple H, X-Pac, Road Dogg, Mr. Ass, and of course, Stephanie McMahon-Helmsley.

MATT: We filmed at this old building in this run-down area in Brooklyn. The director came to us and said, "We want to shoot you up on that balcony, dancing to the track, and then you jump off."

"Are you joking?" I said.

It was probably a twelve-foot drop, onto one of those air pillows that stuntmen use. "No way are we jumping onto that little thing."

They came back to us a few minutes later and showed us another stunt gimmick, which was about as thick as a mattress.

"This is the biggest thing we've got," the director said. "Can you guys do something?"

It was another one of those times where we were backed into a corner. "We'll give it a try," I said, thinking, *Man, this is going to hurt.*

I did an elbow drop and Jeff did a Swanton. We shot it twice, and as I predicted, we were both real beat-up afterward.

JEFF: Everybody thinks I love to jump off ladders, just like people like to wake up in the morning and have breakfast. After you've jumped off ladders so many times in the ring, people expect you to do it like it's no big deal. It's really been a battle for us to get away from that, to try to create a different image, where people still think we're cool, but at the same time, where we can stop killing ourselves.

MATT: The first year we were in WWE, we were going full bore every night, on TV and on house shows. We were working with Too Much and we would do dives off the top turnbuckle, we would do leg drops, Swantons, and the Event Omega. There were days when I could barely walk. *Oh my God,* I'd think. *I have no idea how these guys do this, night in and night out.* Then I realized that they don't do all the crazy stuff that we do.

I woke up one morning and I couldn't straighten out my arm. My ankle was killing me, and one of my knees was screwed up. *I'm almost crippled,* I thought, *and I've only been working in WWE for six months!*

JEFF: Because we get in the ring and do these very acrobatic moves, people think we're invincible. Well, we're flesh. We get hurt just like anybody else.

You have to learn how to turn it down. You've got to give people a good show, but you can't kill yourself. And if they complain, to hell with them. Let them kill themselves night after night and then they can sit in a wheelchair ten years later.

CRIBS

JEFF: When we started doing well, I decided it was time to move out of the house I lived in with Daddy and Matt. I was so fired up to have my own place, I went out and bought myself a double-wide modular home. I had an area of our land picked out for the longest time—it's where I had my motorcycle track when I was a kid. I always thought, *That would be a great place for a house.*

At first Daddy was against it, but he's grown to appreciate what I've done. He bought me a great Christmas gift—it was a picture of my house and the property taken from an airplane. That showed me that he understands how much I love this land.

When I first decided to set up house, Matt couldn't understand it. He was dead set on buying a house in Raleigh in order to be closer to the airport, which I thought was just ridiculous. "Dude, an hour's drive ain't shit," I said to him. "We need to stay here to look after this land in case anything happens to Daddy."

That really hit him hard. He had a huge change of mind and heart, and decided that he would build a house on the Hardy land.

The difference is, he's putting up a big mansion—he wants people to ride by his house and say, "That dude makes some money!" But I've got all these other interests—like dirt bikes and sculpture and music—and that's where I'd rather put my money.

My house is eighteen hundred square feet, which is all I need. I've never needed a big house. I think it's kind of crazy to spend a lot of money on a big house when you don't have a family. Especially when you're never home. I don't need to have a big house so that I can impress people.

If something ever happened where I couldn't wrestle anymore, I wouldn't want to have an enormous house that I'd have to pay for. I just don't need the responsibilities that come from owning a big house. I wanted something I could pay for just like that, then move on to other things. I'm much more carefree about material things. I don't need a two-hundred-dollar heated toilet seat to make me happy.

Which isn't to say my place isn't loaded with all kinds of toys and gimmicks. For instance, I just love artificial plants. Being on the road, I can't really take care of live plants, so I kind of went crazy with the artificial ones. My house is covered in them from floor to ceiling.

I've also got a collection of life-size Japanese fiberglass sculptures. They look kind of like the Bob's Big Boy guy. I've got one of Charlie Chaplin, Laurel

& Hardy, and Marilyn Monroe—which looks nothing like her. There's a Chef, a Butler, and one that's called a Bimbo Girl. I started collecting them before I bought the house. I was in an antiques shop and I thought they were the coolest things. I told them to get me as many as they could—I'm still waiting on the Blues Brothers, which are excellent.

There are also a few hundred of my Aluminummy sculptures all over the place. I began making my Aluminummies when I was little. I really wanted He-Man and the Masters of the Universe figures, but Mom and Dad couldn't afford them. I started trying to make my own using tinfoil.

As I got older, they became more extravagant and artsy, using different kinds of tubing and metals. I've made hundreds of them, of all shapes and sizes. I've made life-size Aluminummies, a ten-foot aluminum version of Willow. I got a little out of control and built a thirty-foot Aluminummy named Neroameee, from Nero, which is my middle name. It's outside, standing over my studio.

Of course, I've also got a whole mess of animals running around my place. One of my guest rooms has been taken over by Imagi, my coatimundi. It's a South American raccoon, and he's crazy!

I had to put tin on the walls just so he couldn't tear through them. It's basically his room now. He has a cage, but I rigged up a bamboo tree so that he could climb and play around. Coatimundis are very agile animals.

I've also got a boxer named Liger, after my hero, Jushin "Thunder" Liger, and a prairie dog named Witty. He is the sweetest little animal. He's got a big cage, but I love him too much to leave him in there all the time, so I let him run around the house even though he tears things up. My couch is ruined from his little claws.

I've got so many plans for this place. It's going to be very unique. I'm still trying to turn it into what I see in my head. I want to build a moat with a drawbridge, like a haunted castle.

My house is in the middle of the field where Daddy grew tobacco. Matt and I worked this land since we started walking. It's incredible, but I've been connected to this earth since I was born. I know that when I die I want to be cremated and spread over this land.

When we were little, I used to say to Matt, "Man, I'm ready to get out of this place." And I did it. I got out and had my fun, but what I found out was that this is it.

I love my place more than anything. When I go out on the road I always have to tell myself, *Dude, it's going to be over soon.* Maybe the biggest thing I've learned in my years as a wrestler is that Dorothy was right—there's no place like home.

THE BIRTH OF
TEAM EXTREME

MATT: It had become clear that the team of Lita and Essa Rios had run its course. Essa wasn't going anywhere, bless his heart. He was a very nice guy, but his English wasn't very good, and he preferred to work *lucha* style than fit in with the WWE brand of wrestling. At the same time Lita was starting to get some real pops, so WWE decided to make her the Hardy Girl.

When they at first asked us about incorporating Amy into our team, I was a little hesitant. I felt that we only really started picking up steam after we had gotten rid of Terri. By the time of *WrestleMania 2000*, we were genuinely over. We had developed a big fan base, a big part of which was girls. The guy fans hadn't turned on us just yet. That happened later, after the TLC match when they started pushing us as these sex symbols, the Backstreet Boys of WWE.

I never wanted any of that to begin with. We didn't change our stuff, it just kind of happened. There were a couple times when they asked us to keep our hair out of our faces so the women could see our pretty faces. Jeff played into it a little more than I did. I tried to keep my aggression.

It was nice that they respected us enough to ask us how we felt about it. I was cool with it, but I wanted to make sure that we were careful not to turn away the strong female audience we had built. So when they proposed the idea about Lita, I suggested that instead of making her our valet, it would be cool if she came in as a female version of a Hardy Boy.

We began building a story line to that end. I had a *SmackDown!* match against Essa, which actually led to a scenario that I got a little heat for. We were on the outside, I was going to try to hit him, and he used Lita to shield himself. As I turned around to swing at him, he shoved her toward me and I ended up hitting her. When I got to the back, Michael Hayes was hot!

"I can't believe you hit a girl on *SmackDown!*" he said.

"Nobody told me I couldn't," was my answer.

Over the next few weeks, they kept showing Lita sitting in the back, watching our matches. We were in a program with Trish Status and T&A—Test and Albert—and one night they were beating the shit out of us. Trish was down there, slapping us, and Lita ran in and tackled her. They wanted her to do something to make an impact. She had been mimicking Essa's moves, so when she asked me what she should do, I said, "You're a mimicker. You should mimic us. Can you do a leg drop?"

"I've been off the top," she said. "It's no problem."

Lita set Trish up and went to the second rope. She jumped off and landed with her ass right on Trish's face. It was crazy! Christian used to call

RIGHT: *Jeff, Dad, and Matt—*
Little League champs
BELOW: *Matt and Jeff—*
Extreme at an early age

ABOVE:
Willow the Whisp and Ignis Fatuus— aka Jynx

NEAR RIGHT:
OMEGA Mania

FAR RIGHT:
"Right now, he's mine"—Razor Ramon welcomes Jeff to the WWE— Youngstown, Ohio, May 23, 1994

THE OMEGA HEAVYWEIGHT CHAMPION IS HAUNTED BY A SINGLE DEMON...

...ONE OPPONENT WHO DOGS HIS DREAMS...

...AND TORMENTS HIS NIGHTMARES.

SURGE V S WILL O'THE WHISP

OMEGA PRO WRESTLING COMES TO WALLACE!!!
SATURDAY, APRIL 25 at 7:30 PM • NAT'L GUARD ARMORY

ABOVE: *Jeff and Matt—in the infamous Daisy tights—pledge D-Generation X, April 15, 1999*

OPPOSITE: *$100,000 Superstarz—Backstage at No Mercy, Cleveland, Ohio, October 17, 1999*

We have a thirst that cannot be quenched. —The New Brood

LEFT: *Matt and Lita celebrate Matt's European Championship victory—Denver, Colorado, April 24, 2001*

BELOW: *Matt Hardy—the longest-reigning American-born WWE European Champion—San Jose, California, May 21, 2001*

OPPOSITE: *Jeff stands high above the Squared Circle—SummerSlam, Raleigh, North Carolina, August 27, 2000*

Bubba Dudley feels the force of the Event Omega—Royal Rumble, New York, New York, January 23, 2000

LEFT: *Team Extreme in action—Louisville, Kentucky, September 5, 2000*

BELOW: *Taking out the Taker—Atlanta, Georgia, June 10, 2002*

OPPOSITE: *X-Pac prepares for the Swanton Bomb—New York, New York, June 25, 2001*

ABOVE: *"Xpand Your Imagination"—Atlanta, Georgia, June 10, 2002*

OPPOSITE: *Brother vs. Brother—Vengeance, San Diego, California, December 9, 2001*

LEFT: *Father and Sonz—The Hardyz at Home—Matt, Dad, Jeff*

BELOW: *3 On A Ski—Matt, Lita, and Jeff—Smith Mountain Lake, Virginia, June 2001*

my leg drop the "Leg-O-Drop," and that was the "Ass-O-Drop." She just murdered Trish with it!

Amy was still very green, but she did her all to try to lead Trish through matches. They worked together a lot, and they had a very good chemistry. It's so hard for two women to go out there and really entrap the audience in the same way the men do.

"Don't take this the wrong way," I said to her one time, "but I think you get much stronger reactions from the crowd when you interfere in one of our matches, as opposed to when you work in a women's match."

"Oh, I agree completely," Amy said.

That's definitely been a huge aspect of Team Extreme's success—we go out there and get them emotionally attached, then Lita comes in, does a spectacular hurricanrana or moonsault, and the crowd totally blows their load. It benefits everybody, and in the end, that's the name of the game.

FULLY LOADED

DATE: *July 23, 2000*
LOCATION: *Dallas, Texas*
ARENA: *Reunion Arena*

JEFF: From that point on, Lita was part of our group, which we dubbed Team Extreme. At first they were calling us "the Extreme Team," but I hated that. *Team Extreme* just rolled off the tongue.

MATT: Lita coming aboard was just another step in our evolution as WWE Superstars. When we first started, we were a couple of young jobbers, then with Michael Hayes, we began getting more aggressive. With Gangrel, we picked up a little bit of a goth vibe. With Terri, our softer, more compassionate side started getting exposed. Finally, with Lita, we became like a cool hangout crew, which was probably the closest to our real personalities.

JEFF: The three of us continued in a program with Trish and T&A. It was a good match, because even though Test and Albert were new to the tag-team scene, they were open-minded. They were young and willing to try new things, just like we were.

We fought one another in various combinations on *Raw* and *Smack-Down!*—ultimately setting up the first-ever Six Person Intergender Tag Team Match at *Fully Loaded.*

We were the opening match, so the crowd was already pretty into it, but when Matt tagged Lita in, man, the place just exploded! There was one truly awesome spot in that match, where we hit a three-on-two suplex on Trish and Test.

Lita was definitely the showstopper. She gave Test a hurricanrana and a cross body off the top onto Albert, but then she got cheap-shotted by Albert, setting up a vicious powerbomb from Test. That was the kind of thing that got Lita so over, mixing it up with the guys. That's what made Lita Lita. She did very well wrestling the other women, but her work with the guys made her the WWE Superstar she is today.

In the end, she went at it with Trish, hitting her with a superplex and a moonsault for the pin.

MATT: It was the first real six-person intergender match, which was a big deal at the time. That's one of ways that we've been so revolutionary, doing matches that had never been done before.

I'm a firm believer that anything goes in wrestling—whether it's a Hardcore Garbage Match or an Intergender Tag Team Match, whatever—as long as there's a strong build to it and all the pieces fit together. You should never throw shit out there just to do it. As long as there's reason behind a match, it'll have meaning for the audience. Unfortunately there have so many times when we did gimmick matches for no apparent reason.

I'm such a logical person. I love for everything to have a reason. The more meaning and the more reasons behind something, the more you get out of it in the long run.

JEFF: Matt has always worked extra hard to make our matches as innovative as possible. Sometimes it's things that have been done by three guys, but never in our kind of two-guys-and-a-girl combination, things like triple suplexes, triple DDTs, and triple clotheslines. I love when we did stuff like the two of us giving somebody a vertical suplex, then Lita does a cross body on them, cool stuff like that.

SUMMERSLAM

DATE: *August 27, 2000*
LOCATION: *Raleigh, North Carolina*
ARENA: *Raleigh Sports & Entertainment Center*

MATT: We were so excited about *SummerSlam* because we were finally going to go over and win the tag titles. The only question was how we could possibly top the Triangle Ladder Match from *WrestleMania*.

The TLC concept was the office's idea. They gathered us together and said we were going to have a TLC match. "What?" I said.

"You know—tables, ladders, and chairs."

"Tables and ladders and chairs?" Edge said. "Oh my!"

The idea was that each of those elements represented each of the three teams. The Dudleyz were known for using tables, we were famous for our ladder matches, and Edge & Christian had been whacking everybody with steel chairs—their "con-chair-tos."

JEFF: I knew we had a task on our hand trying to top the Triangle Ladder Match. We couldn't figure out what we would do for the finish. How could we possibly top the table on the two ladders?

MATT: I wanted to do a spot where Bubba and I went through four tables—two stacked on two—but Bubba refused. "I don't feel comfortable doing that," he said to me. "We're going to get killed."

"Dude, I'm telling you," I said, "we can do it!"

"But if one of us hits first, the other one's dead!"

"Well, how about if I go through two tables myself?"

"No," he said. "I'm going through the tables—that's my bump."

We did a false finish where everybody was down, and Edge & Christian were going up. Lita ran in and pushed the ladders and they both nutted themselves. As she left the ring, I started going up the ladder, which D-Von then flipped over, and I took a killer bump backward through a two-table stack.

Lita came back to check on me— "Matt, Matt, are you okay?"—and Edge speared her onto the floor. She took a good bump; her head hit the ladder that was lying there and it just about knocked her unconscious.

JEFF: We were trying to all outbump one another. Christian did the same big bump every match—the ladder gets shoved sideways and he takes a bump over the top rope to the floor. Every match. We always had to get that spot in.

MATT: It was, of course, Jeff's idea to hang down from the belt at the end, fifteen feet above the ring. We were all worried that the thing wouldn't hold.

JEFF: The production guy told me I had to hook my arm through it, that would be the only way I'd be able to hold on. "That thing is rubber," he said. "I don't know if you'll be able to hold it with your hands. It'll rip your fingers off."

"Oh, I can hold it," I said. "I'm cool with my hands."

"Are you sure?"

So I went up there and grabbed it in my hands and started swinging around, going "Hey! Look at me!"

MATT: We had the match all figured out—Bubba was going to be taken out, I was going to be taken out. Edge & Christian were down, but not completely crashed and burned. It was going to be Jeff up there holding on and Edge & Christian would pull the ladder out from under him and he would jerk down the belts.

Then Michael asked us how we'd feel if not only Jeff was hanging up there, but one of the Dudleyz was up there with him.

"I'm going to be taking that big bump," Bubba said. "How about D-Von?"

"I ain't hanging up there," D-Von said. He's totally scared of heights.

JEFF: D-Von was terrified. He said to me, "As soon as they move the ladder, start kicking, because I don't know how long I'm going to be able to hold on."

I started kicking at him, but he was freaking out: "Don't kick me! Don't kick me!"

MATT: D-Von was so scared up there, but he sucked it up and took the bump. It turned out to be a bump and a half, because he dropped down and landed flat on his back, God bless him. It was awesome.

The day before the match we were told that Edge & Christian were going over. "Vince thinks everybody knows you guys are going to win," Michael Hayes told us.

"That's not a bad thing," I said. "They want us to win. We're *supposed* to win. It's the finish to the story."

"Sorry, but Vince doesn't want to do it. You'll win the belts next month."

It was so aggravating. After all, we didn't win the belts at *WrestleMania* with the promise that we'd go over at *SummerSlam*.

JEFF: Now that we weren't winning, we had to figure out a variation on the finish. We needed a way to allow Edge & Christian to grab the belts without sacrificing the spot where D-Von and I were swinging up there.

MATT: I was lying up against the barricade. I actually adjusted myself so I could watch the finish. Edge & Christian moved that ladder, and instead of Jeff and D-Von bumping, they were both holding on. Everybody in the building was on their feet! Jeff and D-Von started kicking at each other, and when D-Von fell and took that bump, man, the crowd just exploded. Because they just knew that we were going to win it. The Hardy Boyz were bringing the belts home to North Carolina!

Then Edge & Christian slid in there, threw that ladder at Jeff, and he dropped down. Man, it just totally took the wind out of everybody's sails. Everybody started booing, not like "We hate this shit," but in a "we're very disappointed" way. They wanted us to win so bad.

JEFF: TLC I was such a breakthrough. It's probably still the best of the TLC matches, just because it was the first of its kind and it was so strong in terms of the overall psychology.

MATT: The first ladder match was more of a stunt show, very highspotty. It's still awesome—if I could go back, I wouldn't change a thing. Same thing with the first table match with the Dudleyz. We were hungry! We wanted to make the Hardy Boyz, Edge & Christian, and the Dudley Boyz into household names. And by God, we did it. I truly believe that that time will always be remembered as one of the greatest tag-team eras in the history of the business.

MATT & JEFF & EDGE & CHRISTIAN & BUBBA RAY & D-VON

MATT: We worked hundreds of matches with the Dudleyz and Edge & Christian, and as a result the six of us have become inextricably linked together. But the relationships between us are completely different. I like both Bubba and D-Von, but we don't have the same bond that I have with Edge & Christian.

JEFF: I feel really close to Edge & Christian—they're both such great guys. Matt and Christian have a lot in common—they are both completely obsessed with the business, and they've both felt stuck in their partners' shadows, though that's not mine or Edge's fault. We are always talked about as the stars of the teams, the ones that ought to move on and become big singles stars.

On the other hand, Edge and I are as close as Matt and Christian. I love that guy. He's straight-up and really sincere, a true friend. He's always been a huge supporter of my art, from my Aluminummies to my writing. He actually came up with the word *emoetry*. I know that he would have loved to make music, but I think he probably feels that it's too late to get involved in rock and roll.

People come up to me all the time and say how much they loved our matches with Edge & Christian. Knowing that you're part of history feels really good. Because those matches will never be forgotten. They're kind of unforgettable, if I do say so myself. I'd love for the four of us to reunite at some point and do the best Hell in a Cell of all time.

MATT: With Edge & Christian, we're similar in every way, shape, and form. It's a little different with Bubba Ray and D-Von. I'm not saying that as a negative thing—it's just that I see more eye to eye with Edge & Christian than with those guys.

Working with Edge & Christian was so easy, because we were all on the same wavelength. When we first started working with the Dudleyz, it took some time for the four of us to become fully comfortable with one another's styles. It also took awhile for us to speak freely among ourselves, and to

151

understand one another's viewpoints and opinions. In time, though, we developed a great working relationship with those guys.

The fact is, each of our three tag teams became a great help to the other two teams. We all made one another.

JEFF: I'm definitely a lot tighter with D-Von than I am with Bubba Ray. We have a secret handshake that we do every time we see each other, which these days is only at Pay-Per-Views. He's a sweet, good-hearted guy. There's a sincerity in his eyes that I love. Personally, I'd like to see the Dudley Boyz back together as a team. Splitting them up was totally nuts.

MATT: Simply put, if I wasn't in wrestling, I would be friends with Edge & Christian, but I'm not sure if I would be friends with Bubba and D-Von. On a business level, we get along famously—D-Von's a sweetheart, he's a very nice person. And Bubba is always full of entertaining ideas on how to make the crowd react.

But the truth of the matter is that if Edge and I weren't wrestlers and he lived down the street from me, we'd definitely be friends. If *Bubba* lived down the street from me, we probably wouldn't hang out.

"THAT'S JUST THE KIND OF MOTHERF***ER THAT I AM!"

DATE: *August 28, 2000*
LOCATION: *Greensboro, North Carolina*
ARENA: *Greensboro Coliseum*

JEFF: The night after the TLC match, *Raw* was in Greensboro. Edge & Christian came out to brag about being the tag champs. They talked about the Hardy Boyz not measuring up, and to prove their point they brought out a midget Matt and Jeff. They came out with little stepladders and Hardyz T-shirts. They threw the guns—it was pretty funny. Then they brought out a couple of midget Dudley Boyz, complete with a tiny table.

MATT: We came running out about thirty seconds into E&C's thirty-seven-second pose. It was great—I threw the little Playskool table into Christian's face from about ten feet away. Man, I murderized him! Jeff hit a

Poetry in Motion on Edge off one of the stepladders, and then we pulled two real ladders out from under the ring. We were set to hit the Event Omega on Edge, but Christian pulled him out just in the nick of time. It was a terrific segment.

After the show we all decided to grab some food. I was in the parking lot, on my cell phone, giving Christian directions, when these kids started asking me for autographs.

"Give me just a second," I said, and finished my conversation. Just as I hung up, Edge pulled up and asked where we were going. I set my phone down on my bag and gave him some quick directions.

When I turned around to give the kids their autographs, only a few of them had stuck around. I signed a couple of autographs, then I started putting my stuff into my car. *Hold on,* I thought. *Where'd my phone go?*

I looked in my bag. It wasn't in there. I looked in my car. It wasn't in there. I looked all around my car and it wasn't anywhere to be found. Fortunately I carried two phones in those days—one for business calls and one for personal use. The bad news was that the one that had gone missing was the personal phone, which had all my WWE buddies' numbers in it.

I used my business phone to call my other phone. "Hey man," a voice said, picking it up. "You dropped your phone on the ground. Then I got in the car with my buddy. We're a couple miles away, but we're driving around. We'll come bring your phone back."

I had a bad feeling about it, but I said, "Thanks a lot. I'll wait for you over here where the wrestlers park."

Ten minutes passed, so I called again. "This is Matt," I said. "Are you back over here yet?"

"Yeah, man. We're getting ready to pull in the gate right now. Give me just a second and I'll bring your phone back to you."

I waited another couple of minutes. Nothing. I called back. "Where are you? I'm in a rush tonight. I've got to get up early."

"I'm standing in the parking lot," he said. "I'm right in front of you."

"I don't see you anywhere," I said.

"I've got both my hands up in the air. And my middle fingers."

Damn! I knew it. I was screwed. I called back and said, "Look, dude. Let's make a deal. How about you bring the phone back and I'll get you tickets to tomorrow night's show in Fayetteville. You want to meet The Rock, I can hook it up. Come on back. What's your name so I can leave the tickets for you?"

Without thinking, he gave me his first and last names.

"Listen to me, you son of a bitch. I've got your name now. I've already called the police and they're going to trace the signal. The cops are going to hunt you down and then they're going to arrest you for stealing my shit."

"Nooooooooooo!" My new pal started freaking out, getting all nervous and paranoid.

"Why'd you do it? Why'd you take my phone?" I asked him.

"Because you didn't want to sign my autograph," he said. "And besides, that's just the kind of motherf***er I am."

"All right," I said. "It's on you, man. I gave you a chance and you blew it. Good luck with the cops."

I hung up on him, then called the phone company and canceled the phone. It turns out that between our little back and forth, a bunch of wrestlers got some strange calls. He called Christian, Edge, and Bubba, saying random things like "Where's the food at?"

UNFORGIVEN

DATE: *September 24, 2000*
LOCATION: *Philadelphia, Pennsylvania*
ARENA: *First Union Center*

MATT: Since we got screwed out of the titles at *SummerSlam,* we had to drag out our feud with E&C for another month. As disappointed and angry as I was about not winning the titles as we were promised, I've got to admit it worked out okay—the *Unforgiven* cage match turned out to be one of my all-time favorites. The psychology was strong, plus it had a few spectacular spots.

JEFF: I got knocked out of the cage early in the match. I had made it to the top, but Edge crotched me and I went sailing onto the floor. That left Matt inside, all by himself, and Edge & Christian really beat the hell out of him.

MATT: They were double-teaming me, but I managed to make it to the top of the cage. I was ready to climb down when Edge & Christian superplexed me down onto the mat. I landed right on my lower back, so every bump I took after that just *killed* me.

155

JEFF: Meanwhile, I was stuck outside the cage! It was so frustrating, but I was doing everything I could to stay involved—when Christian climbed out, I threw a ladder right at his head.

MATT: That match was the first time I had gigged in my WWE career. Vince has always been smart as far as his use of blade jobs. He's always avoided overdoing it, except when it really forwards a story, like when Steve Austin juiced during his *WrestleMania* match with Bret Hart—the image of Austin bleeding in the Sharpshooter definitely helped create the Stone Cold image.

One time that blading is absolutely appropriate is in a cage match. If the premise is that the steel cage is a brutal weapon, then it's only logical that someone would get cut in there. Since we were following a classic match like TLC by only a month, we wanted to make our cage match as dramatic as possible. We wanted one of each team to blade, but after the production meeting, Michael Hayes told us that there would be no gigging. "Vince is dead set against it," he said.

The four of us went to Vince and laid out our case—it was such an important match and we wanted it to be intense. "I see your point," Vince said. "One of you can gig. But I don't want a bloodbath out there, okay?"

I went to Mick Foley for advice on the best, safest way to gig. He even made the blade for me!

It went perfectly—I had color all over my face, but not so much that it was a splatter fest. The important thing was that it helped push the story. In the end, that's all that matters.

JEFF: I kept trying to climb back into the cage, even though I had already been eliminated. Finally I made my way back in, hitting Edge and Matt with a crazy corkscrew moonsault from the top. That was so cool—the crowd popped big for that, everybody coming to their feet as one. Not to blow our own whistle, but Team Extreme was really over at that point!

Once I was in the cage, Edge nailed me in the head with a chair, giving him a free shot at climbing out. But Matt and I quickly followed him up to the top and gave him our own rendition of the con-chair-to, which sent him plummeting back-first onto the mat.

MATT: "I hope I'm not too scared to bump at that height," Edge said.

"Don't worry," I told him, "when you're unconscious, you won't be afraid to bump."

We were pretty stiff with the chairs, trying to get the maximum sound and effect for the finish. Edge went down hard and we hit the floor and finally—finally!—we were WWE Tag Team Champions again.

It was a very emotional moment for me, because I had begun to think that we were never going to win the tag-team titles again. We'd been screwed around so many times, I was beginning to lose hope.

THE NEW TNN

DATE: September 25, 2000
LOCATION: State College, Pennsylvania
ARENA: Bryce Jordan Center

MATT: I was in bad shape after the cage match. I was limping pretty badly in the back, so somebody gave me a couple of pain pills, which genuinely helped me out. We had a three-hour drive to State College, and I don't know if I could've made it otherwise.

I'm very lucky, because I don't have an addictive personality. There have been occasions when I've had to take a few pain pills, but I know myself well enough to know that I can take them when I need them with-out getting hooked.

Those things have a place if you use them right, like if you've got a long drive, or you need to get a good night's sleep. Unfortunately, so many peo-ple can't control themselves and get addicted. It really depends on your personality.

People talk about guys that have to take pills because they're in con-stant pain. The truth is, if you've got an injury and you hurt all the time, you shouldn't be wrestling. If I was in so much physical pain that the only way I could survive was to take pills, I would quit.

Monday night was the very first *Raw* on TNN. We knew we would have to work, but they promised us it would be something really simple, more or less the equivalent of having the night off. But when we walked in—all four of us were so beat-up—they asked us if we would have a ladder match.

Great, I thought. *I couldn't even get out of bed this morning.*

I think that was the point where ladder matches started to become abused as a way to hotshot the ratings. Edge said we shouldn't agree to do it, but I said I didn't mind doing it because it was such a prestigious posi-tion to be in.

"It's not that I mind doing it," I said. "It's just that I don't know if I *can* do it."

Edge voiced his concern to a few people, and they said, "Well, you guys don't have to have the caliber of match that you had at *SummerSlam* or *WrestleMania*. Just go out and do a basic ladder match. It doesn't have to be that spectacular."

That was just horseshit. They knew we weren't about to go out there and sacrifice our legacy by giving the fans anything less than 100 percent.

"I'll do what I can," I said, but I knew I shouldn't be wrestling that day. I should have been at home, in my bed. I had two bruised ribs that felt like they were cracked, and my back was totally killing me.

JEFF: I was also all banged up from the cage match, though not quite as badly as Matt. The match was fine, even though we only had a couple of hours to put it together. There wasn't a lot of thought put into it, and to be honest, it didn't have a hell of a lot of heart in it either. It was definitely passable, but it just didn't have the magic or energy of our previous matches.

MATT: When I look back at that ladder match, it's definitely not among my best performances. But it's amazing what adrenaline can do for you.

Basically, we got through it. There was one spot where Edge & Christ-ian were going up, so I threw a ladder at them and knocked them both off.

Unfortunately the ladder came right back down and hit me on top of the head, busting me open.

It was a good cut, nice and long and wide, right there on top. I went back after the match and saw this doctor. He's this guy that is really out there. He's got a ranch somewhere out in the woods, and he's always inviting wrestlers to come stay there. I've always thought that he invited wrestlers out there and turned them into animals, like in *The Island of Dr. Moreau*.

Anyway, when I saw that the doctor was on-site, I was immediately ready to run: "Um, do I really need stitches?"

"You know what I like about you North Carolina guys?" he said. "You're good ol' tough country boys. Well, I'll tell you what I'm going to do. I'm going to sew me up a good ol' country boy."

He's rambling all this stuff, and as I'm asking him, "What are you going to use to numb it?" he sticks his needle in there. *Owwwwww!*

"I don't use anesthesia," he said. "I'm all natural. Besides, a tough ol' country boy like you doesn't need any. Don't worry. I'll be through here in just a minute."

Man, he put in twenty stitches and every one hurt like hell! I had been hit with a fifty-pound ladder, my head's all bruised up and bleeding, and this wacky doctor is sewing it up with no anesthesia. Between that and the fact that I was still hurting from the cage match the night before, I was in as bad a shape as I've ever been in my career. Of course, I did what I always do—I toughed it out.

NO MERCY

DATE: *October 22, 2000*
LOCATION: *Albany, New York*
ARENA: *Pepsi Arena*

JEFF: After we won the tag-team titles, there really wasn't a strong team for us to work with. Commissioner Mick Foley had made a stipulation at the *Raw* on TNN ladder match that if we beat Edge & Christian, then that was their last shot at the titles. That's what led to our feud with Los Conquistadors.

MATT: Los Conquistadors were two masked *luchadors* from the eighties who returned to the WWE roster just around the time Edge & Christian were banned from going for the tag titles. They had limited English—all they could say was "*Sí, señor!*"—and looked suspiciously like Edge & Christian wearing gold jumpsuits and masks.

JEFF: Edge & Christian wanted to get two other guys to wrestle as Los Conquistadors, but Vince made them do it every time. He didn't want to have a couple of guys out there screwing the bit up, and in the end, it was going to be them anyway. They weren't very happy about that, because it meant that they would have to work twice on every show.

There were a couple of vignettes where E&C were shown backstage with Los Conquistadors in an effort to prove that they weren't them. The Conquistadors in those segments were actually played by two very cool indie wrestlers from UPW, Chris "Fallen Angel" Daniels and Aaron "Hardkore Kidd" Aguilera. But whenever Los Conquistadors were in the ring, it was Edge & Christian under the gold hoods.

MATT: The Los Conquistadors angle was a pretty funny gimmick—*el hilarioso!* They eventually earned a shot at our tag titles at *No Mercy*. In the end, I hit Conquistador Uno with the Twist of Fate and then tried to unmask him. But as I pulled the mask off of Edge—I mean, Uno—there was another one underneath! I couldn't believe it, and in my shock, Conquistador Dos hit me with the Unprettier for the pinfall—1-2-3!

What's interesting about that is that Dos—Christian—was hurt in the middle of the match. He went to do his Jimmy Jump, where he jumps on the second rope and springs out, but as he jumped, his mask turned and he couldn't see where he was landing. He fell on his side, jamming his neck and shoulder, so he had a dead arm for the remainder of the match. When he hit me with the Unprettier, it was with his one good arm.

When we got to the back, he was in bad shape. Now Los Conquistadors have the titles, but Christian's hurt and can't do anything.

The next night, we all got together to figure out how to play it—it was Vince, Michael Hayes, writer Brian Gewirtz, Mick Foley, Edge, Christian, Jeff, and myself. The story line was that E&C would pay impostors to be Los Conquistadors on *Raw* so that they could beat them for the titles.

Someone said, "This is a lot to do in one night."

"Please," I said, "let's just do this, so we can get out of it and move on."

JEFF: What we did was this: Edge found Christian lying on a broken table in the back, saying that the Dudleyz had powerbombed him and now he was too injured to take on Los Conquistadors for the titles.

"No problem," Edge said confidently. "I'll take on both of the Conquistadors by myself."

Edge battled Los Conquistadors until one of them hit him with a Swanton Bomb and made the pin—1-2-3! Los Conquistadors peeled off their masks and—ta-da!—it was us!

Commissioner Foley got involved and he broke out double-secret footage of E&C scheming with two impostor Conquistadors, which of course was in complete defiance of his mandate against them getting another title shot against us. That said, he admired their creativity, so he banged his gavel, allowing Los Conquistadors' victory at *No Mercy* to stand. But he also admired *our* creativity, so he allowed our win to stand as well! Therefore, we were WWE Tag Team Champions for the third time!

TIME STANDS STILL

JEFF: In November, we were asked to star in a commercial for a new Nintendo 64 game, *The Legend of Zelda*. We were so excited! The fact that they wanted us in a commercial showed us that WWE realized how popular we'd become.

The concept behind the promotion was that a gamer has seventy-two hours to save the world, just like the hero in the actual video game. Everyone in the world stops what they are doing to see if he wins or loses, including your friendly neighborhood Hardy Boyz.

MATT: The setup for the commercial was pretty basic. We were in the middle of a match, I set the guy up with a Twist of Fate, and Jeff goes for a Swanton. As he dove off, he stopped in midair—like time had stopped.

Then it cut back to me and I said, "He's only got seventy-two hours to save the world."

It was another one of those times when they left the decisions up to us—which one of you guys want to do something off the top, and which one wants to read the line? Whoever did the bump had to do it over and over again, so I said, "Well . . . Jeff is famous for doing the Swanton Bomb. It's a very popular move!"

RIGHT TO CENSOR

MATT: A couple of weeks after Los Conquista-Hardyz won the titles, we had to drop the belts to Right To Censor—Bull Buchanan and the Goodfather. That whole Right To Censor gimmick was Vince's baby, poking fun at our archenemies, the Parents Television Council. Well, the Godfather—excuse me, The *Good*father—was very uncomfortable about being a heel, so Vince wanted to reward them with the tag-team titles.

"You guys are so over with fans," he told us, "having the titles isn't going to make you more over. But if we give them to RTC, it will give them the heat they need."

We should have had the tag titles for a good long reign. If we could have been seen as fighting champions, it not only would have made us look like a great team, it would have made the titles seem more important. But Vince looks at things though the lens of sports-entertainment—titles or no titles, the people were still going to cheer for us.

JEFF: We went from wrestling Edge & Christian and the Dudleyz to working with Right To Censor. No offense to those guys, but it was kind of a letdown. We had set such a high precedent. Every week we were having great match after great match. Then, when we went into our program with RTC, we had to work twice as hard just to put on a decent match.

MATT: It was frustrating. The Goodfather was totally old school. He wasn't about to work in our style. Bull Buchanan is a great guy, but he was no Edge or Christian. He kept jumping up on the ropes, and I finally said to him, "You're huge, man. You don't need to do that. Leave the high-flying to us."

So Jeff and I would go out there every night and take a bunch of bumps off of our bump card just to make the matches as passable as possible.

JEFF: The highlight of our feud with Right To Censor was an elimination match at *Survivor Series*—us and the Dudley Boyz vs. Edge & Christian and RTC. It was another one of those times when Michael Hayes came to us and gave us a choice. "One of you guys win," he said. "The only finish we want is that one of the Hardyz survive."

Matt and I flipped a coin and I won. It was a pretty standard *Survivor Series* match, which ended when I hit a Swanton on Christian, eliminating him. Then Val Venis did a run-in, accidentally clotheslining the Goodfather, enabling me to pin him and become the sole Survivor.

THE RADICALZ

MATT: It was one of those angles that started with something that was only planned for one night. There wasn't any thought put into it—it just happened. We were doing *Raw* in Ames, Iowa. Lita went to go into the locker room, and as she reached for the door, the Radicalz—Chris Benoit, Dean Malenko, Eddie Guerrero, and Perry Saturn—walked out, slamming the door into her head. She went down, and Malenko said, "Maybe we should help her up."

"Just leave her," Benoit snarled.

As they walked off, we came out of the locker room.

"Oh my God! Lita, are you okay?"

The Radicalz turned around, we exchanged a few words, and they started kicking the crap out of us. That led to a match—the Radicalz vs. us and Chris Jericho.

They came up with an angle where Dean started wooing Lita—his gimmick at the time was that he was a big ladies' man. The long-term plan was to have Amy wrestle Dean at the *Royal Rumble*, I would help her win, then we would kiss. They asked us what we thought about it, and we were both cool with it. The problem was that they had no idea what we were going to do to get to that climax.

JEFF: The next week we were in New York doing *SmackDown!* at the Garden. Amy and Dean did a series of vignettes that ran throughout the show, showing them going out on the town.

MATT: We were only involved in the opening and closing bits. First Dean came into our locker room to pick Amy up for their "date." Then we shot the closing segment in this seedy joint just a few blocks away from the arena. Lita and Dean were in a hotel room. "How does your wife feel about you being a sneaky two-timing bastard?" she asked him. He told her not to worry, then turned out the lights.

"I like the lights on," Lita says, so Dean turns them back on, only to find me and Jeff standing there. I hit him over the head with a champagne bottle, Jeff threw the bed on him, and then we beat the holy hell out of him.

"I promised you a night you'd never forget." Lita laughed as we left him there.

JEFF: After we left, Amy and Dean spent the rest of the night taping their segments with Bruce Prichard. Before we shot the hotel-room scene, Bruce came to us and said, "Whatever you do, don't bust Dean open, because we've still got to do all the other pretapes."

From there, we faced Dean, Perry, and Terri in an intergender elimination match at *Armageddon* in Birmingham. It ended with Dean getting Amy to tap with the Texas Cloverleaf, keeping their program going for their blow-off match at the *Royal Rumble*.

"YOU CALL THAT EXTREME?"

JEFF: In the middle of our feud with the Radicalz, we were asked to be in another commercial, this time for Chef Boyardee overstuffed ravioli. When you get offered things like commercials, it feels so good—it's like confirmation of your WWE Superstardom. If you get gigs like that, then you know you've got some status within the company.

Also, there's a little bit of a payday, which is ultimately the bottom line. Wrestling's not a typical job by any stretch of the imagination, but it's still a job. And you never know how long it's going to last. So if you're the flavor of the month, you've got to get what you can.

MATT: Bruce Prichard came to us at *Raw* and said, "I need you guys to do me a big favor. We've been doing some business out in California with this independent promotion, Ultimate Pro Wrestling. Since you're filming your commercial on Thursday, how about you appear at their Wednesday-night show in Santa Ana?"

We said, "No problem," even though we weren't all that thrilled with the idea.

On Wednesday we flew from Charlotte—where we taped *SmackDown!*—to L.A., then drove out to the show and met Rick Bassman, the owner of UPW. "Here's what I'm thinking," he said. "You guys work a match with our top tag team, the Ballard Brothers, and put them over."

"Whoa, whoa, whoa," I said. "I don't know the Ballard Brothers. I don't mind working with them, but we're doing this as a favor. It'd probably be better if we went over."

In the end, we changed it to a six-person intergender match, us against the Ballards and a female indie wrestler named Lexie Fyfe.

We were the main event, obviously. Afterward Bassman wanted us to stay and sign autographs for a while, so we didn't get out of there until after midnight. We had a limo to take us to Big Bear Mountain, which was where the Chef Boyardee shoot was going to be. It was a good three-hour drive, but the limo driver got lost along the way, so we didn't get to our hotel until 4:30 in the morning. Then we had to be up at 6:30 to start the commercial.

JEFF: The premise was that these two guys were snowboarding: "Dude! Look at the snow. It's gonna be an extreme day!"

They do a jump off a hill and land in the ring. "You think that's extreme?" we said. "*This* is extreme!"

And then we start beating the shit out of them. We did all our signature moves—Twist of Fates, Swantons, Spin Cycles.

The two other guys were played by a couple of wrestlers that were actually pretty heralded workers on the independent scene—Chris "Fallen Angel" Daniels and Frankie Kazarian.

After we shot all the in-ring material, we had to film us eating ravioli. We had to act like it was the most delicious thing we've ever put in our mouths, but it was ice-cold and totally gross. They need to shoot from every angle, so you eat it, then spit it into a bucket. We shot it at least twenty times. And the bucket full of half-eaten, chewed-up ravioli—it was nasty!

MATT: There were two different versions of the commercial, one where I said the tag line—"This stuff definitely feeds the need"—and one where Amy said it.

We spent the whole day shooting, and by the time the sun had gone down, it was freezing. God, it was cold! It was brutal. We were in our wrestling gear, which is like street clothes, so that wasn't too bad, but they wanted our hair to be wet. They kept pouring water on our heads, but it was so cold, our hair would freeze up after ten minutes. It was real bad. We all got pretty sick.

JEFF: After the shoot ended we hopped on the red-eye to Chattanooga to tape the Christmas-night episode of *Raw*. Matt called Michael Hayes before we got on the plane to let him know that we were going to grab a few hours' sleep when we got into Chattanooga, so we'd get to the building a little later than usual.

MATT: We fought Dean Malenko and Chris Benoit that night. In the match I tackled Dean, messing up his already hurting knee, and he took a few weeks off for surgery. The fact of the matter was that Vince wanted Dean to put Amy over, and Dean wasn't too happy with the idea. I think he figured that he'd be out for six to eight weeks and that when he came back, they'd have forgotten all about the angle.

The next night we were in Nashville, and I had a kick-ass match with Benoit for the Intercontinental title. When you're in the ring with Chris Benoit, you have to bust your ass, because he only has one gear—full steam, straight ahead. He doesn't do anything half-assed.

JEFF: There was a definite clash of styles between us and the Radicalz, both in terms of wrestling technique and where we saw the story line going. It was the exact opposite of working with friends, like Edge & Christian. It's so easy to work with those guys because we can talk freely among ourselves and really say what's on our minds.

We weren't as relaxed with the Radicalz. We couldn't speak freely with them, we couldn't say, "This is what we think should happen . . ." When that happens you sometimes find yourselves backed into a corner, and you're forced into doing things that you really don't feel comfortable doing.

MATT: With Edge & Christian, we all saw things in the same light. But Dean, Perry, Eddie, and Chris, they'd been in the business a lot longer than us and had a very different view of how things are done. It was okay for a while, but if you're working with people you don't see eye to eye with, it becomes a big hassle. After a few weeks, we just wanted to get out of it.

THE KISS

DATE: February 19, 2001
LOCATION: St. Louis, Missouri
ARENA: Savvis Center

MATT: During the angle with Lita and Dean Malenko, there were tentative plans that would have had me becoming so jealous that I freak out and turn heel. I think Stephanie McMahon, who was heading up the creative department at the point, was pushing for that. She really wanted to split us up. But we weren't ready yet. We thought there was plenty of life left in Team Extreme.

Once we made the Chef Boyardee commercial, the plan to break us up was put on the back burner. The commercial was set to start airing in mid-January, and so they had to keep us together.

JEFF: When Dean came back in the beginning of February, we picked up the angle right where we left off. It was pretty funny, because I'm sure when he took off, he was thinking, *Whew! Thank God I got out of that one. Now I won't have to put over the girl.* And now he had to put over the girl!

They asked us if we thought we could stretch out the angle until *WrestleMania* and we all agreed, "Absolutely not."

It would've been one thing if there was a clear picture of where the angle was going, but it was very much one of those things where they were making it up as they went along. And the truth is, we weren't all that comfortable working with those guys. It was a real clash of personalities and wrestling styles.

We just wanted to get through it, and the sooner the better. It was decided that we'd tie it all up at *Raw* in St. Louis.

MATT: When they presented the idea of an on-air romance to us, they worried that we might have a problem with it, but we were fine with it. We both felt comfortable enough that the fans would accept us as a couple.

I think they felt that two people who see each other in real life would be more realistic than a gimmick couple like Spike Dudley and Molly Holly. Plus, the possibilities for physical contact between us is pretty limitless. A gimmick couple can be professional and do what they don't normally do with each other, but there's definitely a line that's drawn. Especially when one of the couples has a husband or wife that's home watching it happen on TV.

By this point, a lot of people in the WWE knew that we were together, but we had always made a point of not being too blatant about our relationship. That day in the arena, Amy and I were outside the dressing room, and I said, "Okay, let's go ahead and figure exactly how we're going to do this so that we're on the same page out there." Obviously we'd kissed several times before in real life, but we wanted to be sure that it looked right on TV.

There we were, rehearsing our big love scene in this corridor, making sure that if anyone walked down the hall, we would act like we were just hanging out. We didn't want people to think we were really back there making out.

When it came time for the match, Dean really pulled out all the stops, acting like a total dickhead. The thing about Dean is that he's a great technical wrestler, but he could never get serious heel heat on himself, because in WWE, that comes from your persona more than anything else. When it comes to wrestling, you can't really touch him, but he's just kind of bland when it comes to being a WWE type of character.

But in this match he really turned it up and got a much better reaction than he'd been getting previously. It might have been because he didn't have to sell for her, except for the three seconds at the end.

Dean picked Lita up for a slam, and as he swung her around, her feet hit the referee, knocking him unconscious. That was my chance to make the save! I ran in and cracked Dean with a chair, and slid out of the ring. Lita got on top for the pin—1-2-3! I got back in the ring and we started jumping up and down, celebrating. And, in the heat of the moment, I kissed her.

Lita just started at me with this surprised look. *Uh-oh,* I thought, *Maybe I shouldn't have done that.*

I went to walk up the ramp, and Lita spun me around and laid the big one on me. The crowd just went totally, completely nuts.

I know Vince and WWE executive producer Kevin Dunn were both worried that the kiss wasn't going to work, that it would look forced. When we got to the back, they both thought it was the greatest thing ever. "That was excellent. Great job!"

"The Kiss" became a classic moment. It even made the *WWE Desire* video.

Amazingly, our real relationship didn't become public knowledge after our on-air relationship began. A lot of people had thought we might be involved, but we never allowed for anything more than speculation. The way we'd interact together backstage was the same as the way Jeff and I work together. Okay, it was a little better than that, but in theory, we just acted like close friends and business partners.

One of the most twisted things about this business is how truth and fiction are blurred. There's reality and then there's WWE reality. There's probably a lot of people that don't know if Jeff and I are really brothers.

When you watch WWE, you don't always know what to believe, which is how they like it.

My relationship with Amy has been a slow build. We just knew if it was more of a gradual thing it would be a lot more acceptable to the rest of the locker room. I never had guys giving me a hard time about it. There have been cases where a girl comes to work there, and all of a sudden she's sitting on one of the boys' laps, making kissy face, and they never hear the end of it.

When we went to work, we were there to work. What we did on our own time, we did on our own time. We didn't want to rub our relationship in anybody's face or make a big issue out of it. People assumed what they assumed, but nobody said anything about it to us. A lot of that has to do with the fact that they respected us as workers, so they respected our privacy as people.

JEFF: When Matt's in the back with Amy, there are times when I can see that he's trying to be one of the guys, and not being himself. I think he loves her to death, but he's not the kind of guy that is comfortable showing his emotions, let alone saying the three little words too easily. He's like our daddy in that way—Dad won't ever say that kind of stuff, especially to Matt and me. Even though I know he loves us, he's just the type of person that has a hard time letting it out.

But there's no getting around the fact that Matt couldn't ask for a more perfect girlfriend, as far as having a passion for the business like he does.

MATT: The easiest way to describe my relationship with Amy is like having a best friend that likes all the same things I like—except she's a pretty girl that I have sex with. I think she liked me more than I liked her in the beginning. I admit it—I'm not the kind of guy who falls in love easily. I've always been the loner type. We didn't have a mom and our dad wasn't very open with his feelings. I knew that he loved me, but in the end, I have to take care of myself. I was of the mentality that I'm all I have in the world, and that's fine. I can do it alone and I'll be cool.

Plus, Amy was so not like the girl I envisioned myself with. We joke about it because I always saw myself with the stereotypical hot blond bombshell. As opposed to a girl with a big tattoo on her arm. At first, I thought, *Her tat-*

too is so big! I wish she didn't have it. It was a little hard to get around. It's funny, because I don't even see it anymore.

What really sealed the deal for us was how well matched our personalities are. You would think working and traveling together all the time would create some tension, but we get along beautifully. It definitely helps to travel with somebody you can get along with. If you don't see eye to eye, if there are issues or complications, it makes an already stressful experience all the more aggravating. But if you're lucky enough to travel with somebody you're compatible with, you can do all the things that you both like to do.

The work and the travel can be stressful, but not our relationship. Being with Amy is one of the things that helps relieve that stress.

THE ROAD TO WRESTLEMANIA X-7

DATE: *March 5, 2001*
LOCATION: *Washington, D.C.*
ARENA: *MCI Center*

MATT: We were doing *Raw* out of Washington, D.C. We walked into the MCI Center and there was Paul E. Heyman. Man, that was a weird moment!

ECW had had financial problems for ages and Paul E. had been forced to declare bankruptcy and come to work for WWE. That was the night he started doing commentary, taking over for Jerry Lawler, who had walked out the previous week after his then wife, the Kat, got fired.

JEFF: We were looking at the format and it had us vs. the Dudleyz. Michael came over to us and said, "You guys are winning the titles tonight."

There was no buildup, they just sprang it on us. But after winning the titles three times, it just wasn't as big a deal.

MATT: When you do something for the first time, obviously it's very exciting. Your names go into the record books. You're established as having made a mark on the business.

The second time we won the titles—in the *Unforgiven* cage match against Edge & Christian—was extremely emotional for me, because I really thought we were never going win the titles again. It felt like we had truly achieved something.

When they told us that we were going lose the titles to Right To Censor because we didn't need them, it was just sickening. That was the moment that I realized that in order to move ahead in this business, you have to be totally selfish. If you sit back and don't say anything, they go, "Okay, I guess he's satisfied. We'll just keep him where he is."

The fact is, everything about this business is a work except the money and the miles. All that matters is the amount of money you can make, and the length of time you can go without killing yourself.

Anyway, by this time we'd had so many successes that didn't involve winning the belts that the importance of the titles had really diminished for me. When they told us we were going to win, I just thought, *Okay, Whatever.*

JEFF: Matt and I had a little heat between us that night. We were planning our strategy when Lita had to go out for her WWE Women's Championship match against Ivory and Right To Censor. "Well, we're not letting you go out there all by yourself," Matt said.

"What about our conversation?" I asked.

"This is more important," he replied. "Come on. We'll talk about our match later."

Matt and I brawled with Steven Richards and Val Venis as Lita and Ivory went at it in the ring. At the end, I went to run the guardrail and take out Val, but I accidentally hit Lita. Ivory got the pin, which pissed Matt off.

All was cool between us by the time our match came around. The finish had Edge & Christian doing a run-in. D-Von went to get the table, Christian chaired him in the back, and when Bubba went to chase Christian, D-Von

took the Twist of Fate from Matt and I made a quick cover—1-2-3! Once again, the Hardy Boyz were the WWE Tag Team Champions.

MATT: We only held on to the titles for two weeks. We were in Albany for *Raw,* and we were supposed to have a rematch against the Dudleyz, but unfortunately, somebody—Edge & Christian, obviously—had canceled their plane reservations. When they no-showed, E&C stepped in and challenged us.

JEFF: I hit Edge with a moonsault, but just as I went for the pin, Rhyno— Edge and Christian's "good friend"—ran in and hit me with a vicious gore, allowing Edge to make the cover for the win.

MATT: Later that night, the Dudleyz arrived and Edge & Christian were forced to defend their titles. That match saw the WWE debut of Spike Dudley, who interfered and cost E&C their just-won titles!

All of this was set up for TLC II at *WrestleMania X-7.* There was actually some debate, because Edge wanted Rhyno to make his debut at the Pay-Per-View, which Bubba and I were both fully against.

The plan for *WrestleMania* was that Lita, Spike, and Rhyno were going to all do run-ins during the match. Our argument was that Lita and Spike are both on TV, so the crowd knows who they are. What if Rhyno comes out and nobody reacts to him?

We went to Vince and said we thought Rhyno should debut that night. That way people would be familiar with him because he'd have been on TV for a couple of weeks prior to *WrestleMania.* In the middle of this debate, Rhyno said, "Well, I do get a hell of a reaction in Albany."

I thought, *Who is this guy?* Once I got to know him, I realized he was totally kidding. Rhyno's a good guy.

"AN ALIEN SHAKING HANDS WITH THE PRESIDENT"

DATE: March 26, 2001
LOCATION: Cleveland, Ohio/Panama City, Florida
ARENA: Gund Arena/The Boardwalk Beach Resort

JEFF: World Wrestling Entertainment officially acquired our longtime archenemy WCW on a Wednesday, so we all knew about it just before we went back out on the road for house shows. Needless to say, the locker room was buzzing about it. It was the biggest thing to happen to the business in years, maybe ever!

That Monday we were in Cleveland for the final *Raw* before *Wrestle-Mania*. Vince gathered all the wrestlers together. "As I'm sure you've all heard, we just bought WCW," he said. "I just want everyone to know that this will not affect any of you. Nobody's jobs are in danger. The brands will be completely separate. Our plan is to bring the WCW brand up to WWE's level of excellence, and then at some point we can have a Super Bowl of wrestling."

No matter what Vince said, there was definitely a feeling among the boys that things would never be the same.

MATT: That Monday—March 26, 2001, to be precise—was maybe the most incredible night of wrestling TV ever. The "Monday Night Wars" officially came to an end as *Raw* kicked off with Vince watching *Nitro* and announcing that he'd bought his own competition! It was a surreal moment, watching *Raw* at the monitor in the back and seeing *Nitro* broadcasting on our show! It was just too weird! I sat there thinking, *There's nothing left that can surprise me.*

JEFF: Halfway through *Raw,* Vince came out to the ring and went off on a long speech about finally beating Ted Turner's ass. All of a sudden Shane McMahon came out on *Nitro* and said that he beat Vince to the punch and that *he'd* bought WCW! Man, when Shane walked out into the WCW ring it was like watching an alien shake hands with the president—it was something I'd never thought I'd see.

175

MATT: We had the lucky task of following that mind-blowing segment. It was a six-man tag, with us teaming with Chris Benoit against Team ECK—Edge, Christian, and Kurt Angle. It was basically more setup for TLC II at *WrestleMania*. It was a good match, but I think we all knew that everybody at home was still preoccupied with the WCW business.

The finish was cool—Benoit made Christian tap to the Crippler Crossface, then I got Edge with a Twist of Fate. Rhyno ran in and gave me the Gore, and when Lita came into the ring to see if I was okay, he gored her as well.

WRESTLEMANIA X-7

DATE: April 1, 2001
LOCATION: Houston, Texas,
ARENA: Houston Astrodome

MATT: Right before *WrestleMania X-7* we were informed that, once again, Edge & Christian were going to win the belts. "Trust me on this," Michael Hayes said. "You guys don't want to win."

"Hell yeah, I want to win it!," I said. "It's *WrestleMania*! We've never won at *WrestleMania*!"

"Whoever wins those titles at *WrestleMania* are going to get destroyed by Kane and Undertaker within a week or two," Michael explained.

"I don't care! I want to win at *WrestleMania*!"

I was hot! It was another injustice, just like when we didn't win at *SummerSlam*.

JEFF: The day of the match, we were all in the back, working things out. Michael was there, jotting things down so that they would be able to shoot the match for TV. I came up with a very cool spot called "the Frogger." I was going to go from the corner, onto one ladder, and to another ladder, and then to a third ladder. As I was standing on top of the third ladder, reaching for the belt, Bubba was going to move the ladder out of the way with my feet still hooked onto it. Then I was going to swing back to the corner, where Edge was going to spear me from off the turnbuckle.

MATT: The other big spot was going to be me and Bubba and getting pushed off the twelve-foot ladder and falling through four tables set up on the floor. Before the match we got together to talk about exactly what we were going to do. We were debating which spot should come last. Edge

thought the last spot should be the Frogger—Edge spears Jeff off the turn-buckle, then either he or Christian goes right up and grabs the belts.

My point was that the last spot should be Bubba and me on the twelve-foot ladder, fighting for the title, then Rhyno comes in and shoves the lad-der, sending us through four tables, set up on the floor outside the ring.

"That's no good," Edge said. "Nothing's going to get a bigger pop than that spear off the turnbuckle. If I do that, then you guys do the table spot, then the finish is going to a total anticlimax."

That go me so hot! "Since you guys are going over again *and* you're heels," I said, "how about you *be* heels? You do that spear off the top—which isn't heellike at all—and then we leave the last thought in every-one's mind that one of the babyface teams was going to win, if it hadn't have been for that damn Rhyno."

I wanted to put in people's minds that either me or Bubba was going to win the titles, but Edge & Christian's third man caused those two to crash and burn, enabling the heels to win. If Edge would've speared Jeff off the ladder and then have gone up and gotten the belts down, that would've been a totally babyface move.

"Plus," I said, "people have seen you do the spear off the post before. But they've never seen two guys going through four tables simultaneously."

JEFF: It became pretty heated. It almost turned into a fight.

"Let's take a vote," Edge said.

Of course everyone started chickening out: "Umm . . . I can see both sides."

"Fine," Matt said. "Let's ask Michael."

MATT: We agreed that we would let Michael have the final say. We ran it by him, and he said, "Well, boys, I like both spots. Matt, I agree with your point about the strong heel finish, but I'm worried that Jeff's Frogger spot—which sets up Edge's spear—could go wrong."

"What do mean it could go wrong?" Jeff piped up. "It's not going to go wrong! Why do you think it's going to go wrong?"

"It's a pretty complicated spot," Michael explained. "The level of diffi-culty is pretty high."

"No, it isn't! It's going to go fine!"

"Okay," Michael said. "Show it to me."

Jeff tried it three times and screwed up every time. He never got it right.

He was so hot! "It doesn't matter! I'll do it right in the match!"

Bubba and I went to Paul E. and told him our scenario. I said, "Don't you think the table spot should go last?"

"Absolutely," he said. "Without a doubt, that's the way it should go."

Then Edge went to him and told him *his* idea for the finish.

"You're right," Paul E. said. "Without a doubt, that's the way it should go."

That is Paul Heyman to a tee—he tells people what they want to hear.

Then, as if things weren't tense enough, Jeff came close to boycotting the match. He wanted to climb up the ladder and, rather than doing the Swanton, just cross his arms and do a deadman fall backward through the table that Spike and Rhyno were on. We all thought that was completely crazy!

"What are people supposed to think when you go up there?" I asked him. "Are they supposed to think you're up there, getting ready to do the Swanton, and then a sniper shot you and you just fell backward through the table?"

He didn't find that quite so funny.

Edge was hot. "Jeff, you're doing the Swanton. Period!"

"This might be the last time you guys ever fight one another," Michael Hayes said. "You're welcome to put some new stuff in there, but we definitely want to see a big Swanton off the ladder."

"Fine," Jeff said. "I won't say anything else."

JEFF: They made me feel like a damn fool, just for suggesting a spot. They all lit into me. It was crazy out of line, and it really bothered me.

Sometimes those guys get jealous because I always get great pops, and they feel like they have to do anything they can to get theirs. They hate that I'll just do one thing—a Swanton off a ladder, whatever—and that will be the spot that's the most remembered.

MATT: Finally it all got settled and it was time to go. We were initially told that we were going to have twenty-five minutes, but right before the match it became twenty-two minutes. Our plan was that the finish itself would take ten minutes.

We were getting ready to go to our go-home spot, which was where we were going to set all three ladders up; all six of us were going to go up and everybody was going to go down. That was going to trigger the run-ins. Then, during the match, we got cut down to eighteen minutes. I was the one who got the word, so I'm buzzing everybody: "We've got to go! Let's go home!" Everything between that point and the go-home spot was automatically ixnayed. I was trying to tell Bubba, "We're going home!"

"What?"

"I said we're going—"

Diiiiiiinnnnggggg! Bubba hit me over the head with a ladder, just for filler. Just out of stupidity. I had to get twelve staples, right across the front of my head, just underneath my hairline. It messes up my nice hairdo, too. I have to watch how I comb it because there's a huge scar there. But stuff happens.

Bubba's split me open more than anybody else has. Every time we had a big match, he ended up busting me open. The true art of professional wrestling is to do as much stuff as you can that looks real without hurting people. I feel so great when I throw a punch that looks like I creamed somebody and I don't even touch them. That's what wrestling is truly all about. I mean, it not always going to work that way. Mistakes are going to happen. I've clobbered people and people have clobbered me.

JEFF: When it came time for the Frogger, I stepped onto the first ladder, then stepped on the second one, but it gave way and I fell to the ring. Man, I was bummed—I beat on the mat twice before I climbed up the third ladder.

MATT: We did the finish the way I wanted it—Bubba and I traded blows on top of a twenty-foot ladder, then Rhyno knocked it over, sending the two of us flying over the top rope and through the double stack of tables on the floor. The crowd went totally insane, giving us the loudest, most heartfelt "holy shit!" chant I've ever heard.

I was so proud at how it went down. I'm not right all the time, but on that occasion, I think I was. A month or so later, Edge came up to me and confessed. "You were right about finishing with the table spot," he said. "That was definitely the way to go."

JEFF: After Matt and Bubba went through the tables, all that was left was for someone to grab the belts. There was no way we were going to have another spot that outdid that one. Rhyno put Christian on his shoulders, climbed the ladder, and TLC II was history.

MATT: Afterward we were walking up the ramp and I could tell Jeff was really hot at himself for missing the third ladder. He had been in one of his "I don't care about wrestling" frames of mind, so I thought it was great to see him showing that kind of feeling, like it actually meant something to him. When we got to the back, he apologized for missing the spot. "Don't worry about it," I told him. "It was still great because it was real."

Psychology-wise, TLC II was the best of all the big gimmick matches. We were worried that there was nothing we could do that would come close to the previous TLC. But we knew that the run-ins from Lita, Spike, and Rhyno were going to make it a little different. Considering the fact that we had nine bodies and a bunch of inanimate objects, that match was pretty sound.

Once you build something great, you can never stop. You always have to add to it. There were people who felt enough was enough—how many more times can we see the Hardyz, Edge & Christian, and the Dudleyz—but TLC II was a great match, with a bit of a different spin. But I understand how people felt. If you have an apple and an orange and you put them in paper bag or a plastic bag, they're still going to be an apple and an orange.

REALITY HURTS

MATT: All wrestlers hate when people describe what we do as fake, because nothing we do is fake. Compare it to football. I've taken tackles where you get knocked down hard but it doesn't hurt. Then there've also been times where it knocks you silly. It's the same thing with wrestling. Sometimes the physicality isn't so bad, and sometimes it's terrible. But *fake* is a very unfair word to use to describe wrestling. It's an art. It's entertainment. For anybody to say that it's fake when we're being thrown down and taking bumps, that's just ignorant.

Every night I drop that leg drop and every night it hurts. It hurts me a lot worse than the guy I'm dropping it on! Basically, to jump off the top and land on your ass just plain hurts! That's probably one of the reasons my lower back is always so tight, because the leg drop is such a regular part of my arsenal.

THE TWO MAN POWER TRIP

DATE: *April 9 & 10, 2001*
LOCATION: *Boston, Massachusetts/Philadelphia, Pennsylvania*
ARENA: *Fleet Center/First Union Center*

JEFF: Within the space of two weeks, everything—and I do mean everything—changed. First we bought WCW, effectively turning wrestling into a one-company business. Then, at *WrestleMania,* The Rock went off to film *The Scorpion King,* and Stone Cold Steve Austin, arguably the most popular wrestler in history, turned heel. So in a very real way, we were left with no top babyface.

MATT: Even though they had paired Stone Cold with Triple H, they were fighting an uphill battle in terms of Stone Cold attempting to be a heel. They needed to find somebody that the fans would feel sorry for when Stone Cold beat their ass, and we got the call. They needed strong babyfaces that he could wrestle that they would cheer over him. That's where we came in. The belief was that if we went out there and Steve roughed us up, it would help get some sorely needed heat on him.

JEFF: It was a couple of weeks after *WrestleMania.* We were doing *Raw* in Boston and we were told that we were going be wrestling Stone Cold and Triple H. I was so damn excited. I knew it was a great opportunity.

MATT: The way it went down was that Lita was in the back, talking to Linda McMahon, telling her how much she admired her for being such a strong woman. Unfortunately, Vince overheard their conversation. "If you're such a strong woman," he snarled, "how about you and the Hardy Boyz face Triple H, Stone Cold Steve Austin, and my daughter, Stephanie?"

The idea was that we would squeeze out a victory by Lita pinning Stephanie. Then Stone Cold and Triple H would put a vicious beat-down on us, with the attention focused on Austin. They were hoping that if Stone Cold beat up a defenseless—and very popular—girl, it would give him the heel heat they wanted.

The two heels both got big reactions when they came down, though Triple H was booed much more than Stone Cold. People were having a lot of trouble hating Austin, who up until *WrestleMania* had been their hero.

JEFF: Triple H and Stone Cold really shined us a lot during the match, and the people got into that. That's the secret behind turning somebody heel—they can't look invincible. They have to talk a big game, but when it comes down to it, guys like the Hardy Boyz can whip their ass.

MATT: All the guys had spilled out of the ring—Stone Cold and I were brawling, Jeff and Triple H were brawling. Lita pulled Stephanie in the ring and they started going at it—Twist of Fate, moonsault, 1-2-3!

Lita stood up, victorious. Triple H came into the ring, decked her from behind, and—*wham!*—hit her with the Pedigree. I came in and tackled him into the corner and started beating on him. Stone Cold grabbed a chair, nailed Jeff over the head, then smashed me in the back. I went down and he started sticking me with the edge of the chair, over and over. He stopped for a second to catch his breath, and Lita crawled on top of me to protect me, because Stone Cold Steve Austin would never hit a girl.

But Stone Cold wasn't afraid to go there. He got that psycho look in his eyes and started hitting beating on her with the chair. It was a pretty vicious beating, too. It almost got us kicked off TV in Canada. Nobody could touch a girl for at least a month.

Stone Cold actually caught me a couple times on the knee with those chair shots. He's such an aggressive worker. Some people try to master the art of looking aggressive but making as little physical contact as possible. But Stone Cold Steve Austin is definitely physical through and through.

I was actually Stone Cold's jobber in his WWE debut match back in January 1996. Of course, he wasn't Stone Cold back then—he was the Ringmaster. He was supposed to wrestle Fatu—now known as Rikishi—but he was hurt, so they stuck me in there. It was a good match, with a lot of back and forth. At one point, Steve started punching me and I thought, *What's with him? Did I do something wrong?* I thought I might have hit him with something tight and pissed him off. By the end of the match I had figured out that that was just how he works.

There's a funny story about that match. I was wearing a pair of my turquoise High Voltage tights, with an *H* and a *V* on the butt. Sometime later, there was a picture from the match in one of the old wrestling magazines, with Steve holding me in the Million-Dollar Dream. The caption read, "Steve Austin defeats pre-lim wrestler Hank Varney in one of his first matches." Whoever wrote the article didn't bother to get my name. They just made up a name from the *H* and *V* on my tights. Hank Varney!

I learned a lot working with Stone Cold. It's really important to know how to do flips and take bumps, but to be a good wrestler, you have to have a full package. You can't just do hot spots. You've got to be well-rounded. Things like punching and kicking are a very important part of wrestling. If you want people to believe it's a real fight between two people, you need to be able to throw believable punches and kicks.

JEFF: Once we went off-air, Stone Cold stayed out there and kept beating on us. He was drinking beer and he was smashing us over the heads with the cans. The longer it went on, the more heat it generated. The crowd was like, "Enough already!" They started filling the ring with trash, just like in the original nWo days. It's a shame that wasn't on TV, because that would have been revolutionary for us.

Working with Triple H and Stone Cold was a very important moment for us, just because it was one of the first chances we got to go head-to-head with two of the top names in the business. We were all on the same level, and we definitely held our own in there. It was a good scenario for everybody involved because even though we got the benefit of saying that we won a tag-team match against those guys, the heels got to leave looking strong by destroying us with the chairs. Everybody benefited.

MATT: The next day, we were in Philadelphia for *SmackDown!* We had an early flight, then we checked into our hotel for a couple hours of sleep. Michael called at 11:30 and said, "Don't be late today, okay? Be here on time."

"Why?" I asked. "What's going on?"

"I can't tell you right now," he said mysteriously. "Just don't be late. It's going to be a good day."

Obviously it was it something coming off the night before, but I wasn't sure what it was going to be. We walked into the building, and when I saw Triple H and Jeff's names up on the format sheet as the main event, I realized that Jeff was going to win the Intercontinental title.

JEFF: When I walked in and found out I was going to win the Intercontinental title, I was so happy, but I didn't want anyone to see just how excited I was. Inside, though, I was screaming, *Wow!* That's just how I am. I don't run around showing my emotions, but believe me, it felt great.

MATT: They had decided that our match with Stone Cold and Triple H had played out so well that we should continue working with them for a couple of weeks. It would elevate us while at the same time it would give them heel heat and warm them up for their feud with the Undertaker and Kane.

One of my favorite things about that night was the package they aired at the beginning of *SmackDown!* It was so awesome, the way it showed us dominating Stone Cold and Triple H in the match and then getting beaten down. It was one of those things where you think, *Wow I* am *important.* It really got my heart pumping.

JEFF: The setup was that Lita and Matt were hurt from the night before, and I was there on my own. Stone Cold and Triple H were in the ring cutting a promo about how they had destroyed everybody—The Rock at *Wrestle-Mania,* the Hardy Boyz, Lita—when I ran out and nailed them both with a chair. Then I gave Stephanie the Twist of Fate.

MATT: We both used to do the Twist of Fate, but when it became my finisher, we agreed that Jeff wouldn't do it anymore. I don't do Swantons, Jeff doesn't do Twists of Fate. But in the meeting, Triple H was laying out the plan and he said, "Jeff's going to come in and do the Twist of Fate . . ."

Okay, I thought, not wanting to make trouble. *I hope he does a good one.*

JEFF: It was a pretty big deal, my taking out the two top guys in the promotion *and* the boss's daughter. Triple H demanded a match for later that night.

MATT: I was sitting right beside Vince in the Gorilla Position—the spot right behind the curtain named after the late Gorilla Monsoon—as they did the promo. I was hoping that the crowd would pop every time Steve and Triple H said "the Hardy Boyz." I knew that the crowd reaction would determine our future—if they went bonkers, the program would continue. The Philadelphia audience is a notoriously hard crowd to please, and to be honest, the pops were just okay. Not huge, but not bad enough that Vince would think, *Uh-oh, I'd better kill this angle immediately*. Still, I would've given everything for that match to have been in front of a truly hot crowd, someplace like Chicago, or somewhere in Texas.

JEFF: The match was pretty hot. There was one spot where I was going to run the rail and feed off into a powerslam by Triple H, but it didn't go right, so I threw Triple H into the barricade, went on the apron, and jumped off for a cross body. But Triple H caught me and gave me a nasty powerslam.

For the finish, I got Triple H with a side Russian Leg Sweep, then went up to the turnbuckle to try for a Swanton. But Triple H shoved me and referee Tim White into the corner, dropping me down and crotching me good. Tim got pissed, so Triple H bumped him to the mat, knocking me out. I was still crotched on the turnbuckle as Triple H went to nail me with a superplex, when Matt ran in and smashed him over the head with a chair.

MATT: Triple H had no idea I was there. He thought I was home nursing Lita and licking my wounds.

JEFF: Triple H was knocked out, so I climbed to the top—Swanton Bomb! I hooked his leg just as Tim White regained consciousness, 1-2-3! I was the Intercontinental Champion!

I was so grateful to Triple H. I know how the business is, how the top guys are about putting younger, smaller guys over. It showed me that Triple H genuinely respected me.

MATT: Jeff winning the Intercontinental Championship was a very big deal. It was the closest we'd ever come to really being top-tier players. My getting to come down and blast Triple H, which led to the victory, was so good for me.

After the match, we got to the back, and just as we were getting ready to leave, Paul Heyman grabbed me. "I don't know if you guys know it," he said, "but you've really done something special here. What happened last night and tonight . . . it's the biggest thing to happen to wrestling since the nWo!"

I would've taken that as a compliment if I thought he seriously meant it. But we both knew it wasn't the biggest thing to happen since the nWo. So I just looked at him and said, "Okay. Thanks."

He didn't mean it as an insult to my intelligence. It's just his way of motivating people. But you can't feed me a line of shit and expect me to believe it.

JEFF: Man, winning the IC title was a total rush. I wore the belt around my house all the next week, although I was wishing that it was the classic old Intercontinental Championship belt that so many of my favorite wrestlers—like Ultimate Warrior and "Macho Man"—wore. The best part was knowing that my name was going down in wrestling history. No matter what happens in my career, I'll always be there as a WWE Intercontinental Champion.

TOUGH ENOUGH

MATT: Jeff and I were booked for two house shows in Florida on Wednesday and Thursday, but they asked us to appear on *Tough Enough* before we went down there. WWE executive producer Kevin Dunn thought the *TE* contestants would benefit from hearing our story about how we got into the business.

JEFF: In order to do that we needed to get to the *Tough Enough* training facility in Stamford first thing in the morning, tape our spot, then fly down to Jacksonville in time for the house show.

It was decided that we were going to fly from Philly to Stamford on the company jet—better known as Air McMahon. It was such a rush! We've just spent two days working with the top guys, we're the hot, new elevated wrestlers, and now we're riding with Vince, Stephanie, Shane, and their whole crew.

MATT: We rode to the airport with them in their limo, talking about the old days, just making casual conversation, which we had never really done with them. It was all very friendly, lots of jokes, a little wine on the plane. It really was a fun little experience.

When we got off the plane, we exchanged hugs with everybody: "You guys did great. Have a great time on *Tough Enough*. Can't wait to see you next Monday."

It was the first time we'd experienced anything like it. It really felt good being treated like top guys.

JEFF: It was an honor to be asked to appear on *Tough Enough*, because we knew that only a select group of wrestlers gets invited there.

We went in that day and met the *TE* producer. "Nice to meet you guys," he said, shaking our hands. "I'm thinking the way to open the show is to have you guys in the ring with a ladder, like you're rehearsing a match."

"Why would we be rehearsing a ladder match?" Matt asked.

"I don't know," he said. "We just need something exciting to start off the show."

MATT: The producer wanted me to be on top of the ladder, then Jeff would push it over so I took a bump onto the ground. Not only that, he wanted to film this three or four times before the *TE* crew even came in.

"No way," I said. "I'm not taking bumps off my bump card. I've only got a few left on there as it is."

I could see he wasn't pleased. "What I was hoping for was something where you take a fall off the ladder right when the crew walks in, then you guys can gather yourselves together and say, 'Hey guys, how're you doing?' "

"Well, if you're really set on doing that, maybe we can do something where Jeff shoves the ladder and I just drape myself on the ropes, land on my feet, and then sail back over. But we'll only shoot it once. I've got to work tonight and I'm still a little beat-up from working with Stone Cold and Triple H the past two nights."

So we got in there, Jeff pushed the ladder, and I took the bump just as the *Tough Enough* crew came through the door: "Hey! What's going on? How're you guys doing?"

JEFF: We talked to the kids for an hour or so, telling them our story. Then we worked out in the ring with them for another half hour. Of course, when *Tough Enough* aired, all they showed was the kids walking in the door and there's Jeff and myself in the ring. They didn't even show the stupid ladder spot. I was right not to have done it, because then we would've taken a bunch of bumps off our bump cards for nothing.

MATT: I would love to run a *Tough Enough* camp one day. But I would do it a little differently. First, I wouldn't put the kids up in a plush house. I'd have all them living cramped together in a tiny space.

I would make them set up the ring every day when they got to the training center, and when they were through, I'd make them take it down. Then every weekend I would have them drive long distances to work small independent shows in a high school or an armory. I'd film those shows and follow their progression.

That's how it works at a real training camp. Of course, *Tough Enough* isn't a real training camp—it's an MTV TV show.

Tough Enough taught people to appreciate what we do, but in the end, it's just a TV show. I would love to put what I did coming up on TV. That would give people even more of a respect for the business, letting them see what most wrestlers have to go through to get to where we are now.

We had to kill ourselves for eight months at Dory Funk's Dojo before we ever got the opportunity to be on *Raw,* and that was after years of working independents and doing jobs on TV.

On the first *Tough Enough* season finale, Al Snow told the last four contestants that win or lose, he was glad they'd found something that they loved in wrestling. That got me so hot! The only way to know if you love this business, to know if it's truly in your heart, is to bust your ass for years and years. Al Snow of all people could tell you that, because he worked like a dog for twelve years before he ever came to WWE. Just because you made it through *Tough Enough* doesn't prove to me that you love wrestling. All that proves is that you went on a TV show and were trained to wrestle. What proves to me that you love wrestling is that you bend over backward and sacrifice everything in order to make it to WWE.

It's a different time now. Jeff and I were part of the last generation to truly pay dues. When we first came in, nobody had any real knowledge of what we had done in the past. All anyone knew was that we'd worked some indie stuff and that we'd done WWE jobs from time to time. That's why Taker and Bradshaw put us through a series of tests, to see if we really belonged in the locker room, to see if we deserved to be allowed into the brotherhood.

Times have changed in a big way. On *Tough Enough I* winner Maven's first day as a WWE wrestler, he came back from the ring and his bags were chained up to a pipe on the ceiling. But he didn't get mad or upset because he knew it was coming. Al Snow and Tazz had told him that he was going to be ribbed. So he went and found some bolt cutters, got his stuff down, and never said another word about it. That's not exactly paying your dues in my book.

It used to be there were a hundred little promotions all over the country and you had to work your tail off in order to get to the top. The more shows you could get on, the more your skills would improve and the more your passion for being a wrestler would become obvious.

I look at a guy like Undertaker. He caught a break five years into his career, and since coming into WWE, he has put up with everything the business has thrown his way. There's no way he could have survived all the injuries, all the backstage politics, without having a real passion for our business. I think I have a similar passion.

Wrestling needs people like that, people willing to drive ten hours just to get a little bit of experience, to ensure that the business continues to thrive. If people just want to wrestle so that they can be TV stars and make a lot of money, it doesn't bode well for the future.

PLAYING THE GAME

MATT: Every wrestler's goal is to be on top of the business. To even have a little taste of that is very exciting. No matter what else happens in our career, that's something we can always reflect upon. It's like Steve Austin always said, "If you're in WWE, your only goal ought to be becoming the WWE Champion." If you're a baseball player, you want to win the World Series. If you're a pro football player, you want your Super Bowl ring. If you're a wrestler, the WWE Championship is the very top, the pinnacle of your profession.

The Intercontinental title is just one step away from there, so it's a very very big deal.

JEFF: Winning the Intercontinental Championship was kind of like a dream come true, even if it was just for six days. I knew I had a rematch with Triple H on *Raw,* and I'll be honest—I didn't get much sleep the night before. I wanted to treasure every moment I had being the IC Champ.

MATT: We did a pretape on *Raw* where I jumped Stone Cold from behind. He was so great to work with. "It's fun when you get to do all this cool stuff, isn't it?" he asked.

"It sure is," I said.

"Enjoy it, man."

Austin knew that when you're an integral part of the show, and you are getting to do good work, it makes the job so much more fun. It's great to feel important.

JEFF: After Stone Cold beat up Matt in the back, Triple H told him to take the night off. Triple H hit me with a nutshot and the Pedigree and that was that. After the bell, Stone Cold came out and the two heels started to destroy us. Then Taker and Kane came out to make the save, which set up their feud.

MATT: Triple H and Stone Cold are different in many ways, but they're incredibly great workers. There are lot of little things that they both do really well, which is what has carried them so far. The execution of little things, like the way someone segues from spot to spot, is what makes people buy you as a legitimate Superstar.

For example, when I worked with Triple H in that tag-team match, there was a point where I was pushed back into the corner and we were trading punches. *Boom! Wham! Boom! Wham!*

As he was nailing me, he kept saying "C'mon!" He wanted me to increase the speed of my punches to match his. Triple H knew instinctively how the timing of our punches would make for a more believable fight scenario, even with our size difference.

I enjoy working with guys like Stone Cold and Triple H because different guys bring different things to the table. Stone Cold, for example, works in a style which I think of as "animalistic"—he feels things out as he goes along, he responds to what the crowd is doing, he's very hard to predict. It's almost like a real fight. It can be hard for some wrestlers to handle, because you don't know what direction he's coming from. It's not necessarily smooth, but it's very aggressive, and most important, it always seems realistic.

I had a really great match with Stone Cold a few weeks after our initial tag match. He was in the back arguing with Debra, and she hit him over the head with a cookie sheet. Later on in the show, Lita said to Debra something about how awesome it was that she'd stood up for herself.

Then Debra went to Stone Cold and put a spin on it: "That Lita said you were a redneck and that if I'm married to you I must be redneck trailer trash, too." He got hot and threatened Lita, but I confronted him, which resulted in our match.

Stone Cold was working very tight—he was on top of me in the Lou Thesz Press position, punching the shit out of me. But that's just his working style. He's always very aggressive, even a bit stiff. And considering the position he was in, compared to the position I was in, he needed to be. It was good for me to have a decent match with him and get that rub, but he definitely needed to look strong and tough, especially in a match against one-half of a tag team.

JEFF: People think because of the way we wrestle that we're small, but when we were in the ring with Stone Cold and Triple H, they finally started to realize that we're not cruiserweights. Obviously we didn't tower over them, but it was clear that we fit in the same ring. That was really important for us, especially if we're ever going to be seen as main-event guys.

191

MATT HARDY— CHAMPION OF EUROPE

DATE: *April 24, 2001*
LOCATION: *Denver, Colorado*
ARENA: *Pepsi Center*

MATT: The week after Jeff lost the title back to Triple H we did a two-night stand at the Pepsi Center in Denver. First we had an eight-man tag on *Raw*—Jeff and me, Undertaker and Kane vs. Stone Cold, Triple H, and Edge & Christian.

There was talk of a one-on-one match between Stone Cold and me for the WWE title on *SmackDown!* but that fell through. I was little bummed, but what are you going to do? When I walked into the *SmackDown!* tapings, I looked on the sheet and saw I was wrestling Eddie Guerrero. I asked Michael Hayes, "Do we have anything going for the finish?"

"Yeah," he told me. "You're going over for the European title."

There had been nothing going on between Eddie and myself. It was just made as a match. I think the European title was a way of throwing me a bone because we did so well with Stone Cold and Triple H, and Jeff had won the Intercontinental Championship.

I had Jeff and Lita with me, Eddie had Perry Saturn and Terri, so we had a lot of tools to play with at ringside. The match started with some good back and forth between us, then I went to the top but got crotched by Saturn. Eddie hit me with a Frankensteiner off the turnbuckle for a two-count while Jeff and Perry went at it on the outside. Then Terri got into it, kicking Jeff, but Lita chased her around the apron and into the ring. This of course distracted the ref, and while he was jawing at Terri, Lita gave Eddie her hurricanrana, which set up a Twist of Fate for the 1-2-3! Matt Hardy is your new WWE European Champion!

My philosophy is that I'm not out there to get myself over—I'm out there to get myself, my opponent, *and* the match over. If every segment gets over, then the entire show gets over. And that should be everyone's goal in the end. The match would have been just fine if it had been just the two of us, and in the end, I made a comeback and hit Eddie with the Twist of Fate. But there's no getting around the fact that we got a better reaction with Lita doing the hurricanrana feeding into the Twist of Fate. When you have different tools to play with, you can create combinations that make for a more exciting match than just a straight one-on-one. That weekend I took the title to a three-way dance at *Backlash* in Chicago. It was me, Christian, and Eddie Guerrero, and we were on in the toughest spot on the card, second to last, right before the main event. That match always gets cut for time, and sure enough, we got cut down just before we went out.

The match was good, but considering the talent involved, it could have been a lot better. I hate to say a bad word about Eddie—he's such a good soul—but he was very out of it that day. After that, we went into an angle where Eddie befriended me and started to infiltrate Team Extreme, with his ultimate goal being to steal Lita away from me with his Latino *heeeeeeat*. That was actually one of the most over times we've had, where Eddie was hitting on Lita. It was a story line that gave people a reason to tune in each week.

JEFF: Matt just thinks that because it was all about him. Most of the time I was just sitting there putting my pants on while him and Lita were making out.

MATT: Ultimately, things didn't exactly go as planned. I was supposed to fight Eddie in a *King of the Ring* qualifying match on *Raw* in Minneapolis, but sadly, he showed up in no condition to wrestle. Back in those days, Eddie had a problem with painkillers, and that night, he was in such bad shape that they had to take him off the roster and send him to rehab. Fortunately, he made it though with flying colors and is now doing great.

At the time, though, it was aggravating because there was no closure to this story line that had been going on for a few weeks. But there was nothing I could do. Eddie was gone and the angle was dropped.

Jeff ended up taking Eddie's place in the qualifying match. He got me with a backslide and went on to the next round, where he got beat by Kurt Angle.

THE FORGOTTEN TLC

DATE: *May 24, 2001*
LOCATION: *Anaheim, California*
ARENA: *Arrowhead Pond*

MATT: Those were really strange days in WWE. After our little run with the top dogs, they gave Chris Benoit and Chris Jericho a shot at being the

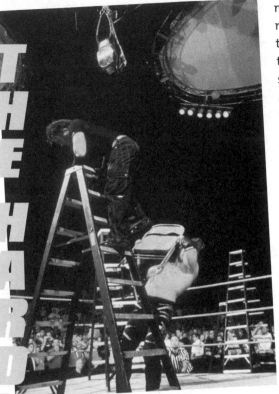

number one babyfaces. It was definitely time to create new stars. I truly believe that one of the things that makes a wrestling company successful is when a guy that is at a high-midlevel position burns a trail to become the top man in the business. That's something that gets the fans so involved, rallying behind someone as they go to the top. That was a huge part of Stone Cold and The Rock's success.

JEFF: Benoit and Jericho won the tag titles in an amazing *Raw* main event against Stone Cold and Triple H. Most people probably remember that as the match where Triple H injured his quadriceps muscle, which took him out of the picture for a good eight months.

The next night, we were in Anaheim for *SmackDown!* and Vince made Benoit and Jericho defend the title in a Fatal Four-Way TLC match against us, Edge & Christian, and the Dudleyz.

We all refer to that match as the Forgotten TLC, and for my money, it's one of the best. When they first told us that they wanted to do it, we were a little upset. It felt like they just wanted to throw something together to pop the ratings. As is always the case when that happens, I worried about how it would affect our legacy. It was just like the night *Raw* debuted on TNN and they asked us to have a ladder match just one night after our cage match with Edge & Christian.

As it turned out, TLC III ended up being a phenomenal match. All eight of us really busted our asses and tore the house down.

MATT: We had a couple of awesome spots—Jeff climbed the monster ladder and leapfrogged over another into a leg drop, putting Bubba through the announcers' table. Then D-Von and I exchanged blows atop two ladders in the middle of the ring. I did a Twist of Fate on him off the top. It was sweet!

As I went back up to go for the belts, Jericho tried to hit me with a chair. I blocked it by kicking the chair into his face, sending him off the ladder and onto the ropes. He bounced off the ropes into the ladder I was on, sending me out of the ring.

On the negative side, that match was where Chris Benoit first injured his neck, going though a table after I moved off in the last split second. But in the end, Benoit managed to get up the ladder and pull down the belts so that the two Chrises retained the tag titles.

By June, though, ratings hadn't skyrocketed and the company pulled back on the push. Benoit and Jericho were in a Triple Threat title match with Stone Cold at *King of the Ring*, and Benoit reinjured his neck, taking him out for a year.

WORK RATE

MATT: It's been said that Jeff and I are pioneers of the cruiserweight style, but I really hate being labeled a cruiserweight. I'm not saying I'm a super heavyweight, but to me, a cruiserweight is two hundred pounds and under. People don't realize it, but I'm basically the same size as Ric Flair and Bret Hart—six-foot-one, 235 pounds.

Where I think we've been influential is in terms of work rate, of putting on fast-paced, intensely athletic wrestling matches. The evolution of what we do can be traced back to Flair, even though he worked in a very different style. He basically did the same few spots over and over again, but he always busted his ass to put on an entertaining match.

Shawn Michaels and Bret Hart were the two pioneering forces in what I call the Work Rate Era. The Hit Man was the first guy that wasn't a monster to be a truly credible WWE World Champion. Like Flair, he fooled people into seeing him as bigger than he really is. He did a few more spots and was a little flashier, but the two of them were actually quite similar. I remember Bret saying in an interview that if you've seen one Ric Flair match, you've seen them all. Well, the same can be said for any Hit Man match, because his comeback was always pretty much the same—Atomic Drop, clothesline, Russian Leg Sweep, forearm off the second turnbuckle.

The secret of what made both of them so great was that they knew how to put their signature moves into different combinations, in such a way that the crowd didn't see them coming. I'm a big believer in wrestlers utilizing trademark moves. That's what the fans are waiting to see.

After Bret came Shawn Michaels. He was the first major-league main-event Superstar to incorporate an acrobatic style into his arsenal. He did high cross bodies to the floor, he did moonsault bodyblocks, he did flips off the top rope. What was even more innovative about Shawn was his size. Not only was he smaller in height than previous World Champions, he only weighed two hundred pounds.

Shawn brought a new kind of flash to wrestling. He had a totally unique charisma, a natural sense of theatricality and flamboyance. Shawn was *the* revolutionary force in creating what is today's WWE.

He didn't invent the style—it had been prevalent in Japan and Mexico, plus guys like Dynamite Kid had been doing that kind of wrestling for some time—but Shawn brought it into the mainstream of American professional wrestling.

Eventually heavyweights like Stone Cold Steve Austin began incorporating a high work rate into their matches. Even though there was a lot of punch-kick-punch brawling, the intensity of today's main-event matches is much stronger than back in the Hulk Hogan days.

To me, the future of wrestling marries a very high work rate with well-drawn characters that people care about. There should still be weight divisions so that cruiserweights can continue to work a more athletic style of wrestling, but those guys need to have fully developed characters as well.

That remains the most important thing—a character that people attach to. In the end, that's what gets people to yell and scream and pop during a match. You can have all the sheer wrestling talent imaginable, but without a compelling character, it doesn't mean a thing. But combine the two and the world will fall at your feet.

LIGHT-HEAVYWEIGHT

DATE: *June 5, 2001*
LOCATION: *Grand Forks, North Dakota*
ARENA: *Grand Forks Events Center*

JEFF: When the Light-Heavyweight Championship first came back into play, I saw it as an awesome opportunity for me. I knew I could really put on some great matches working in that style.

Matt, of course, wanted no part of it. "I want to be a heavyweight," he said, which is fine, but that doesn't mean that the light-heavyweight title

was pussy. That belt has been worn by some of the best athletes in wrestling history, from Ultimo Dragon and Jushin "Thunder" Liger to X-Pac and Jerry Lynn.

The *SmackDown!* match where I won the Light-Heavyweight Championship from Jerry Lynn was a good fast-paced TV match, with lots of hot near falls. I hit him with everything—a somersault leg drop, a spinning heel kick, and a Whisper in the Wind—but I couldn't get anything more than a two-count. Finally Jerry tried for a superplex, but I pushed him off and got him with the Swanton.

I dig Jerry, he's a cool guy and an amazing athlete. The only problem I had working with him was that he always wanted to do too much, even on house shows. "Man, we don't need to do all that," I wanted to say to him, but I had to respect that he was older and he knew what he was doing. I've always been kind of like that, though. I just listen. But, to be fair, we had some pretty great matches.

MATT: When Jeff won the Light-Heavyweight Championship, I came running into the ring with Lita for a big celebration. Then we went to the back and did a little vignette where we were leaving the building, saying how cool it was that we were both singles champs—Jeff had the light-heavyweight title and I was the European Champion.

Cut to Edge & Christian watching us, going "We could be singles champions if we wanted to," and giving each other devious looks back and forth. That was pretty much the beginning of the end for those guys, setting up their breakup.

JEFF: I ended up dropping the light-heavyweight title to X-Pac a couple of weeks later. It was at Madison Square Garden, the night after I beat him at *King of the Ring*. The match was short but sweet, with Pac pinning me with a backslide and his feet on the ropes.

But X-Pac winning the title wasn't the big news out of the Garden. The Invasion had begun . . .

INVASION

DATE: *July 22, 2001*
LOCATION: *Cleveland, Ohio*
ARENA: *Gund Arena*

MATT: We all knew that without WCW and ECW around, things were going to be very different. Nobody was hot on our heels, and worse, there was no alternative to our product. We're number one regardless of what we do, and that's not necessarily the best thing for the business. I want WWE to be number one because we're *the best,* not because we're all there is.

JEFF: After a few months, it was decided that WCW would not be a separate brand. In fact, they were going to become part of our show. The first WCW wrestler to "invade" WWE programming was Lance Storm, which was very exciting for the smart marks, but most of our audience didn't have a clue who he was! Next came Hugh Morrus, followed by Booker T at *King of the Ring*.

That was a bad omen—Booker came out of the crowd and interfered in the Triple Threat match by putting Austin through the announcers' table, but he was a little overexcited and wasn't as careful as he should have been. Steve hit the table at an awkward angle and fractured his hand as he tried to stop the momentum.

MATT: After *King of the Ring,* we did both *Raw* and *SmackDown!* at Madison Square Garden. The opening match on *Raw* was Test and Rhyno for the hardcore title. They were battling in the back, and just after Rhyno got the pin, Mike Awesome ran in and powerbombed him across a ladder. He was the first WCW guy to win a WWE title.

The next night we had a Tag Team Table match for the Dudleyz' titles. Jeff eliminated D-Von with a Swanton through one table, then Bubba powerbombed him through two tables on the outside when Sean O'Haire and Chuck Palumbo, the WCW Tag Team Champions, came running into the ring from out of the crowd. Chuck nailed me with a superkick as Sean hit Bubba with a fireman's carry spinebuster. As I was lying there, Sean hopped up on the top rope and got me with his Seanton Bomb.

JEFF: A handful of WWE guys started coming down the ramp—Rhyno, the Goodfather, Bull Buchanan, and Haku—so O'Haire and Palumbo tried to get out of there through the audience. As they hopped the barricade, they got ambushed by a dozen more WWE Superstars, led by the Acolyte Protection Agency (APA). They chased Chuck and Sean back into the ring and started beating the living shit out of them—Bradshaw really lit into O'Haire. He whaled on him as the crowd went nuts! Then the APA put them both through tables—hard. It was Faarooq and Bradshaw's way of saying "Welcome to WWE, boys!" Those guys definitely felt the brunt of the WWE locker room's frustration with the Invasion.

MATT: Things had been going so great. I was feeling genuinely excited about the future—we had just worked with Stone Cold and Triple H, Jeff won the Intercontinental Championship, I won the European Championship. It seemed like we were both going to get a legitimate shot at elevating ourselves. But once the Invasion happened, it sent us right back to the bottom of the ladder. There were so many guys in WWE that had been busting their asses to get ahead, and then all of a sudden everybody's push was thrown on the back burner so that they could concentrate on the Invasion. It was an aggravating time, but something we had to simply ride out. The wrestling business is notorious for that. Sometimes you just have to be patient and wait till your turn comes up again.

JEFF: It got very crowded in the back. There were twice as many wrestlers occupying the space.

MATT: The next *Raw* featured Booker T vs. Buff Bagwell, and it will go down in history for more than just being the first-ever WCW match on WWE TV—quite frankly, it was one of the worst wrestling disasters of all time! It was awful!

The people that support us are die-hard WWE fans. To them WCW was the enemy. So when they decided to put on a WCW match as the main event on *Raw*, I had the feeling that the crowd wasn't going to rally behind it. I was right—they did anything but rally behind them.

The sheer displeasure of the people in the Tacoma Dome that night was incredible. It was similar to the level of crowd intensity during the Hulk Hogan vs. The Rock match at *WrestleMania X-8*—but in a completely negative way. The fans were as hostile as I've ever seen them, chanting "This match sucks!" and booing like maniacs. To make matters worse, it was a truly terrible match. There could not have been a worse choice than Buff Bagwell, who represented all that was wrong with WCW TV.

JEFF: From that night, the fear set in—WCW was not working as everyone had hoped it would. Vince had underestimated just how much WWE fans despised WCW. It's funny to realize that when the Invasion started, WCW was supposed to be the babyface promotion. But the audience had been trained to hate WCW no matter what, so they quickly turned the story line around and made the Invaders into heels.

MATT: A quick fix was needed and it came in the form of ECW. They realized that the only way to make the WCW thing work was to take some of the WWE Superstars and inject them into WCW.

ECW didn't have the same stigma with our audience as WCW. In fact, the ECW's cult following was very much on our side in the "Monday Night Wars." Most of their roster had become part of WWE, guys like Rhyno, Tazz, and the Dudley Boyz. So they signed Rob Van Dam and Tommy Dreamer, paired them all with the WCW wrestlers, and the Alliance was born.

JEFF: Once the Alliance became part of our show, every match became an interpromotional match, and it didn't take long for that to lose its excitement. It was something wrestling fans had fantasized about for years and the reality was a huge letdown.

MATT: It was a very confusing time, not only for the fans but for the wrestlers as well. It didn't matter if you had been a heel or a babyface in WWE. All of a sudden we were all babyfaces and all the Alliance wrestlers were heels.

JEFF: After ECW joined the Alliance, the *Invasion* Pay-Per-View began coming together. Lita and Trish were booked to face Stacy Keibler and Torrie Wilson in a bra-and-panties match at the Pay-Per-View, but the real winners were me and Matt! They added heat to the match on *Smack-Down!*—Lita and Trish had a match, and afterward Matt and I were talking in the back. Stacy and Torrie came up behind us, introduced themselves, and gave us both kisses!

"What was that all about?" Matt asked.

"Those chicks dig us," I replied.

As if that wasn't enough, later in the show I won a victory for our side by taking the hardcore title from Mike Awesome. I got some help from Edge & Christian, who did one of their trademark run-ins and whacked him with a con-chair-to, setting up a Swanton Bomb and the 1-2-3.

We had a tag match with the Dudleyz—who were in the Alliance—on the next week's *Raw*. RVD interfered, hitting me with the Five-Star Frog Splash. That set up our hardcore title match at the Pay-Per-View.

The fans had been looking forward to seeing me vs. RVD for the longest time. They knew our styles were pretty much in tune with each other.

I first worked with Van Dam in May 1997, when Jerry Lawler brought him onto *Raw* as part of his whole feud with Paul E. and ECW—he called it "Extremely Crappy Wrestling." I was still just a job guy back then and Howard Finkel introduced me as being from Virginia.

I wore my hair back with a red bandanna, and these old-school red spandex tights. I'll never forget how Lawler made fun of me. He said to RVD, "Take care of this little Jon Bon Jovi wannabe!" The match was a total squash. I oversold everything, and Van Dam pinned me after hitting a Five-Star Frog Splash and a split-legged moonsault.

We didn't click back then. He was kind of a stuck-up ass-hole, and he acted like he didn't have much respect for me. He was okay after the match. Paul E. was cool, though. He came over and said, "Thanks, kid. You put him over real well."

By *Invasion,* we'd become better acquainted, and Rob was much mellower than he was back then. RVD has his own psychology, which is very similar to mine, and very different from Bubba's or Matt's. When I work with a guy like William Regal, the discussion is usually me saying "Okay. Yes. Whatever." But me and Rob really get into it because we're both on the same page.

Before the match, we had a backstage vignette. Matt was telling me that RVD is that damn good, and that I'd better finish it quick, or else it was going to get ugly. "Fine," I said. "That's just the way I like it."

Then Van Dam came in and knocked Matt out with a chair shot. "You're next," he told me.

It was a great match, full of highspots. There were a few classic moments—the two of us running the rail at each other, with me winding up in the crowd; my giving Rob an awesome sunset flip out of the ring; Rob sending me flying off the stage with the Van Daminator. The finish was cool, too. Van Dam laid the hardcore belt across my chest and hit the Five-Star Frog Splash directly onto it.

That night it really felt like our match was the one people were most excited about. I like to think it lived up to its potential.

PLAY BALL!

JEFF: In August we were asked to do a commercial for the 2001 *No Mercy* Pay-Per-View. The premise was based around the World Series, because *No Mercy* is WWE's October event. The idea was that Kane would be running the bases, and the WWE Superstars foil the other team's attempts to tag him out. I'm a big baseball fan, so I was pretty excited. It sounded like a lot of fun.

MATT: I got to the set—Jeff was late, as usual—and the director said, "What we had in mind was that as Kane gets to second base, you do Swanton Bombs off of ladders and put a couple of guys through tables."

What?! "We didn't sign up for a TLC match," I said. "First off, I don't do the Swanton Bomb. Second, this is a baseball field! It's real solid, hard-packed dirt! To be honest, we don't feel too good about this."

"Okay," the director said, even though I could tell that it wasn't. "If you're not comfortable with it, it's completely up to you." Translation: If you don't want to do it, we'll just tell one of the WWE higher-ups and you'll get in trouble.

"How about this?" I said. "What if we put these guys on tables and we give them both leg drops. That'd probably be the safest thing. But we're not going to do it more than once, because it's going to hurt—it's going to hurt us and it's definitely going to hurt the guys we land on."

Fortunately, the director was totally cool with that idea. The two guys we were going to put through tables were both workers from Ultimate Pro Wrestling in Los Angeles, Tom Howard and a guy named—believe it or not—Smelly.

Jeff finally showed up and, being Jeff, said, "I'll do the Swanton if you want me to."

"Dude," I said, pulling him aside, "what I'm going to do—and what I'd advise you to do—is leg drops on these guys, and let them take the impact. Don't give them a safe leg drop where you're going pop back and hit your head on the baseball field.

"Not to sound like a dick, but tonight it's either going to be me or it's going to be him. And it damn sure isn't going to be me. I recommend you do the same."

"All right, man," Jeff said. "That's what I'll do."

We set it up, and before they rolled camera, I said to Smelly, "This is probably going to be pretty rough, so I'll just apologize ahead of time."

I set Smelly up on the table so that when I landed, my hamstring would be right on his face and my butt would hit right in the middle of his chest. That way the table would break in such a way that I would basically just be sitting right on top of him. With a legitimate leg drop, I would hit and then pop backward.

Well, I dropped off the ladder and *Wham!* I drove Smelly right through the table. He went down hard. It actually knocked him unconscious. They had to use smelling salts to get him up. "Sorry, man," I said as he finally stood up. "I told you it was going to be rough."

Jeff, on the other hand, jumped off the ladder and gave Tom Howard the basic calf-to-the-throat leg drop. He hit, went through the table, then tumbled backward and knocked *himself* out. It was hilarious!

I thought to myself, *Why did Jeff do that? Is it because he's such a humanitarian that he would rather kill himself than hurt the other guy?* I don't think so. I think the main thing was that Jeff just didn't want to listen to what I had to say. It was an act of defiance. Plus, he doesn't pay attention. He thinks, *I'll just do it my way and it'll be fine.*

JEFF: I tried to aim, but I missed. Really.

MATT: Still, they got it in one take.

JEFF: It's a problem we have—everyone's always asking us to jump off of ladders! I'll probably never get away from it. People are always going to expect me to be the crazy risk taker.

MATT: The problem with being seen as the highspot guy is that you can only go so far with it. Also, being a daredevil will unquestionably end your career early. Poor Shawn Michaels. He busted his ass night in and night out in those hard rings, and it took ten years off of his career.

There's a classic story about the night Shawn hurt his back in the famous casket match with Undertaker at the 1998 *Royal Rumble*. After the match, Triple H came to the back and told Vince, "Shawn's hurt."

"Is he hurt bad?" Vince asked.

"Well," Triple H replied, "he's definitely not hurt good."

SUMMERSLAM

DATE: *August 19, 2001*
LOCATION: *San Jose, California*
ARENA: *San Jose Arena*

JEFF: The 24–7 hardcore rule was pretty damn stupid, but it worked out good for me a few weeks after *Invasion*. Van Dam was representing the Alliance in a *Raw* match against Kurt Angle. Late in the match, Mike Awesome, Tommy Dreamer, and Raven interfered on RVD's behalf, so I came running out to make the save. Kurt got Rob with the Angle Slam, then I hit the Swanton for the win.

We had a tag match on *SmackDown!* the next night—me and Chris Jericho vs. Rhyno and RVD. Rob pulled a ladder out from under the ring and set it up on the ropes. He hit the ladder with an ax handle, seesawing it into my face. After the match, I said that if Van Dam likes ladders so much, maybe we should raise the stakes on our *SummerSlam* hardcore title match and make it a ladder match!

It was a crazy violent match, very ECW in style. It was the first time I'd actually juiced on WWE, but I didn't do a very good job of it. I didn't take any aspirin before the match, which supposedly thins the blood so you get a lot of color.

There's several different ways to juice. The old-timers used to put the blade in their mouth, which is crazy! Like we said before, the most common way to do it is tape it onto your finger or your wrist. The way I did it was I had the referee put it out there for me. "I don't want to wrestle with that in my fingers," I said.

MATT: I wasn't a huge fan of that match. I like matches where people bust their ass and do a lot of innovative stuff, but also I like it to have logic behind it.

There were too many instances where Jeff and Rob used the ladder for nothing other than the spot. If you don't hurt your opponent and then try to win, you lose me. It's like watching a movie and seeing a boom in the shot—you think, *Oh. This is fake.* There were too many spots in that match where I said, "I'm not buying this for a second."

JEFF: Matt and Amy are always talking about what makes a match "realistic." But how can you say what's realistic around this place? Sometimes I think they break things down too much. Sure, logic comes into play, but it's silly as hell to start thinking that what we do is real. My favorite example is getting shot into the ropes. If I were to really get shot into these ropes, I wouldn't spring right back!

I loved the hardcore ladder match. It was an awesome match, even though Matt thought it was stupid and had no logic. There have been matches where I just wanted to take the ladder and throw it in the ring right away. But no one wants to do it because they can't get away from following the basic ladder-match story line. "We can't bring it in yet," they tell me. "That's too early. We've got to build up to it."

There are also times in a ladder match when you have to take your time going up the ladder because the other guy is not in the right place at the right time. There's really no other way to do it.

The one thing that was wrong with the match was that the finish didn't come off like we planned it. Rob was on top of the ladder, so I climbed up and powerbombed him off. As he lay there I went back up and tried for the belt, but Rob moved the ladder and left me hanging. He was supposed to take me down with a spinning heel kick off the top, but he missed, so I dropped down and climbed up there again. Rob pushed the ladder over before I could get the belt, sending me into the ropes, then climbed up to regain the title. I don't care what Matt thinks. It was a great match.

STAND BACK!

DATE: August 27, 2001
LOCATION: Grand Rapids, Michigan
ARENA: Van Andel Arena

MATT: For me, the one best thing about the Invasion was that my good buddies Shane Helms and Shannon Moore—a.k.a. Three Count—had been picked up from WCW. Shannon got shipped off to Heartland Wrestling Association for development, while Shane was brought onto the active roster. It was just like the old days for me, riding with Shane. He's definitely one of my very best friends.

When he came up with the Hurricane gimmick, they wanted to give him a little something to help him get over. When they came to me and asked if I'd mind dropping the title to him, I said, "Hell no!"

It was the night that Shane debuted as the Hurricane. That afternoon, we were talking about the match and Vince came over to give us his ideas. "Matt, when he walks out onto the stage in his costume and his face paint, you'd probably chuckle, right? You'd think he was a little silly."

Right before we went out for the match, Vince was sitting in the Gorilla Position and he said, "When the Hurricane comes out in his getup, you'll probably chuckle, right?"

Gee, I thought, *I'd better chuckle.* I told Vince not to worry.

We got out there, Shane's entrance music hit—"Stand back! There's a Hurricane coming though!"—and I did exactly what Vince wanted. I chuckled.

It was a decent-enough TV match. I had most of the offense, then Ivory ran out with a tire iron and took out Lita. I pulled Ivory into the ring by her hair, but she smacked me in the ribs with the tire iron, setting up Shane's Eye of the Hurricane finisher for the victory.

We had some ideas for a feud between the Hurricane and myself, but it wasn't to be. The four of us had a mixed tag the following week, with Ivory beating Lita, and that was that. I never got my blow-off with him, which was too bad, because Shane and I had some great ideas.

Nevertheless, I had held the title for a little over four months, making me the longest-reigning American-born WWE European Champion. Only Davey Boy Smith, the British Bulldog, held it longer.

MATT: We did *Raw* in San Antonio on September 10, then drove all night to Houston for the *SmackDown!* taping. There was a writer from *Rolling Stone* magazine traveling with us, writing a piece about Amy. His name was Harry Thomas, but Jeff kept calling him Harry *Potter*. Because he was with us, the office had paid for our rental car, so we had a big Ford Excursion. It was a fun ride. We spent the night cutting up, doing crazy stuff like rapping and making up song lyrics.

JEFF: We were checking out some new entrance music, seeing how we liked it.

MATT: WWE was also paying for our hotel that night, so we stayed at the Hilton on the south side of Houston. That morning, Amy and I were in bed sound asleep when the phone started ringing. Amy picked it up and it was Shane. He said, "Hey, are you guys watching TV?"

Amy was still half asleep and out of it. "What are you talking about?"

"Just turn on the TV. My girlfriend just called me. There are planes flying into buildings. Turn it on."

Amy hung up the phone and lay back down. I said, "Who was that?"

"It was Shane. He said something about planes crashing into buildings."

I turned on the TV and we saw what was happening. Of course, we instantaneously woke up. I called Shane back and said, "What all's happened? What's going on?" And that's when the second plane hit.

JEFF: It seems like everybody has a story about picking up the phone and someone telling them to turn on the TV. I'm sure it happened all around the world. My girlfriend called me when it started happening. All I was thinking about was getting *SmackDown!* over with and getting home. When she called, I was like, *"Whaaat?"* I turned on the TV and pretty much spent the rest of the day staring at the news.

MATT: Amy and I were just frozen. It takes a lot to affect me, with everything I've seen and been through, but that did it in a really major way. I didn't want to leave that room. I didn't want to go anywhere. I was just stuck to the TV. I sat there watching the footage over and over and over again. So many thoughts were running through my head: What's going to happen next? How many people died today? Was there anybody in there that I knew? We fly four times a week. What's our life going to be like now?

I knew that this was going to change everything.

JEFF: I was just numb, especially after the plane hit the Pentagon. Then the Towers went down. Everybody was running, all that shit was falling. It reminded me of when the tidal wave hits in *Deep Impact*. It was weird, because I kept seeing scenes from movies in my head, like *Daylight*, where all those people are trapped in the Lincoln Tunnel.

MATT: It was around noon when we got a call from WWE. They said, "We're not sure what's going to happen tonight as far as the show goes."

JEFF: I was really pissed off. I mean, what the hell? The worst thing I'd ever seen had just happened. Even later, when we heard we were going to do *SmackDown!* on Thursday night, I was still so freaked out.

MATT: Some of the WWE crew was in the Hilton with us, but a bunch of people were staying out by the airport. That night, though, everybody migrated to our hotel. There was a restaurant and a bar downstairs and we all gathered together and spent the night talking, having a few drinks.

JEFF: It was good to be there with all those people, because we really are like a family in a lot of ways. And so many WWE people have roots in New York, like Tazz, Tommy Dreamer, and Lilian Garcia. Her husband worked in the World Trade Center, but that day he forgot his cell phone and turned around and went home! It was one of those times when you could really feel the closeness among the boys. Later that night I wrote a song called "September Day."

MATT: Even if Vince had wanted to do the show that night—and I'm sure he wouldn't have—they had shut the whole city down. Eventually it was decided that we were going to do *SmackDown!* on the thirteenth.

That day I walked into the Compaq Center with Lance Storm. "I don't think we should be here," he said. "I just don't feel right about this."

Nobody did. Wrestling was the last thing on any of our minds. Everybody just wanted to get home and be with their loved ones.

JEFF: We were all hanging out in the back, and Vince made a little speech. "Our job is to make people smile," he said. "The terrorists want us to give up, and we're not going to let that happen."

I was still pretty frustrated about being there, but when I saw the crowd that showed up, I thought, *Well, if these people want to see wrestling, I'm glad I'm here to give it to them.*

MATT: *SmackDown!* was the biggest live assembly to happen after the attack. It was two days later and there were twenty thousand people there. It was hard not to think, *What if they bomb this place?*

I knew that we had to move on, but it was hard for the boys in a lot of ways, especially when you consider that our job is play fighting. Thousands of people had just been killed and America was under attack from a terrorist organization. We still had no idea what was going on, or what was going to happen next.

JEFF: The show opened with Lilian singing the National Anthem. I'll never forget that as long as I live. It was just so powerful, so moving. Tears were rolling down all of our cheeks; it was incredible. When the people started clapping, I knew we were doing the right thing.

MATT: I wanted to go hug every member of the crowd. It was really a special moment. We weren't there as performers, we were there as Americans. We wrestled Lance and Shane that night. None of us were really into what we were doing, but in the end I was glad that we did it. In a way it was kind of like America saying "We *will* go on."

I'm proud to have played an important part in that. Everybody was feeling so patriotic, but Bradshaw was just totally full-on.

"We're running this show tonight because we're gonna show you that you cannot break, you cannot even bend the fiber, the backbone of the United States of America," he said. "There's gonna be some critics. There's gonna be some critics that wonder why we run this show. I wanna make this perfectly clear: *Go to hell*. We're doin' this show because we love America. All we have to give you for tonight is this, is this evening. If I had to, I'd give my life, readily, for this country. I have relatives who have done that, who are buried overseas, who are buried in many different places. I would do the same thing 'cause I love this great country . . . You guys who are out there, we're gonna find your ass. We're gonna make whatever country's hiding you into a stinking parking lot. God bless this country, God bless this great state I live in, and God rest the sorry son of a bitch that did this. We will find you."

A lot of people thought he was a little over-the-top, but I loved it. We'd never been through anything that devastating before and it really made me appreciate being an American like no other time in my life.

JEFF: That night they were saying how flights were going to be back on schedule the next afternoon, but we were like, "Puh-lease! We're not getting out of here for days!"

When *SmackDown!* was done, we talked it over and decided, "Let's drive home."

MATT: We just wanted to get home so bad. We had that rental car and we didn't care where we were supposed to drop it off—we were going to take it to Raleigh.

I was determined to do all of the driving. Amy was in the front with me, and Jeff and Shane crashed out in the back.

Man, I smoked it! Jericho, Edge, and Christian were driving together to Tampa, where they all live, and we called one another every hour on the hour, just to make sure everybody was okay. I got a little sleepy around Atlanta, but I refused to hand over the wheel. It was another example of my competitive nature, even against myself. I swore I was going to drive every inch and that's exactly what I did.

We ended up getting home at around three o'clock the next afternoon. I had driven twelve hundred miles in a little over sixteen hours.

JEFF: They canceled the house shows for that weekend, but we had *Raw* in Nashville on Monday and *SmackDown!* in Memphis. Matt and Amy flew up there, but I was still scared. I know I have an overactive imagination, but I kept picturing people on the plane getting their throats slashed. So I ended up driving to Nashville by myself.

MATT: Amy, Shane, and I flew together on Sunday night. The airport was like a ghost town. Man, it was eerie. We took a Southwest flight and there were only twelve people on the plane. Just going to the airport, you couldn't get the image of those planes crashing into the Trade Center out of your head.

JEFF: You think about the terrorists or guys like Timothy McVeigh. There's so many mad minds out there.

MATT: Before 9/11, I didn't pay much attention to current events. I knew the basics of government and law and so forth, but I didn't care. My attitude was, as long as I'm not affected by it, everything's fine. But then everything changed, and I started reading more, studying the newspapers, and just learning about the world around me. I just found myself becoming involved and interested. From then on, I wanted to make sure that whatever hotel we were staying in had CNN.

JEFF: We'd watch the news in the locker room and in our hotel. I was really struck by this fire crew from Texas who went up to New York to help out. We were all united as Americans. It used to be that there were people in places like Texas and North Carolina that just hated New York, but that totally ended on 9/11. And when you look at it like that, you can't help but think that it made us stronger. It was a terrible thing that happened, but there was some good that came out of it.

MATT: I heard someone on the news describe it as a "hinge event," where the world just makes a complete and total change. That made me think about hinge events in wrestling history, like when Stone Cold and DX got hot, or when Vince bought WCW. When that happened I thought, *Oh my God, I can't believe this is happening. From here on in, everything is going to be completely different.*

JEFF: A couple of weeks later we were all on a charter flight from Winnipeg to Minneapolis and the U.S. had just made its first bombing raid in Afghanistan. Bradshaw got up in front of everyone and said, "Fellow WWE Superstars. I just want to let you all know that we just bombed bin Laden's ass in Afghanistan." And we all cheered and applauded.

MATT: It wasn't until October 14 that we finally went up to New York City for a Sunday-afternoon house show. We got into town on Saturday, and that night we took a cab down to Ground Zero just to see it. The WWE people who got to go down there for an official visit were the top-tier guys, like Vince, Austin, and Triple H. Man, I really wanted to go down there and lend a hand, or just show my support. It turned out that Chris Kanyon has a cousin in the New York Police Department, and he arranged for us to make a trip down to Ground Zero. We do a lot of appearances, we meet kids from Make-A-Wish, that kind of thing. But this was special.

JEFF: It was Chris, Matt, Amy, and myself. We were talking to all the people working down there, firemen, cops, construction workers. They were all so cool. We signed their hard hats, took some pictures. It was so great that we could help brighten their day a little bit. It's cool as hell being able to do something like that because we are who we are and we do what we do.

MATT: They all had such a positive vibe. We asked how things were going and they said, "Well, it's slow but we're getting there. Slowly but surely, we'll get back to normal."

In a lot of ways New York's so hard and so callous, people have an attitude there like no place else. But if the attacks were to have happened anywhere else, I don't know if another city would have made it through. It was a blow to all of America, and New York is the leader of the pack. After all that happened, you realize what a great city it is. They took it, they lived through it, and they're standing tall.

JEFF: We're up in the New York area at least three or four times a year. We always stay by Newark Airport when we wrestle up there, and whenever we drove into the city or out to the Meadowlands, it was always cool for us to look across the river and see that skyline. You know, I'm just a little country-boy redneck from North Carolina, but it'll always be a real heartbreak for me not to see the Twin Towers standing there.

SEPTEMBER DAY

A thought of who did this—A thought of how could they?
Flying away . . . They steered astray.
An act of ignorance—Unthinkable thought since . . .
They flew away—Steering astray . . .
Straight into America's financial heartbeat—
Innocent lives that died—Your souls are so alive—
. . . You won't stop America.
A city of many—A nation more—Building away—Rebuilding
*   today.*
A piece of History—We define Bravery—Building away—An
*   invincible day.*
An act of ignorance—More spiritual since . . . They flew away . . .
*   Steering astray.*
You won't kill America's—Overall heartbeat—
Innocent lives that died—Your souls are so alive—
. . . You won't kill America.
A thought of where is he—A thought of him killing me . . .
All the life that's in this world—
All that dies within this world—
Is a part of God and His Creation.
All the terror you have poured—
Represents your Holy War—
HOLY SHIT!—I SCREAM!—Vis-ioning—How you die!
—How you die!
—How you die!
—How you die!
A thought of who did this—A thought of how could they?
Flown away . . .
September Day.

PART 3
MOMENT OF TRUTH

THE MILES

JEFF: Flying sucks, quite frankly. Airports are such a hassle. We fly so often, it's amazing how many nightmare experiences we've had.

The day after Easter last year—April 1, 2002—was a particularly grueling and miserable day, but it's a perfect example of the hell we often have to go through in order to do our jobs. We had an 8 A.M. flight to Charlotte out of Raleigh-Durham Airport, then from Charlotte we'd fly to Albany, New York, for *Raw*. We left the house at 5:45, but when we got to RDU, everything was crazy because there were thunderstorms all over the East Coast. There were delays everywhere. It turned out that our plane hadn't gotten in until late, and so the flight crew had been up all night and didn't have the amount of sleep they're required to have. So our flight didn't leave until 8:45. We got to Charlotte, and of course we missed our connection.

The only thing we could do was go to Boston, and from there fly to Albany. But it was three hours before that flight left, which meant we wouldn't get to the arena until at least 4:30, when we're supposed to be there at noon. Matt called WWE and they said to go ahead and do it. We spent the day hanging around in the airport, and about forty-five minutes before the flight, they told us, "Sorry. The Boston flight's canceled."

MATT: We had to get back in line, and when we got to the counter, I said, "Look, we have to be in Albany by nine. Get us as close as possible and then we'll just drive from there."

We ended up getting on a flight to Newark that was about to take off. We ran to the gate, and we were the last two people to get on board. Of course, that meant that the luggage compartments were all filled up, so we had to check our bags.

We landed in Newark at around three, and needless to say, Jeff's luggage didn't make it. But we had no time to wait because it's a three-hour drive from Newark to Albany, about a hundred and sixty miles. We rented a car, got on the Garden State Parkway, and traffic was completely stopped. There was nothing moving. I called Michael Hayes and said, "We might be a little later than anticipated."

Eventually we got through the Garden State Parkway. I did a hundred miles an hour up the New York Thruway. We finally showed up to *Raw* at seven that night, after leaving our house at 5:45 in the morning.

JEFF: I wrestled in my street clothes that night, and at the house show the next day. I had to borrow boots from Justin Credible. We're lucky, because our outfits are kind of like our regular clothes, so I was able to get away with it. If we wore tights, I would've been screwed. But it was the first time I ever went out without my black pants, white belt, and white boots. The airline finally got my luggage to me at 4 A.M. Wednesday morning, a few hours before we left to go home.

MATT: If there's time between shows, I would rather drive than fly. I'm up till three or four in the morning most nights, it's just how my body clock works, so I know that I'm not going to go straight to bed after a show. It makes much more sense to drive all night, then sleep in the next day.

Back before we split crews between *Raw* and *SmackDown!* it used to be me and Amy in the front, with Jeff and Shane in the back. Man, those two used to go at it and Amy and I would have to tell them to be quiet or else we'd pull over. Sometimes Jeff will refer to us as "Mom and Dad." Yes, that's us—Mom and Pop Hardy.

JEFF: Shane gets very serious about wrestling, and I love to provoke him and make him crazy. He gets so hot. He'll get totally torqued and then I have to say, "Okay, Shane. You're right."

MATT: They'd get into the funniest arguments. Jeff has a habit of asking "What do you mean by that?" about the most insignificant things. Most people would give up after a point, but not Shane. He never lets something drop, he just keeps going and going.

Unforgiven 2001 was in Pittsburgh, with a house show the night before in Reading. There was a group flight scheduled for the morning of the Pay-Per-View, but we decided to drive.

We were booked for a four-way tag at Unforgiven—the Hardyz vs. the Dudleyz vs. Lance Storm & the Hurricane vs. Spike Dudley & Big Show. We did a run-through at the house show and it set off a colossal—and hilarious—shouting match in the backseat.

There was this one spot where Jeff and Shane were in the ring, then Bubba grabbed Jeff from outside on the apron. As Shane went to hit Jeff, Jeff was going to move and then Bubba and Shane were going to have some interaction. The idea being that after that little miscommunication, Shane and Bubba would have a little bit of heat when they got in the ring together.

When we got in the car after the house show, the two of them started arguing about what they wanted to do, with Jeff wanting to do something off-the-wall and Shane having a strong logical spot in mind. Jeff wanted to flip out of the ring and dropkick Bubba off the apron. Then when Bubba tagged in, he and Shane would be starting from absolutely nothing—they've never even touched before, and now, halfway through the match, they're supposed to start a brand-new story.

If it was just Jeff and me, I'd just have said, "Okay, fine. I'm not going to argue anymore." But Shane kept hammering on the point: "What do you want it to mean? Do you want it to mean something or do you want it to mean nothing?"

JEFF: That really stuck with me. I said it over and over again, mimicking Shane. "Do you want it to mean something or do you want it to mean nothing?"

MATT: We were driving down the Pennsylvania Turnpike and they were just going at each other for close to an hour. They asked me, "What do you think?"

I said, "Well, logically . . ."

To which Jeff said, "In your opinion . . ."

He was different when we were growing up. Jeff used to listen to what I had to say, but that was before he became a household name.

WCW TAG CHAMPS ...SORT OF

DATE: *October 8, 2001*
LOCATION: *Indianapolis, Indiana*
ARENA: *Conseco Fieldhouse*

MATT: We showed up for *Raw* and the format said we were wrestling Booker T and Test, that week's WCW Tag Team Champions. "What's the finish?" I asked.

"Undertaker is going to interfere and give Booker the Last Ride," I was told, "then you guys are going to win the titles."

Alrighty, then. It was cool to get the WCW tag-team titles, even though we didn't really win them in WCW—it's still in the record books.

JEFF: We were the WCW Tag Team Champions, but it didn't feel any different. We were WWE wrestlers working with other WWE wrestlers; calling it the WCW Tag Team Championship was just a gimmick.

One of the biggest problems with the Invasion was that there were way too many championship belts floating around. It reached a point where the titles were literally dropping like flies and nobody but the biggest Internet marks were able to keep them all straight.

219

SURVIVOR SERIES

DATE: *November 18, 2001*
LOCATION: *Greensboro, North Carolina*
ARENA: *Greensboro Coliseum*

MATT: It was decided that we would begin teasing a potential rift between Lita and myself, kicking off at *No Mercy* in St. Louis. We opened the show with a WCW tag-team title defense against the Hurricane & Lance Storm. Later that night there was a pretape where I ran into Stacy Keibler backstage right before her lingerie match with Torrie Wilson.

"You're a guy," Stacy said, "and I was wondering what you think of my lingerie."

She opened her robe and I looked her up and down. Slowly. "It's, uh, good," I said. "It's real good. You look great."

I stared at her as she walked away, then Lita came over: "Hey Matt. Whatcha looking at?"

"Um, nothing," I stammered, then told her she looked great, as always. I gave her a kiss, and as we hugged, I had a "whew!" look of relief on my face, like I was lucky I didn't get caught checking out Stacy.

It went over great. The crowd cracked up and everybody in the back thought it was a terrific piece of business. So the next night on *Raw* we did a bit where I went to the women's locker room looking for Lita, but instead found a topless Trish Stratus.

She wrapped herself in a little towel as I sputtered something about how I was looking for Lita. "I don't know where she is," Trish replied. "I was just going in for a shower."

She left me standing there with a big horny grin on my face. Lita came in and asked what I was doing there.

"I was looking for you," I said, sounding like a kid with his hand in the cookie jar.

"Okay," Lita said, then told me she was going to take a shower.

"Why don't the two of us find a secluded area and take a shower together?" I said, and we scurried out of there!

There was talk of doing another "Horny Matt" bit at *SmackDown!* where I would ogle Stephanie, but it never came to be. The angle pretty much just faded away.

A week or so later Amy and I got called into the principal's office—that is, Vince's office—for a little talk about our future.

"We're both of the same mind-set on this," I told him. "Amy and I would love to continue working together, but we both think the time has come for us to go out on our own."

Basically I was trying to say that I wanted to split from Jeff, but in the nicest way possible. Vince was cool with that, so from there, it switched from me having problems with Lita to me having problems with Jeff.

JEFF: The Invasion came to its sad conclusion at *Survivor Series,* which was being held in Greensboro. Things had gotten unbelievably complicated and confusing. We spent a couple of weeks as the WCW Tag Champs while the Dudleyz—who were in the Alliance, don't forget—held the WWE titles. After the Dudleyz lost their titles to The Rock & Chris Jericho, we lost our WCW Championships to the Dudleyz.

Got it? Next Rocky & Y2J dropped the WWE belts to Booker T & Test, who we then beat on the *Raw* before *Survivor Series.* The end result of all this was that we would face the Dudley Boyz in a Tag Team Title Unification Cage Match at the Pay-Per-View—we had the WWE titles and they had the WCW titles. Whoever won would be the undisputed Tag Team Champions. Whew!

MATT: Jeff could've climbed out of the cage, but instead he went for a Swanton onto D-Von, who was set up on a table in the middle of the ring. But D-Von managed to get off the table and Jeff knocked himself out, giving Bubba an easy 1-2-3.

They stretchered Jeff out of there, and on the *SmackDown!* a couple of nights later, I acted like he blew it, accusing him of being a glory hound.

"I couldn't resist," Jeff said. "I'm sorry, man. I made a mistake."

"You made a choice," I told him. "A selfish choice. It cost us the most important tag-team match in the history of this business. You weren't thinking about the team. You were thinking about yourself."

From there, they had me acting like a total dick toward Jeff and Lita in an effort to turn me heel. It really felt like we had hit a dead end as far as our development was concerned. Those months were probably my most miserable time in the wrestling business.

JEFF: In the end, I think we blew the Invasion. It's so sad, because once it happened, there was no going back and doing it again. The Invasion was something that had only existed in wrestling fans' dreams, and when it became a reality, it turned out to be a colossal letdown.

VENGEANCE

DATE: *December 9, 2001*
LOCATION: *San Diego, California*
ARENA: *San Diego Sports Arena*

JEFF: After the Invasion disaster, it was decided that Matt and I were going to finally break up, starting with a match between the two of us at the December Pay-Per-View, *Vengeance*. That was cool, because we were both definitely ready to go out on our own. The problem was, they wanted to pair me with Lita! I thought that was just stupid.

MATT: We were in Cincinnati, working with the Dudleyz and Stacy Keibler. I was going to accidentally elbow Lita during a match, and we needed to do a pretape where Jeff was touching her face, asking if she was okay, then I was supposed to walk in and act jealous.

When it was time to shoot that vignette, Jeff was nowhere to be found. He had been there earlier—he was around when we discussed the match—but then he just disappeared. Nobody knew where he was. He had lost his cell phone, so we couldn't call him. There were actually some people who were worried that he had gone to a hotel room and overdosed on drugs.

Everybody was looking for him. Vince came up to me. "Matt," he said in a serious tone, "where's your brother?"

"I haven't a clue," I answered honestly. "You know as much as I do."

"Have you been in contact with him at all?"

"No, Vince, I haven't."

"Is this strange of him," Vince asked, "to just drift off and not tell anybody where he is?"

"Actually, Vince, it's not. Not in the World According to Jeff."

He showed up just before show time. He claimed that he had gone off to look for his cell phone, but he really went back to his hotel and fell asleep.

JEFF: It was six o'clock at night and I had nothing to do, so I left. Then, all of a sudden, they wanted to do a pretape. When I got back, Stephanie called me into her office, like she was the damn principal, and freaked out. I admit, I fucked up by leaving. But in my defense, they didn't tell me they were planning to do a pretape with me. Usually they'll let you know early in the day.

"Where did you go?" Stephanie said. "We needed you!"

"I went to my hotel room," I explained. "I had left my cell phone in a taxi and I was waiting for the taxi service to return it. I was only gone for an hour."

"I think you need to be fined," Michael Hayes said.

"Go ahead and fine me! Do you think I care about that? Michael, I've never left the building in the last three years. This is crazy how you all are freaking out like this."

It just showed me how little they understand me. For all the other guys, money's a big deal. But I could care less about it. They can't control me and I think it drives them all crazy.

"Look, I'm sorry," I said. "Plain and simple. I'm sorry and I won't do it again."

They never fined me for that. Another time I got fined a thousand dollars for blowing off a house show.

MATT: Michael was extremely hot. He sat Jeff down and just went off. "You've got all this talent and you're throwing it all away!"

Jeff sat there, taking it in, but not reacting at all.

JEFF: Michael Hayes gave me a talking-to, like he was my dad or something. "Don't spit in the face of God," he said. "You've been given a gift and to turn your back on wrestling would be disrespecting God."

Don't hand me that! I thought. *You don't know my passion. You don't know what my heart's telling me.*

I was so hot, but I chose not to say anything. I just bottled it up inside and tried to redirect those energies into my music.

One of my biggest problems in WWE is that there are all these fifty-year-olds that still think they're the hippest guys around. Michael Hayes made rock records back in the day, but that was twenty years ago! He has no clue what's cool in 2003! He once told Rob Van Dam that his singlets looked like hell, that nobody thought airbrushing was cool anymore. First off, Van Dam's gear is the shit, his stuff is so awesome. Second, this was coming from a guy who still walks around in tight blue jeans.

Lita and I ended up doing the pretape seconds before it aired. Stephanie kept telling me, "We want you to caress her face more. More caressing."

It was very awkward and upsetting. It was something I really didn't feel comfortable doing.

MATT: I think that was the point when it started becoming obvious to everybody that Jeff didn't give a damn anymore. He'd missed a couple of house shows, he'd disappeared from TV. He would come to TV and go sit up in the top of the bleachers by himself.

Jeff simply couldn't care one way or the other what was going on. I had no problem breaking up the team, but as we worked against each other at house shows, I came to the conclusion that the fans didn't want to see us fighting each other. If we went our separate ways and I became a heel on my own, then maybe we could've pulled it off, but otherwise it was an uphill battle in terms of getting the audience to care. Plus it was just so overdone—why do two partners always have to fight each other in order to break up?

It all came to a head the day before our match at *Vengeance*.

We had an early-morning flight to San Jose for an afternoon house show the day before the Pay-Per-View. The night before, I started coming down with a nasty stomach virus, and I felt just terrible. I got hardly any sleep, and I didn't eat anything all that whole next day.

Jeff was supposed to fly out there with Shane and me, but he missed the flight. We were supposed to have a run-through match for our *Vengeance* match.

This wasn't the first time he missed a house show before a Pay-Per-View. He skipped the show in Columbia, the night before we fought Hurricane & Lance Storm at *No Mercy*. His coatimundi got out of its cage and was stuck up in a tree, so he stayed home.

JEFF: Man, I just totally freaked when my raccoon escaped. I was so worried. So I called in and told WWE agent Arn Anderson why I wasn't going to make it. He said, "Say that again?"

MATT: Because Jeff wasn't in San Jose, I wrestled Test. That was about the last place I wanted to be, feeling the way I did, but I went out there and had the match. It was a struggle. It was all I could do to take a bump.

After the match I lay down for a while in the back, but I wasn't feeling any better. The plan was to take a group flight to San Diego that evening so everybody could get a good night's sleep before *Vengeance*. Amy and I went to the airport, and right as we got there, I needed to throw up. Immediately. But there was no bathroom in sight, so I just hurled into a bush outside. We walked in and I couldn't help myself—I just kept throwing up as we walked through the terminal. *Blaaaaagh!* Right on the floor!

I was looking for a bathroom, but there just wasn't one close enough. I threw up on the escalator, and the vomit got all caught in the grooves on the steps. It was pretty horrible! Finally I found a bathroom and I went in there and cleaned myself up—there was puke all over my coat, on my shoes, on my luggage.

We got to the gate, and Jeff was sitting there, writing in his notebook.

"I was running a little late," he said, "but the power went out in the American Airlines terminal, so they couldn't print my ticket."

All the guys started to arrive, but Jeff never got up to say hello, or apologize for missing the show. He just sat there like he hadn't done anything wrong. He had real heat with a bunch of guys about that.

When we landed in San Diego, Jeff decided to stay at a hotel with P.J. (Justin Credible).

"Do I need to pick you up before the show?" I asked him.

"No, man," he said. "I'll just come to the building with P.J."

The morning of the Pay-Per-View, I still felt like shit from the stomach bug, but I got to the building at around 11 A.M., because when we go live from the West Coast, we have to start the show at five. A little while later, P.J. showed up at the arena, and surprise surprise, he didn't have Jeff with him.

"Sorry, man," he said. "I tried to get him out of his room, but he wouldn't come. He said he'd just take a cab later."

Jeff showed at 2:30, which gave us just a couple of hours to work out our match. The whole time we were talking, he was drifting off and totally not paying attention.

My whole mind-set for the match was if it was going to be the start of a program between us, I didn't want us to go all out. I wanted to make it a good first go-around, not a spectacular blow-off match.

People expected us to have a blockbuster classic, like Bret Hart vs. Owen Hart, but we weren't ready to give it to them. I was so sick that even if I had wanted to go out and give them a spectacular match, I don't think I could have. And Jeff was in a state of mind where he couldn't have given them that match either.

We went out there and Jeff's heart was clearly not into it. He was barely giving it any energy at all. I kept calling moves to him, telling him to pick up the pace. "C'mon, Jeff! Let's go!"

It was already a difficult point in our career. None of us liked the creative direction we were headed in, and then on top of that Jeff started fading on us. It was definitely the most frustrating period of our time in WWE.

After that match, we got back to the Gorilla Position and I was hot. I shoved Jeff hard: "What is wrong with you? It was really important that we did good out there and you don't give a shit!"

"Go ahead!" Jeff said. "Hit me!"

"I'm not going to hit you! Why don't you care anymore?"

We were completely in each other's face. Michael came over and tried to separate us. "Don't do it here, guys," he said.

Then Stephanie walked by and asked, "Is there a problem?"

"To hell with this," I said. I went back to the locker room and threw up.

Jeff had me so frustrated and so aggravated. He's my brother and I'd love for him to do well. But if we're doing business together, then what he does reflects on me. I'm the older brother, and in a lot of ways, I've always taken care of him. If they made a movie of our lives, I'd be the babyface. Because when people are out there yelling for Jeff to do a Swanton, or chanting "Lita! Lita! Lita!" they don't realize that I'm in the back telling everybody what to do.

The next night they wanted to add some more heat to the angle, which was when they decided to really push some romance between Jeff and Lita. Jeff was very uncomfortable with that whole concept.

JEFF: It was a stupid idea, wanting me to kiss Amy. It was a power trip. They just wanted to try to make us do something they knew we didn't want to do. I looked right into Stephanie's eyes and said, "I'm not going to do it."

MATT: When we said no, we were told that we were going to be off TV for six to eight weeks. It wasn't a punishment, exactly. I think they had come to realize that the fans weren't interested in seeing Team Extreme feud, and if we disappeared for a couple of weeks, maybe they'd forget it ever happened.

"I don't really want to be off TV," I said, "but I'd be willing to do it if you think it's going to lead to something good when we come back."

It was a combination of factors, really. Mostly it was down to the fact that we were overexposed. We had a match on every TV show, week in and week out. We had burned up every possible combination of things we could do. Say we were in a story line with the Dudley Boyz—which we usually were—we could have a match with another team and the Dudleyz could do a run-in. The Dudleyz could have a match and we would do a run-in. We'd do a promo and the Dudleyz would interfere, then they'd do a promo and we'd interfere. It was out of control and was beginning to get a little boring.

JEFF: It seemed like we'd wrestled everybody there was to wrestle. They told us that they were going to create a few new tag teams while we were on our hiatus. That way there would be new combinations when we returned. They actually did put together a couple of new teams—some of which didn't last too long, like Tazz & Spike Dudley, and others which worked out pretty well, like Billy & Chuck.

FEAR FACTOR

MATT: Team Extreme taped its appearance on *Fear Factor* in December 2001, right after *Vengeance*. We were part of an all–WWE Superstar episode, alongside Test, Jacqueline, and Molly Holly.

I watch very little TV besides wrestling, so when they asked me to do *Fear Factor*, I had no idea what it was. They explained that it was a hugely popular show where six contestants attempt three physical or mental stunts that are either too difficult or too disturbing to complete. If a contestant cannot finish the stunt within a certain amount of time, or if they chicken out, they are eliminated. The winner gets fifty thousand dollars, but because we're "celebrities," our winnings would go to a charity of our choice.

JEFF: We had to stay in California after the Tuesday-night *SmackDown!* taping. When we agreed to do *Fear Factor* we didn't realize that it took three days. It was one of those weeks where we worked Saturday through Friday, took a red-eye home, slept all day Saturday, then went back to work.

MATT: I was a little aggravated when I realized what we had gotten into, but I'm so glad we did it, because *Fear Factor* turned out to be a blast.

JEFF: We were all taken out to a pier, where we met the show's host, Joe Rogan. The WWE representatives requested that Team Extreme be kept physically apart on the show. The thinking was that we'd be split up on WWE TV by the time *Fear Factor* aired, and they didn't want to confuse the fans. So when the show opened and all six of us were walking down the pier, they spaced it out so that Matt, Amy, and I weren't in contact.

The object of the first stunt was to grab hold of the bottom rung of a rope ladder hanging out of a helicopter. Then the helicopter would fly out over the water and circle as we tried to climb the ladder. They explained to us that the way the helicopter was moving increased your body weight by three times.

MATT: We all thought Jeff would get the best time on this stunt. He's like a monkey. He climbs a ladder like nobody's business.

JEFF: Everybody said I was the odds-on favorite going in because I'm the fearless guy. Having spent years saying that "Fear is just a four-letter word," now I had to live up to it. All the other contestants pumped me up to be the winner, but my elbow was hurting and I was tired as hell from wrestling all weekend.

MATT: Amy went first. She tried to pull herself up onto the ladder with her arms, but figured out that the easiest way to get up there was by flipping up and using her legs to pull up onto the ladder. Once she did that she was able to climb it pretty quickly, coming in at 1:55. Unfortunately, the other girls learned the secret, so they both beat her time.

I was still feeling queasy from the flu, but when it came to my turn, I just put my feet through and shot up the ladder. I set a goal of doing it in one minute. I came close—I did it in 1:01.

Jeff had been acting all cool, but he was a little intimidated by my time. "I don't know if I can beat you, man," he said. "Maybe I should just do it all with my upper body."

One of things the producers tell you is to try to swerve your competitors, like giving them a little bit of misinformation after you do your stunt. So when Jeff suggested that he try getting up there with just his upper body, I said, "I wish I'd have done that. I think I would have been much faster."

"Yeah, man," Jeff said. "That's what I'm going to do."

JEFF: I decided that I would try to do it in a different way. I really thought I could do it. I felt confident I was going to make it, but then my arms completely cramped up.

MATT: Jeff grabbed on to the ladder and tried to climb up, hand over hand. He quickly learned that it was just about impossible to do it that way. It took every bit of strength he had. Imagine pulling yourself up a ladder with just your arms when your body's three times its regular weight.

JEFF: I struggled and struggled, trying to pull myself up using my arms and my upper body. By the time I got my foot on the bottom ring, my arms were just about dead. I *did not* want to go in that water, but I literally had no strength left in me.

MATT: He made it about four-fifths of the way up the ladder before his arms gave out on him. He almost made it into the helicopter, but he was completely blown out and fell off the ladder. It was a pretty good drop, too—maybe thirty-five feet into the water.

JEFF: It was not one of my prettier falls. I was out of control. I swallowed so much water. When the boat came to get me, I was choking for air.

MATT: It was funny, because we had all been joking about letting go of the ladder so we could go home. "As I climbed up there, I kept seeing myself getting on the red-eye," Test said afterward. So when Jeff fell, I figured he was going straight from the water to the airport!

JEFF: I know everybody figured I was going to get the hell home as soon as I was eliminated, but actually, Beth flew out to L.A. and we had ourselves a little vacation.

MATT: The *Fear Factor* producers refer to the second stunt as "a mental challenge."

They brought us to downtown L.A., and we had no idea what was going on. We were kept secluded in a trailer for a while, then they walked us into a Mexican restaurant that doubled as a strip club. And not a very good strip club either, judging from what the signs said: LAP DANCES: $1.

The usual *Fear Factor* formula is that the first and third days are physical challenges, and the second day is a mental challenge. Basically, that means the second day is the disgusting gross-out stunt. Sometimes they do things like put people's heads into a cage with rats or a coffin filled with snakes and worms. Other stunts involve eating really horrible stuff, like buffalo testicles or pig rectums.

As we walked through the restaurant, Test caught a glimpse of the things they had set up for us. "Dude," he whispered, "we're going to have to eat stuff!"

"Don't look over there!" they said. The producers don't want you to know what the stunt is until the last minute so they can get your reaction on film.

They had what looked like a craps table set up, with three big dice and ten repulsive ingredients, including fish sauce, pig intestines, bile, cow eyes, and everybody's favorite, rooster jewels. The dice had the various ingredients listed on them instead of numbers. Each of us got to roll the three dice, one at a time, then all three ingredients got mixed in the Blender of Fear with ground pig brains. Then we had two minutes to drink it all down.

Everybody was freaking out, but I wasn't worried at all. Mentally, it was a no-brainer—nothing can gross me out. The only way I wouldn't win is if my body physically rejected it. Either way it was going to make great TV.

Molly went first. She got fish sauce, cod-liver oil, and bile. It wasn't a great experience for her. She took a couple of sips and then came close to having a total mental breakdown. Her mind would not let her put that slop into her mouth. Test and I were leaning on each other, cracking up, hitting each other on the back. We felt bad for Molly because she tried as hard as she could, but there was no getting around the fact that it was funny as hell.

Next was Jacqueline. Her shake consisted of veal brains, spleen, and something called durian, which is the worst-smelling fruit on earth. Seriously. Jacqueline is legitimately tough, as tough as any WWE Superstar, and she proved it right there. She downed every drop of that nasty stuff.

I could tell from the look on Test's face as we watched Jacqueline that he wasn't going to make it. When it came to his turn, he rolled the dice and got bile, cod-liver oil, and rooster jewels. Test tried to chicken out without even tasting it, but Rogan broke his balls until he took a sip. *Then* he chickened out.

"That's it for me," he said. "I'll see you guys later, I'm catching the red-eye home."

Not only was I lucky enough to go last, I'm also a wise man. I saw that the two worst things you could get were the bile and the fish sauce. I realized that if you threw the dice very carefully, you could avoid both of them.

I rolled the dice and got two spleens and animal fat. I thought of it as a protein shake—a stinky pink protein shake. It was pretty bad. It had a raw, fatty smell. I started drinking it, and for the first few seconds it was a piece of cake. Then the stench and the taste set in and it was just terrible. But I kept going until it was all gone. I was determined that I was going to devastate that shake—one way or the other, I was going to get rid of it. I was lucky in that I got so much of that slop on *my* face and on my shirt that I probably didn't end up drinking as much as Jacqueline did.

JEFF: Man, I don't know if I could've drunk that gross shake—I probably would've puked!

MATT: After the show aired, people came up to me and asked, "Oh my God, how did you drink that stuff on *Fear Factor*?"

"Well," I said, "growing up, my dad did all the cooking. Compared to that, it was no problem."

That night Amy and I decided to have dinner at Wasabi, which is a great Japanese restaurant in Universal City. We were strolling around the Universal City Walk Mall when we spotted Test and Stacy Keibler walking arm in arm. There had been speculation that they'd been seeing each other, but Test always denied it. Well, we cold-busted them! It was tremendous!

"Hey guys," we said, laughing, "what are you doing here?"

"Er, um, nothing," Test sputtered. "Stacy was in town and I decided to stay on."

"You didn't make the red-eye, huh?"

"Um, um, no. Okay, well, see you guys later," Test said, and the two of them skedaddled out of there, only now they weren't walking so close together. It was so funny!

For the third stunt, we flew up to the mountains outside of Los Angeles. There were six tall wooden poles set up, staggered three feet from one another. Each succeeding pole was about a foot taller than the previous on. The first one was maybe forty feet high, and three yellow flags were attached to the top with Velcro.

As soon as I saw the poles, I knew the stunt was going to involve walking across them. The object was to grab a flag from the first pole, then one by one, attach all the flags to the sixth pole.

It was miserable out there. It was forty degrees and raining, and then to top it off, they threw in some artificial rain just to make it that much harder.

I was hooked up to a harness that was attached to a kind of bungee cord. I pulled off the first flag, walked all the way across the six poles, and put the flag on the last pole. I walked back and grabbed the second flag, walked across to the last pole, and as I was bending down to put it on the Velcro, I fell off.

It was extremely hard for me to bend down. It would be hard for anybody to bend down when you're up so high, standing on a pole, but like I said before, I've got Jimmy Legs. Squatting down is not exactly one of my strong points. If I bend down with my feet close together, my hips don't go straight out. I'm a genetic mutant!

Okay, then, I thought. I climbed back up and walked across the poles again, thinking, *I can't fall, I can't fall, I can't—Ahhhhhhhhh! I'm falling!*

I was hot! I was cursing a blue streak as I climbed back up there! Needless to say, they had to edit that out. I finally got the second flag on there on the third trip across. Then I climbed back up, grabbed the last flag, walked over the poles and got it on the first try. My total time was 7:08, which wasn't nearly as good as I'd hoped for. I was really hot at myself. I thought I should've been able to do it in three minutes!

"Trust me," Joe said, "Seven minutes is not as bad as you think."

The show has a group of stuntmen that do all of the stunts—they drank all the various combinations, they did the helicopter gimmick, and so forth. Off-camera, Joe told me that the *Fear Factor* stuntman's best time for the poles was close to six minutes. Not only that, he couldn't do it without falling off a couple of times.

I still felt like I had delivered a poor performance. "If Jacqueline's going to beat me," I said, "tonight's her night."

Jacqueline made it up to the top of the first pole, but as she tried to jump onto the second pole, she lost her nerve. She stood up there for a couple of minutes as Joe egged her on to keep going, but in the end, she gave up. Matt Hardy is your new *Fear Factor* champion!

The only thing that put a damper on the whole thing was that Jeff had blown it on the first stunt. If it had come down to the two of us at the end, it would have been much more competitive and exciting.

JEFF: I would have loved to have competed against Matt in the last stunt. That was all me, right there. I don't have Jimmy Legs, so I probably would have kicked his ass!

MATT: Overall, *Fear Factor* was a good experience. It was nice, being able to give fifty grand to the American Cancer Society. Plus it was an opportunity to be myself on TV. It was a chance for people to see me and say, "This guy is a real competitor."

THE CLEANSING

MATT: Since 1996, Jeff and I and all of our oldest wrestling buddies have made a point of getting together every New Year's Eve for the Cleansing. We start by getting the fire going. We'll bring a few soft drinks, some chips, and hot dogs that we cook over the fire. As we eat, we hang out and talk about what's been going on in our lives for the last couple of months.

Eventually we get serious and start the Cleansing. We used to do it starting with the one who has the least to say and ending with the one who talks the most, so Shannon would start and Marty would go last, because when it comes to talking about the bad that's happened during the year, no one can top Marty. The past couple of years we've changed it up a little and gone in order of age.

After we all take a turn talking, it becomes almost like a communion. I buy a solid loaf of bread and some grape juice. Once we get through talking, I pour everybody a little juice then pass the bread around. Everyone breaks off a piece and we all eat and drink at the same time.

We try to keep it the same group of seven. Joey Matthews came one year, but it didn't feel right. We all agreed to protect the original ritual.

The 2001–2002 Cleansing was pretty heavy, because we'd all fallen out with Jason. I think with him there, we all had a hard time being as open and honest as we wanted, but we tried. It's sad, because each year the meeting loses a little of the purity it had the first couple of years, but it's still something that I really look forward to. I really do believe it helps us to put away the last year and then start fresh again.

JEFF: I was really late to the 2001 Cleansing. I really didn't want to go. The only reason I did was out of guilt and a sense of obligation. I'd have felt horrible if I hadn't gone, because we all used to be so close. But the fact is, I've really drifted away from those guys. Plus, I know how crazy Matt would have been if I didn't show up—he would have tried to make me feel so bad.

I came up with this whole punishment gimmick—I told them I biked all the way there as a way to punish myself for being so late, but in actuality, I only biked a mile or two. I parked my car at a convenience store and then rode my bicycle down to where they were. It's funny, because it really did turn out to be torture—it was freezing cold, I got chased by dogs, and it was much further than I thought.

I walked up to where they were in the woods and watched them for a while. I was waiting to hear them mention something about me, but they hadn't started talking yet.

Then I came down and told them how sorry I was for being late and how I rode my bike to punish myself. It was a crazy gimmick, mostly just to amuse myself.

They busted on me awhile, and then we started talking around the circle. Shannon went first, then I spoke a few minutes, about how I wanted to do an album this year and really throw my music out there and get it going.

Finally Matt got up and said, "I feel that we're all successful." I know he was just being nice, but damn! He should be proud of what he's accomplished, but it's bullshit! I sat there thinking, *We're not all successful.* You're *successful!*

When we first started doing the Cleansings, we spent the majority of our time talking about making it in wrestling, becoming WWE Superstars. Matt and I had been doing more and more jobs, and it really felt like we were getting close. But now it's so different. Matt and Shannon and I are definitely doing well, but the other guys aren't and probably never will be. Marty's in his late thirties, and Jason had his shot and blew it—his head got real big and he got so messed up.

Right then and there, I realized that the Cleansing had lost its original meaning, and that this was going to be my last time. Not only that, I don't want to go sit out there until four o'clock in the morning, cold as hell. I'm just not into that anymore.

BACK IN BUSINESS

MATT: The relationship between Jeff and me really improved during our time off TV. We continued to work together at house shows, which is a lot less of a high-pressure situation. We were able to see our friends and enjoy ourselves doing what we really love—going out there and wrestling in front of a crowd.

JEFF: Man, I loved having all that free time at home. It gave me some real time to recharge my batteries, and more importantly, it helped my relationship with Matt. The two of us hung out together more than we had in ages, which was awesome.

MATT: We came back at the *Royal Rumble* and we were supposed to return to TV the next day. When we showed up at *Raw*, they said, "Sorry, but we don't have anything planned for you."

"Oh," I said. "Well, thanks for telling us."

We came back full-time in February, beginning at *No Way Out.* It was a Tag Team Turmoil for a shot at the titles at *WrestleMania X-8.* We did a run-through the night before at the house show in Green Bay and we won the match. Unfortunately, we weren't so lucky at the Pay-Per-View and the APA got the win.

JEFF: Billy & Chuck won the titles in the weeks leading up to *WrestleMania X-8*, but they decided that instead of just having them wrestle the APA at *WM X-8*, it would be a Four Corners Elimination Match, with us and the Dudley Boyz joining in the fun.

The last two teams were Billy & Chuck and us. They beat us—Billy whacked me with one of the belts, setting up the 1-2-3—and it looked like we were set to enter into a program with them.

MATT: It was my least favorite of our *WrestleMania* appearances for any number of reasons. The previous two *WrestleMania*s were the Triple Threat Ladder Match and TLC II, both of which were semimain events. This time our match was just thrown together the week before and there was nothing special about it, especially considering our *WrestleMania* history.

Also, it was in Toronto. Nothing personal against Canada, but it's not high on my list of favorite places to be. It's usually a fun week leading up to the Pay-Per-View, but for some reason it just didn't have that big-time *WrestleMania* feel.

Maybe it was my personal dissatisfaction, because we weren't involved in anything as important as we had been in previous years. It felt like we were in a filler match, and to be honest, that kind of sucked. We had been part of the most exciting Tag Team Division in wrestling history, but for some reason, it just faded away. It was sad. Once I realized that the tag-team scenario was never going to be as special as it had been, I was determined to strike out on my own as a singles wrestler.

THE DRAFT

DATE: March 25, 2002
LOCATION: State College, Pennsylvania
ARENA: Bryce Jordan Center

MATT: After *WM X-8*, there were still tentative plans for us to feud with Billy & Chuck, but the brand extension splitting the *Raw* and *SmackDown!* rosters put an end to that. Jeff wrestled Billy in a singles match that night, but then we got drafted to different shows.

JEFF: Whether it's as singles or as a team, Matt and I have always been very good at putting guys over. We can make people look good. That's because we know the value of selling.

They've definitely used us to get guys over. I think we're responsible for getting Billy & Chuck over. We had some killer matches with them when they first got together. We got beat every night and it made them look like a strong, serious team.

MATT: The day of the brand extension draft was one of the weirdest in WWE history. They were trying to keep things very hush-hush, and everyone was walking around on pins and needles, worried about their futures.

We had no idea where we were going. The main thing we were concerned about was that Amy and I were on the same show. We just wanted to be on the same schedule. If one of us was on *Raw* and the other was on *SmackDown!* then one of us would work from Friday to Monday and come home on Tuesday, while and the other one would work from Saturday to Tuesday and come home on Wednesday. That would leave Thursday as the only day that we'd get to see each other.

JEFF: Amy and Matt were convinced that they were going to be separated as a kind of punishment. We all knew that some teams were going to get split up, but once they separated the Dudleyz and the Acolytes I knew we were staying together.

MATT: I was actually hoping that they'd break us up. Both Jeff and I had been waiting for a chance to be on our own and prove ourselves as singles wrestlers, and the only way that was ever going to happen was to split up the Hardy Boyz.

JEFF: There were a few guys, like Stone Cold and The Rock, who knew where they were going, but for the most part, the wrestlers were as surprised as the fans. We only found out that we were all on the same show after *Raw* went off the air. They showed the first ten selections as part of

Raw, followed by a lottery after the show ended. Amy was the number ten draft pick, so that was on TV, but then the rest of the picks were revealed on the Internet. Matt was lucky number thirteen and I was number fifteen.

MATT: When they told Amy that she was going to be the number ten draft pick, she just felt bad for me and Jeff. That definitely bummed me out a bit, but now that WWE is more about entertainment than wrestling, there was no point in being offended.

The draft was designed entirely for entertainment purposes. It wasn't really an accurate reflection on who's the better wrestler or who's more popular—it was part of a story line. None of it had anything to do with someone's position in the company.

JEFF: I was happy we were sticking together. I thought that Team Extreme could be an important part of the new *Raw,* especially if they gave us some new issues.

MATT: Overall, the brand extension was a good thing for WWE. It created opportunities for some very talented guys to get elevated into the next level, guys like Edge and Booker T.

That said, I think it's very important not to just concentrate on the top guys, but on the entire roster. Everybody in WWE needs to be part of some kind of story line in order to make the show as strong as it can be. If we make two strong brands then it doubles the amount of shows we can do, in terms of house shows and eventually Pay-Per-Views. It also creates the possibility of having a major Super Bowl of wrestling somewhere down the line.

JEFF: The split was not an instant success, for any number of reasons, from injuries to creative differences. But it's like Vince said when they told us what was going to go down: "It'll probably be one step back to take two steps forward."

MATT: The worst thing for me was that all of my best friends—Shane, Christian, Jericho—were going to be part of the *SmackDown!* brand. We had been on the road together for a long time, and I knew I was going to miss having those guys around.

The other thing that sucked was that Billy & Chuck took the Tag Team Championships with them to *SmackDown!* Since we weren't able to pursue the titles, there seemed to be no real reason for the Hardy Boyz to continue on as a team.

With all that going on, I decided that the time had finally come to truly focus on becoming a singles wrestler. I turned up the voltage on my training and my in-ring work. I put my mind to really busting my ass, just waiting for my opportunity to come a-knockin'.

"THE NEXT BIG THING"

MATT: We were given the lucky task of working with Brock Lesnar in his first significant program. They wanted us to teach the new guy how things work in the ring. Our job was to help him to have good matches with people that the crowd cared about, to make him look like a credible monster that could do damage to established Superstars. In short, to make him truly look like "the Next Big Thing."

JEFF: The first time we encountered Brock Lesnar was after a match against Boss Man and Mr. Perfect. We beat them clean—Twist of Fate, Swanton—then Brock came to the ring and took us both down with a couple of clotheslines. He hit a sideslam and the F-5 on Matt. Then I went up to the top to try for a hurricanrana. But Brock caught me in midair and gave me three vicious powerbombs. *Wham! Wham! Wham!*

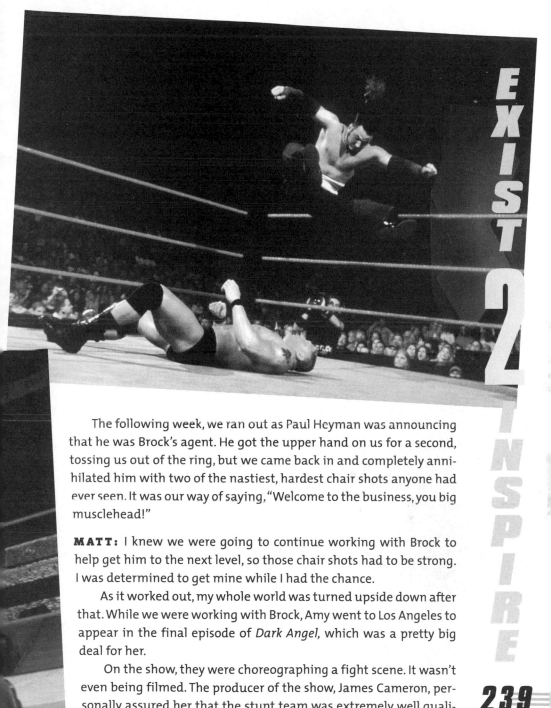

The following week, we ran out as Paul Heyman was announcing that he was Brock's agent. He got the upper hand on us for a second, tossing us out of the ring, but we came back in and completely annihilated him with two of the nastiest, hardest chair shots anyone had ever seen. It was our way of saying, "Welcome to the business, you big musclehead!"

MATT: I knew we were going to continue working with Brock to help get him to the next level, so those chair shots had to be strong. I was determined to get mine while I had the chance.

As it worked out, my whole world was turned upside down after that. While we were working with Brock, Amy went to Los Angeles to appear in the final episode of *Dark Angel*, which was a pretty big deal for her.

On the show, they were choreographing a fight scene. It wasn't even being filmed. The producer of the show, James Cameron, personally assured her that the stunt team was extremely well qualified to work with her and do wrestling moves. She was supposed to be attached to safety cables, but they told her that they just wanted to work a few things out and that they'd hook her up when they shot the scene. Amy got up on one of the stuntwomen's shoulders to rehearse a hurricanrana . . . and was dropped on her head.

She immediately knew something was wrong. Her arm was completely dead, so she asked if they could call a doctor. They told her that there wasn't a doctor on the set, but there was a massage therapist. Eventually she scraped herself up, but she still couldn't move her arm. "I really think I ought to go to the hospital," she said.

They kept treating her like it was no big deal. "How about you go to your hotel room and we'll send our physician there?"

The doctor came to her room and gave her some ibuprofen for the pain, but as far as he was concerned, she was fine. *Okay,* Amy decided. *It's probably just a stinger and I'll be fine in a couple of days.*

Nobody from *Dark Angel* even asked her if she wanted to go home. Of course, the wrestling mentality is that if you get hurt, you just suck it up and go. So Amy kept working. There was another week left to the shoot. She did all her close-ups with her arm in her belt to take the pressure off her neck.

Two days later, she was still in terrible pain. She was doing shot after shot in the freezing-cold rain, without a coat, her hand in her belt. Finally, she just said, "I'm hurt and these people are trying to dodge the whole subject. I need to go to a hospital."

They brought in another doctor to see her, and he agreed that she was definitely hurt and that she really ought to have a full range of tests. Amy finished the shoot and then flew down to Abilene, Texas, where we were kicking off the weekend's house shows.

When I saw her, she looked so pitiful. She was obviously in real bad shape. We got to the building and Arn Anderson told me that Jeff and I would be working with Mr. Perfect and Shawn Stasiak. "Maybe we'll get Lita to do a hurricanrana in there somewhere," he said.

"She can barely move," I said, pissed off. "Her neck's messed up pretty bad. Doesn't the office know?"

"Sorry," Arn said. "I had no idea. I guess we won't have her do anything."

While we were in Texas, Amy went and had a CAT scan done, and the doctor said there was a lot of swelling back there, but no real damage. He gave here some anti-inflamatories and painkillers and sent her on her way.

That eased the pain, but she kept having problems moving her arm. The following weekend we were out at the Nassau Coliseum in Long Island, New York, and Amy went and got an MRI, which detected some cracks in her neck. They suggested that she get a full CAT scan as soon as possible.

On Sunday we were in Kansas City for the *Backlash* Pay-Per-View. The original plan was that it was going to be me vs. Brock, but the week before, Brock hit me with the F-5 on the stage and it ended up being Jeff vs. "the Next Big Thing" in Brock's official in-ring debut. I think they decided that Jeff would be better at selling for him.

JEFF: Brock beat the hell out of me to the point where the ref had to stop the match. Then he gave me three powerbombs for good measure! The match served its purpose, though—it got Brock over as a total killing machine while at the same time allowing me enough offense to show my heart in taking on the monster.

MATT: After *Backlash,* there was a group flight to St. Louis for *Raw* on Monday, but Amy had a 7:30 A.M. doctor's appointment. So as soon as Jeff's match ended, Amy and I got in the car and hauled ass across the state of Missouri.

We got to the hospital in time for the appointment and the examination showed that Amy's C6 vertebrae was cracked in three places, and that the disk between the C6 and the C7 was ruptured. In fact, the damage was so bad that by continually walking around she was risking permanent paralysis!

The doctor wanted her to see a neurosurgeon to get another, more thorough CAT scan. We made an appointment for two o'clock, then decided to go to the arena to tell the WWE officials what was going on. When I looked at the sheet I saw that I had a match scheduled against Brock, even though I'd been told that I wouldn't be working that night.

I ran into Steve Austin, and as always, he was totally cool and supportive. "Just go take care of Amy," he said. "Let me know if there's anything I can do to help."

We went to the doctor and the tests took longer than I'd expected, so I had to leave Amy there. I showed up at the arena just as the doors opened. Brock and I had a quick talk about our match and then I called Amy on my cell phone.

"It's worse than they thought," she said, barely holding back tears. "They might have to rush me into surgery tonight."

Well, the last thing I wanted to do now was wrestle! I went and found Vince and explained the situation.

"She's not having any surgery tonight," he said. "This doctor just wants to get credit for working on a WWE Superstar."

I had my match with Brock, which went really well. Brock came out to open the show, but I ran down through the audience and attacked him from behind. It was the most offense anyone had scored against him at that point, and the crowd was solidly behind me. Finally Brock got me with the F-5, and then, instead of pinning me, he powerbombed me into the mat. The ref called for the bell, and that was that. I couldn't believe that I got through the match because my mind was with Amy, not in the ring, but everyone in the back thought it was great.

When I got back to the hospital, Amy was in bad shape, both emotionally and physically. The doctor told her that she needed to have surgery immediately. He explained the procedure, which involved going in through the back of her neck. We had spoken to a few people and they told us that if you do the operation that way, the muscles don't heal properly and Amy wouldn't be able to wrestle anymore. When Chris Benoit had his neck surgery, they went in through the front—he had to wear a hard collar for a month or so, but his neck healed to the point that a year later he was able to resume his career. We explained all this to the doctor and he just didn't seem to get it.

"I work on professional athletes all the time," he said.

"Yeah, but not professional athletes like us," I told him. "Our specialist, Dr. Lloyd Youngblood, is in San Antonio, and we definitely want to get a second opinion from him before we do anything."

"I recommend you don't leave this room," he said, "If she gets out of bed, she may walk five steps and fall over dead or she may be paralyzed."

Amy was bawling; she was just terrified.

"Look," I said, "she's been walking around for two weeks and she's not paralyzed yet. I can't see how getting on a plane is going to hurt. Dr. Youngblood understands what we do and I really think we need to hear what he has to say."

I called J.R. to tell him what was going on, then I asked if he could find Stone Cold for me. He had suffered a severe neck injury a few years back, and I wanted to know what he thought.

"Let me talk to that doctor," Steve said.

When the doctor came back into the room, I gave him the phone. "This is Stone Cold Steve Austin. He wants to talk to you."

They were on the phone for a few minutes, but the doctor stuck to his guns. He said the only way he would release Amy from the hospital was if he put her in a halo, which is a major surgical procedure in itself.

"But if I put that on," he said, "the airlines won't let you fly. So you're stuck. She's going to have to have the surgery here."

By this point, Amy was a complete wreck. She basically told me to handle it—she'd do whatever I thought was right.

Oh great, I said to myself. *Her life is in my hands!* But that's part of what being a boyfriend is all about, I guess. I felt so bad for her. J.R. called back a little while later. "I talked to Steve," he said, "and we booked you guys two tickets to fly to San Antonio tomorrow morning. Go down there, talk to Dr. Youngblood, and let's see what we really need to do."

I told the doctor that we were leaving. "You can't keep somebody against their will," I said.

"I don't recommend it," the doctor said, "but if that's your final decision, I'll get the release papers drawn up. But if anything happens, this hospital is not responsible."

We went back to the hotel and spoke to Steve again. "I told J.R. to get you on the same flight as Debra and myself," he said. "If the flight's full and you can't get on, then you guys can have our seats and we'll take the next flight and meet you there."

It worked out so that we all flew together and Steve and Debra took care of us every step of the way. They're both really wonderful people. When it comes to wrestling, Steve is all business. Outside of that, he's a very good-hearted person. One of the reasons he got over so big is because the audience could feel that he was a normal guy, just like them.

Steve came with us to see Dr. Youngblood. It was one of those times when we just needed somebody with some experience to help us out. I've never had to deal with a life-or-death situation in a hospital. What do I know about how severe an injury is and if somebody should or shouldn't be moved? As the doctor explained things, Steve would ask him questions that he knew would help us to understand.

"You have a serious situation," Dr. Youngblood said, "but the other doctor definitely blew it out of proportion. What I suggest you do right now is go home for a few days, take it easy, and then we schedule surgery and get you fixed up. The chances of you becoming paralyzed just from walking around are slim or none. If you were in a car wreck and your head smashed through the windshield, you could be paralyzed, but otherwise I'd say you're pretty safe."

It was a rough situation, but we definitely made the right decision. Amy had the surgery a week later, and hopefully she'll be able to recover enough that she'll be able to continue her wrestling career. Of course, there was no way I wasn't going to be right there with her that day, so I was forced to miss *Raw* in Buffalo as well as the first day of our UK tour in Europe. I left for Scotland on Wednesday evening and went straight to the show. I had a really good match with Brock. The next night we were in Birmingham, England, and I was actually in the main event. I teamed up with Triple H against Brock and Undertaker. It was a great feeling to head-line a show, even if Triple H let me take most of the beating.

The tour wrapped up with the *InsureXtion* Pay-Per-View in London, which saw Jeff and myself going up against Brock and Planet Stasiak. It was nothing special—Jeff hit a Swanton on Shawn for the pin, but then Brock kicked all our asses.

JEFF: A couple of *Raw*s later, we faced "the Next Big Thing" in a handicap match. We actually did some damage on him. We nailed him with the Event Omega, but Heyman pulled the ref from the ring before we could get the 1-2-3. The ref called it a DO, and while Brock was seething Matt hit him with a Twist of Fate and I followed up with a Swanton Bomb.

Heyman stopped us as we walked triumphantly up the ramp. He demanded a rematch at *Judgment Day*—with him as Brock's partner! Needless to say, we accepted.

The Pay-Per-View saw Brock wrestling the whole match as we tried to take him out of commission long enough to get our hands on Heyman, which finally we did. The best part was when Matt pulled off Heyman's Yankees cap and revealed his creepy-looking bald head!

In the end, Brock got me with the F-5 then Heyman tagged in so he could get the cover. I know a lot of guys would rather die than give up a pinfall to Paul Heyman, but it didn't bother me at all. What bothered me is that I knew all the boys would make a big deal out of it, like, "Paul Heyman beat him. Doesn't he care that it made him look weak?" Come on. It's enter-tainment. Everybody knows I could kick Paul E.'s ass.

Matt was so against the idea of me lying down for Paul Heyman. So what? It's didn't ruin my career. Nobody's even going to remember it. All they're going to remember from our program with Brock Lesnar is that we whacked the shit out of him with steel chairs.

MATT: *Judgment Day* was not exactly a highlight of the Hardy Boyz' career. Between the UK tour and the Pay-Per-View, it had become increas-ing clear that Jeff was getting burned out again. J.R. called him on it at TV the next night.

"I admit it," Jeff said. "I'm not feeling very passionate about wrestling right now. I'm really into making music and that's all I want to do. I'm sorry. It's just the way I feel."

J.R. discussed it with Vince and they decided to give Jeff some time off. They wrote him off TV for a couple of weeks and cleared him off the house-show schedule altogether.

"Go recharge your batteries," J.R. said. "Concentrate on your music for a while and then maybe you can do something with *SmackDown! Records*."

It's really amazing how quickly things can change. In the space of just a few months I had gone from having a car full of people—myself, Jeff, Amy, and Shane—to being completely alone.

LOSING HIS SMILE

MATT: When you work for WWE, it truly consumes your whole life. Jeff was twenty-four years old, he'd been wrestling nonstop for close to five years, and it finally became too much for him.

He's a remarkably creative person, and I think the fact that he didn't have creative control over his own career was probably a contributing factor. He was on the road constantly, and he realized eight days a month at home with his girlfriend wasn't nearly enough. All of those things were part of it, not to mention the fact that his body was feeling the effects of taking bump after bump, night after night.

At the beginning of our career, Jeff had been even more of a risk taker. Every time Jeff would get thrown out of the ring, he would land on his back. I said to him, "Don't do that! If you want to do it, do it on Pay-Per-View!"

"It doesn't hurt me," he'd say.

"It doesn't hurt now," I'd tell him, "but it will."

JEFF: My body actually isn't as beat-up as people think it is. I think people think I'm starting to break down because they see me as this crazy bump-taker.

MATT: Jeff was just like me for the longest time. It used to be like whatever Matt would do and whatever Matt would think was what Jeff would do and what Jeff would think. But there came a point when he became his own person and went out on his own limb.

Despite what a lot of the Internet people might think, Jeff isn't addicted to pain pills because of an aching body. He's like me in that he doesn't have an addictive personality. He's just crazy and different.

Jeff's definitely more open to new things, more inclined to experiment. He's the kind of guy who isn't as worried about the consequences as much as I am. I'm such a logical thinker and Jeff's more of an abstract kind of person. But neither of us has an especially addictive nature and I think that's helped us so much.

JEFF: I'll be honest—I've experimented with drugs. I've taken some pain pills. It really takes the edge off, especially when my back is really hurting, but it doesn't last. An hour later, the pain is back. A lot of the guys like to mix alcohol with the pills, but that's too dangerous for me. Plus I hate drinking.

I'm so thankful for what I've got in life, I'm sure as hell not going to screw it up by doing a bunch of drugs. I'm so lucky. Even if I were to die tomorrow, I've been so damn lucky.

It got me so hot when everybody started treating me like I had a drug problem. My performance hadn't changed at all—I was just showing up late for work!

People saw I was losing interest in wrestling and getting into music and they immediately thought, *That Jeff Hardy. He does drugs.*

I can't help it if I lost my passion for wrestling. I said to Michael Hayes, "If you know so much about the signs, tell me what drugs you think I'm on."

"Well," he said, "I think you've been smoking shit."

I got so damn mad! "What is wrong with you people?" I said.

That was one of the things that started driving me further away from the business. People were judging me without even trying to understand me. There was a lot of talk about me, on the Internet and in the locker room, saying that I was lazy, that I was whacked-out on drugs. That really broke my heart because it's so far from the truth. I always give 100 percent when I'm in the ring, even if I'm sick as hell or tired or just not interested. Every time I go out there, I give my heart and soul to the match. Not to mention my body!

Then there was all this talk about how my body's changed. I definitely don't work out the way I used to, but I don't think I look bad. I look normal. I just do a basic regimen. I don't want to be much bigger than two hundred pounds.

I've never been outrageously big. Matt has always been bigger than me. He looks great now. He's in amazing shape. One of the things I've always loved about wrestling is how it allows for all shapes and sizes.

Matt trains like nobody's business, and that doesn't interest me that much anymore. But I definitely try to stay in shape. I get up at eight in the morning and drive my Bobcat, I dig holes, I climb trees—I do physical stuff all damn day.

But there was no doubt that I needed to take a break from wrestling. I was losing my passion, as Matt would say. I think I just needed to do something different. I have other interests, which is unusual in this business.

A few years ago I decided I wanted to try turning my "emoetry" into music. I borrowed Daddy's guitar and started messing around with it. It was something I'd always wanted to do, and it was just so much fun. Pretty soon I was able to play a very simple riff or two, and I wrote a little song.

I bought myself a guitar and started practicing constantly. I'd sit up in my hotel room all night, just playing and playing. I've always loved watching Daddy and his buddies get together to play music. I can sit and watch him play the guitar forever. He tried to teach me, but he's just too fast. It's easier for me to just play around and teach myself.

I met the musicians in Peroxwhy?gen through Shannon Moore. He was out in Heartland Wrestling Association in Cincinnati, and he hooked up with this fantastic band, Burnside6. Their singer/guitarist, Jr. Merrill, is a huge wrestling fan, and a huge Hardy Boyz fan, so he was totally torqued when Shannon approached him with the idea of all of us making music together.

Shannon's been focused on his wrestling career since he's been brought up onto the *SmackDown!* roster, but he's contributed some interesting ideas and very cool beats and programs.

When we first started playing, my band would practice in my living room. Then the guys started bringing their friends over, and all of a sudden I had a house full of headbangers, night after night.

There is just too much going on in my living room, I thought. *I need to get myself someplace where we can practice.*

Daddy had this trailer that he used to use for storage. I walked in and thought of all the things I could do with it, so I bought it from him for eight hundred dollars and started fixing it up. I'd spend my whole week just itching to get home so I could get back to work on it.

I decided to spray-paint the whole trailer, inside and out. I was in the kitchen, painting away, and I got so involved in what I was doing that I passed out from inhaling all those fumes. Man, those fumes will kick your ass. But I love spray-painting—I think I spent over a thousand dollars on paint. I'm still not completely finished with it and probably never will be.

The studio has become the place I want to be more than any other. I bought all kinds of recording equipment, including a drum kit so I can ultimately do everything all by myself. I pretty much spend all of my free time in there, sometimes working through the night without even realizing it. I get a six-pack of Mountain Dew and experiment with different sounds, different recording techniques.

When I cut back on house shows a lot of the other wrestlers started acting jealous toward me, like I'm on vacation and I'm not doing anything. What they don't realize is that I've been working my ass off trying to make my music. The truth is, I would probably have slept more if I'd have been on the road.

The toughest thing for me is that Matt is like the rest of the boys—he just doesn't get it. When we were kids, he was so into music. I invited him over to the studio to try singing with me, or maybe even to lay down a rap—Matt can mad rap!—but he's just not interested. He's totally focused on wrestling and anything else is a distraction. I'm just the opposite—I need distractions from the wrestling.

Matt calls my music "Alternative Alternative," which hurts, because what he thinks means a lot. I offer to play things for him all the time, but I can sense he doesn't want to hear it.

One time he asked me if I was interested in getting money for my music, if I wanted to get paid for doing it. Of course I'd like to make a few dollars from people buying my CDs, but it's truly not *why* I do it. I like money as much as the next guy, but I'm not validated by financial success, especially as far as making art. Wrestling is about making money. That's what defines success.

Making music has got to be inside one's spirit. I know it's a gift because I feel it in my heart. Sometimes it makes my head hurt. The thrill I get from doing music, it's such a rush. When I'm in my studio, I lose track of time. That's why I end up being late for everything.

My goal is to truly develop my own style. I can't really sing country music—I've tried and I can't do it. I've also tried screaming grunge stuff, but that doesn't work for me either. Just like I created my own style of wrestling and poetry and sculpture, I need to figure out my own voice, as a singer, as a musician, as a songwriter.

I'm always trying to be different. I always want to be original. I hardly ever listen to other people's songs now because I just want to make my own without anything interfering with my inspiration. I want my music to be completely 100 percent Jeff Hardy.

RESPECT!

DATE: *July 1, 2002*
LOCATION: *Manchester, New Hampshire*
ARENA: *Verizon Wireless Arena*

MATT: The spring of 2002 was probably the most exasperating and maddening point in my career as a professional wrestler.

I was working hard on every level during Jeff's burnout period. I busted my ass in the gym and got into the best shape of my life. I was getting tremendous responses at house shows, usually among the biggest pops of the night. Nevertheless, it felt like no one was paying attention to the amount of effort I was expending.

When the plan was for Jeff to feud with Taker, then leave TV to make his record, I was told that I would finally be highlighted on my own. I was really excited because I've never had that opportunity. It's always been "Matt and Jeff" or "Matt and Lita," with Jeff and Lita doing the flash moves that make them both so popular. There were plenty of times over the years when I could have been a dick and said, "Lita can stay outside." Instead I've always said, "Whatever gets the best crowd reaction."

But perception becomes reality in a lot of people's minds—even though reality isn't necessarily what's real. So I was pumped about getting a legitimate shot as a singles wrestler.

Of course, here in WWE, nothing ever goes as planned. Jeff ended up getting a singles push, and I was temporarily relegated to *Sunday Night Heat* in order to keep us separate in the minds of the viewers.

JEFF: Initially the idea was just for Matt and me to have a short angle with Undertaker, winding up with Taker beating me into oblivion. From there I was going to take time off to record an album.

But when Stone Cold Steve Austin walked out, they realized that *Raw* needed any amount of star power they could get, so I was told that I would stay on TV.

Since I wasn't going anywhere, I came up with a couple of ideas that I thought would be awesome. I wanted to lift the classic Undertaker gimmick, with the purple cloak and the scary music. Man, that would've been sweet! Then I wanted to run out and steal his motorcycle. I heard that Vince loved my ideas, but Taker shot them both down.

MATT: Basically Taker wasn't getting the heel heat they were hoping for, so once again, the Hardyz got the call. It started in Dallas when Jeff ran into

249

Taker's match with Tommy Dreamer and dropkicked him into a big puddle of puke.

When Taker came to the back to kick Jeff's ass, Jeff was nowhere to be found, and I took the beat-down. The next week, Taker was doing an in-ring interview, talking about how Jeff was going to die for what he did, but I came out with a ladder and said that it wasn't about Jeff, it was about how Taker disrespected me. As I came down the ramp, Jeff came off the top rope from behind. We ended up beating on him with the ladder, which was cool—anytime you can offense on a guy like Taker is good, even if he did kick the crap out of us in the end.

The next couple of weeks saw us getting our asses handed to us in nontitle matches, culminating in Jeff's ladder match for the WWE Undisputed Championship.

JEFF: It's pretty clear that I don't care about wrestling as much as most of the boys in the locker room. That's definitely one of the reasons I felt so much heat on the day of my ladder match with Undertaker for the Undisputed title. They see me not caring about it as much as they do, and yet I'm the one that gets a title shot. I could feel the boys thinking, *Jeff's not working house shows and he's the one that's getting a match with Undertaker.*

It felt like everybody in the whole locker room was against me. It pisses me off, and it hurts somewhat, but at the same time it motivates me. I wrote a song about it: "Increase the Jealousy, It Inspires Me."

I cut a backstage promo before the title match. They told me I needed to make the fans believe that I was going to win the title. "Undertaker can't climb ladders," I said, acting all crazy. "I've been in tons of ladder matches! He's been in none. Therefore, I'm the new WWE Undisputed Champion!"

Everybody thought that was too arrogant, but I thought it was exactly right. If I don't believe I can win a match, why should the people watching believe it?

My biggest matches have all been with a lot of other people involved, like the TLC matches. There's so much going on. It's great doing the singles matches, but sometimes I think, *Oh shit. I'm all by myself out here.*

In the match with Undertaker, I really felt alone. It was up to me to make that match exciting and I think I pulled it off. It's not that I carried Taker—far from it—but I had more responsibility as far as the spots and the pace. It was a terrific fight, and the crowd was so into it. We had them going. They were right there with us.

I got some offense, but for the most part, Taker beat the hell out of me. I wasn't expecting those first chair shots he gave me. That shit hurts when you're not ready, and I didn't know they were coming. It's better when you

can tense up a little bit. The chokeslam off the ladder at the end of the match wasn't pretty. I tried to land legs first, to try to stop some of the momentum. All that did was make it worse. My head snapped hard on the mat just as Taker pulled down the belt.

Taker had said he wouldn't leave me standing, but at the very end, I kept pulling myself up. He rode his motorcycle up the ramp, but I got on the mike and said that I was still on my feet. Taker came back down to the ring, and instead of knocking me down again, he held my hand up and endorsed me as one tough son of a bitch. That was cool, because it showed the fans that even if I didn't win the championship, I did win the Taker's respect. It really worked out great for both of us—it elevated me a rung on the ladder and set Undertaker back on the road to being a babyface.

MATT: The ladder match was pretty competitive. Jeff gave it all he had and it ended up being one of his best matches in a long time.

JEFF: The funniest thing happened after we got to the back. Taker was making like he was completely unaffected by the match, but the second he got through the curtain, he was beaten up and worn down. I sold my ass off all the way up the ramp, but when I got back there, I started jumping up and down like a little kid. I was just naturally high. It's a great feeling when you have that kind of match and you know it was good. The crowd was as hot as they could be, Taker was happy, and no one got hurt. You can't ask for more. Except maybe if I'd won the Undisputed title.

Deep down, the boys respect me. Taker had never been in a ladder match, so the fact that he was willing to put himself in the ring with me doing what is my specialty showed how much he respected me. I was so honored to get to work with him.

Since then, I've had the opportunity to do a couple of promos with Ric Flair, which is so awesome. Being involved with him in any way is such an honor. I really want to work a match with him. I'd also love to take a punch from Hollywood Hulk Hogan. When I started wrestling, it never even crossed my mind that I'd get a shot at working with legends like Flair or the Undertaker. If someone had told me I'd be in a ladder match with Taker for the WWE Undisputed Championship, I wouldn't have believed it.

Most people probably think that I'd prefer to work with somebody like Jerry Lynn or RVD, but the truth is, I like a slower pace. That's why I liked working with Undertaker. He takes his time, and he's so good at facials. I've done matches with endless highspots. Now it's more interesting for me to learn how to slow down the pace.

I recently watched an old match, Matt and myself against Joey Matthews and Christian York from a MEWF show in Maryland. I could not believe how much I did throughout the match. It was crazy. Watching it, I realized how much I've learned since then, how much I've grown. I don't feel like I could survive that sort of match anymore.

The week after my title match with the Taker, I won the European title from William Regal. The director told me to go crazy with my celebration when I won, but I just couldn't do it. I told him, "I'm not going to be happy over this! Not when I was so close to winning the WWE Undisputed Championship!"

I wanted to do a promo after the match where I gave the belt back to Regal. "This doesn't mean anything to me," I wanted to say. "I was an inch away from being the WWE Undisputed Champion. Here you go, Regal. You can have this back!"

Then I thought how cool it would be if I just gave the belt away to a kid in the audience. That would make Regal so upset because the European title truly meant something to him. The writers said no, of course.

That was actually part of a cool little streak going in the summer—I competed for five different titles on six editions of *Raw*. First I took on Undertaker for the WWE Undisputed title. Then I beat Regal for the European title. Next I fought RVD for the IC title—and lost the European Championship in the process. A week later, I beat Bradshaw for the hardcore title—but lost it a half a minute later to Johnny the Bull. Finally, Matt and I reunited to fight The Un-Americans for the tag-team titles.

It would've been nice if I'd have come out of all that with something, but my attitude is that when all is said and done, the belts don't mean shit. What counts is putting on a hot match. That's my real goal every time I go out to the ring.

THE MATTITUDE ERA BEGINS!

DATE: *August 13, 2002*
LOCATION: *Seattle, Washington*
ARENA: *Key Arena*

MATT: When Jeff went into his program with Taker and I got trapped doing *Heat,* I'll admit I was a little disappointed, but they promised me that when the time was right, I'd get moved over to the *SmackDown!* roster.

I continued to work extra hard, having killer *Heat* matches with guys like Raven and Steven Richards, guys that were hardly getting any TV time. We were really lighting it up. The crowds were really responsive. I was able to use the star power that I had from doing the Hardy Boyz gimmick for so long to get the crowd into any match I was in.

It ended up feeding into my current gimmick because I made some comments about how people needed to get over the misconception that Jeff was ten times more popular than I am. People heard that and took it as "Matt thinks he's more over than Jeff." All I was saying was that the fans understood that there were two Hardy Boyz—it wasn't all about Jeff.

There were people in the office, though, who just didn't want to see it. I would make all of these valid points, and they'd say, "Oh, Matt Hardy's self-absorbed and completely delusional about his status." In a way, that's where the Mattitude character was born.

Jeff's style is much flashier than mine. His strengths are in his flying around and flipping out. My strengths are for the more solid transitional stuff, so Jeff would invariably shine brighter than me. That was cool by me, because my attitude is that as long as both the team and the segment got over, it's good for everyone involved. I don't try and highlight myself. It doesn't matter who I'm working with—whether it's Justin Credible or Undertaker, I want whatever match I'm in to be the best it can be. If the segment gets over, then everybody in it gets over.

It's no secret that I put together all of our tag-team matches. Jeff has great creative ideas, but the majority of putting it all in order fell onto me. Usually Jeff would just say, "Tell me what I need to do tonight."

But after years of that, it kind of backfired on me. People began to think that since Jeff got a bigger reaction, nobody cared about me. That became a stigma that I needed to overcome.

All I've ever asked for is an opportunity, and when I finally got one, I took the ball and ran with it.

We did a double-shot out in Seattle a couple of weeks before *Summer-Slam*. There was a pretape segment on *Raw* where Rob Van Dam and *Raw* general manager Eric Bischoff were discussing the fact that RVD had a return clause in his contract, guaranteeing him a shot at Chris Benoit, who had just beaten him for the Intercontinental title and taken it over to *SmackDown!*

Jeff and I stood there watching their exchange, and then I asked, "Hey, why don't I get the shot?"

"Because RVD has the guaranteed shot in his contract," Bischoff explained.

"Then why don't you give me a shot at the guaranteed shot?"

"Well, why you and not your brother Jeff?"

"Hey! I asked first!"

"Fine," Bischoff said. "Let's flip a coin. If it's heads, Jeff gets a match for RVD's shot. If it's tails, Matt."

Bischoff didn't even bother to flip the coin. He just kind of looked at it in his hand and said, "Heads!"

So later that night, Rob and Jeff had their match. A few minutes in, the ref got bumped, and Jeff missed a Swanton when Rob rolled out of the way. As Jeff stood there, I slid into the ring, and instead of helping him beat RVD like everybody assumed I would, I grabbed him and hit him with the Twist of Fate.

The following night I officially became a *SmackDown!* wrestler, but for some reason, I never explained what happened with Jeff. I think the powers that be thought that the very act of Twist of Fating my brother would cause people to boo the shit out of me, but that was not the case. Not the case at all.

It started with Shannon Moore, the Hurricane, and Hardcore Holly having a six-man tag match against Billy & Chuck and Rico. After the match, the heels were beating up on Shannon, so Holly and the Hurricane came back in and cleaned house. Just as they were throwing Billy out of the ring, my music hit—the crowd popped like crazy!—and I slid in under the ropes. I grabbed Shannon and Shane—the crowd wondering, *Whose side is Matt on?*—and we all hugged, celebrating my arrival on *Smack-Down!*

Then they showed us all together in the back as I took credit for making the save. Even though I did nothing at all. It was cool—I acted incredibly arrogant and self-absorbed, yet I didn't come off like a full-blown heel. I was more like a sickeningly conceited babyface.

The next week we were in Fayetteville—definitely Matt Hardy country. What happened was more or less the same thing. It was Shannon and Hurricane against Tajiri and Jamie Noble. Once again, Shannon got the pin, followed by the heels beating him up. Shane came in and cleared the ring, and just as he got the heels out, my music hit. I ran down and started celebrating with them, going so far as to make them hoist me up onto their shoulders, like I was the hero of the match.

We went to the back and I bragged about how the crowd reaction had been great the previous week, but this week it was at least ten times as loud.

"You think the only reason I got that reaction is because we're in Fayetteville, North Car-o-li-na," I said, "but I get that kind of reaction anywhere, anytime. I bet if I go out there again, the reaction will get even louder, because these people damn sure got a love for me."

I went back out to the ring and did my whole entrance, hitting my pose five times, throwing the Version 1 hand sign instead of the Hardy Guns. The crowd went wild, cheering like crazy—which is not what the WWE expected. They thought that by the time I posed once, twice at the most, the fans would start booing.

As I stood there basking in the cheers, Chavo Guerrero came out and cut a promo on me: "We'll see how great a reaction you get when I come down there and beat your ass!"

He came running down the ramp and we had ourselves a match. Just as I got him set up for the Twist of Fate, Kane's pyro went off—this was the week before the Big Red Machine made his comeback after an injury. As the explosions hit, I threw Chavo down and took cover, thinking *Oh shit! Kane's coming!*

The lights came up, but I was still distracted and Chavo rolled me up—1-2-3! I flipped out on referee Mike Chioda. "What are you doing? I didn't lose the match! Everybody in this building knows that if an explosion goes off, the match ends!"

Mike just looked at me like I was out of my mind.

"Come on! This is North Carolina, Mike! This is my hometown, for God's sake. They love me in Fayetteville! This is the biggest travesty since Earl Hebner screwed Bret Hart in Canada!"

The next episode of *SmackDown!* was at the Mohegan Sun Casino in Connecticut. Stephanie set up a Number One Contenders Tournament, with the winner getting a shot at the undisputed champion, Brock Lesnar. I ran into Steph backstage just after the first round ended, with Eddie Guerrero going over Edge. "Do you hear it?" I said, referring to the crowd. "They love me in Mohegan Sun! Obviously, I'm facing Eddie in the next round of the tournament, right?"

"Actually, no," she said. "It's Rikishi."

"I'll face the winner of the Rikishi–Eddie match, right?"

"We'll see, Matt, we'll see."

I stood there stretching, warming up. "Well, I'm ready."

The show progressed, but Steph never told me when I was getting my turn in the tournament. I stormed into her office to try to talk to her, but she was on the phone. I was making hand gestures—"C'mon, I need to talk to you!"—but she refused to pay attention. So I reached out and hung up the phone, cutting off her conversation.

Well, that did it. Stephanie was irate, just completely outraged. "That was important," she shrieked.

"No, *this* is important," I said. "This is my life."

"Oh, it will be your life! If you want Brock Lesnar so bad tonight, you've got him—in a nontitle match!"

I got all excited. "Yes! That's all I need. That's my first step!"

The next segment saw Funaki—the number one *SmackDown!* announcer—in front of Brock's dressing room, trying to get an interview. Paul Heyman came out and Funaki started begging to talk to Brock. I pushed my way in front of the mike and said, "If Brock doesn't want to talk, then I will. Tonight's the beginning of a new era on *SmackDown!* No, it's not the era of Brock Lesner, it's the era of Matt Hardy! No longer will this be known as the era of WWE Attitude. From here on it's the era of WWE *Mattitude!*"

As I stormed off, Heyman turned to Funaki, shaking his head in amazement. "Wow," he said. "You learn something new every day. I had no idea that Matt Hardy had a death wish."

Brock and I had our match, and of course he dominated, though I definitely fought back throughout. At the end, I came close to hooking the Twist of Fate, but Brock blocked it and put me into the F-5 and beat me. As he walked up the ramp, I pulled myself up and started acting cocky, throwing the V.1 hand sign. Heyman saw me showboating and sent Brock back to the ring, resulting in me taking two nasty powerbombs for my trouble.

Even though I didn't win, there's no getting around the fact that that was a very special night that will go down in WWE history, the night *Mattitude* was born!

I took it one step further the next week in Green Bay. I was in the back, watching a video that looped all of my offense from the previous week's match with Brock. I called over Shannon Moore and started bragging about going toe-to-toe with the WWE Champion, explaining how I took Brock to the limit.

"The reason I brought you over here to watch this video is because I exist to inspire," I said. "I saw your match earlier tonight and you looked good, but you still lost. But hey, keep your head up. Listen to my advice, follow my leadership, and one day you, too, may have the *Mattributes* to face the WWE Champion."

Those few weeks were a major turning point in my career. It was the moment when I went from being half of the World Famous Hardy Boyz to being Matt Hardy V.1, *SmackDown!* Superstar.

From the second the word came out of my mouth, I knew *Mattitude* was money. I was in the gym with Scott Matthews, and I said something totally off-the-cuff, about it being a new era of WWE *Mattitude.* Scott just about fell on the floor laughing.

Mattitude is exactly the kind of catchphrase every wrestler wants, because it plays off of something everyone knows, in this case, WWE Attitude. When you have a phrase that's easy to remember, that sticks in the fans' minds, it really helps to get you over. Plus it had an arrogance that played perfectly into my character.

My goal is to find the exact right blend of humour and work rate. The perfect example of a guy like that is Kurt Angle. He's unquestionably one of the most well-rounded wrestlers of all time.

I know how the system works. It's up to you to get yourself over as much as you possibly can. You need to come up with as much creative stuff for yourself as you can, because nobody's going to just hand it to you. I've been very lucky in that I've been given room to really create the Matt Hardy V.1 character. The writers hand you lines and it's up to you to just say them as written, or to do what you can to make them better.

For instance, I came up with the Montreal Screwjob reference for after the Kane explosion in Fayetteville. Bringing up Bret Hart and the infamous Montreal Screwjob is always a touchy bit of business in WWE, so I asked Michael Hayes what he thought.

"I don't know," he replied. "That's a Vince call."

I went in and asked Vince about it. I explained that since my character is somewhat delusional, it would be hilarious if I put my getting beat by Chavo in North Carolina on the same level as Bret getting "beat" in Montreal. He chuckled and said, "That's great. I love it!"

After those first couple of weeks on *SmackDown!* Michael told me that Vince was really high on my character. That's a great feeling, knowing that the Boss is into what I'm doing. From that point on, the writing team began working me into more pretapes in addition to my matches. They don't give away TV time to just anybody.

It's like I've always said, just give me the opportunity to do my thing and I can light up a crowd—whether they're cheering me or chanting "Asshole!"

NEW FRONTIERS

MATT: I love being the Hardy Boyz, but it reached the point where we were almost backed into a corner. In a lot of ways, we've done all that we can do as a tag team. We've won six Tag Team Championships, we've stood toe-to-toe with the biggest names in the business, we've put on matches that I believe will go down in wrestling history as some of the most exciting and innovative matches of all time.

And as long as we were seen as only a tag team, people couldn't seem to take us seriously as singles. We simply had to go our own separate ways. We want people to see that we're more than Matt and Jeff, the Hardy Boyz—we're Matt Hardy and Jeff Hardy, two distinct and individual characters.

JEFF: Now that Matt's on *SmackDown!* and I'm on *Raw*, I can really cut loose on my own. I can express my ideas and my character without him telling me "That's not logical."

Our personal relationship is so much better now that we're working on separate shows. We have a couple of crossover days, Wednesday and Thursday, when we're both at home.

MATT: The professional wrestling business is all about the constant battle to move ahead. You always want to move up the ladder. You want to go from being a great tag team to being the Intercontinental Champion and strong midcard player, and then, eventually, a main eventer. That's the obvious progression. With Jeff, all that is completely possible, but what makes him so different is that he's not worried about it. Jeff is such a free spirit. He's not bound by anything. He'll only do something if it's going to make him happy. He's perfectly willing to sacrifice the good money he makes to go play music for less. Because that's what he loves.

Me, I love this business, I'm going to be a part of it till the day I die. Professional wrestling is as much a part of me as anything else in my life. Once it gets in your blood—I mean *truly* gets in your blood—it's not just an infatuation: it's something you can't get rid of. Whether I'm involved or watching or even just talking about wrestling, it makes me happy.

I'm happily obsessed with wrestling. I meet people and they say, "I'm not going to talk about wrestling. I'm sure you get sick of talking about it." Actually, I don't. I really don't.

Jeff, on the other hand, doesn't fit the typical personality that's successful in the wrestling industry. He is a very different soul. Jeff is Jeff. As long as he has time to hang out around his house and drive the Bobcat and build Aluminummies, he's happy.

JEFF: Sometimes I'm in the locker room and I just feel so different. I'm nothing like anyone else there. You ask anybody in WWE about me and they're going to say, "He's a weird cat." But I think everybody in WWE is weird in some way. You've got to be a little crazy to be a wrestler.

But I can't deny that I'm sick and tired of the politics. Of constantly jockeying for position. Of all the infighting and backstabbing that goes on. All the politics makes me have headaches. It makes me throw up. Literally.

I'm just happy to have a job where I'm on TV entertaining people. I really just love the wrestling—the physicality, the storytelling, the theater. There's nothing that's quite as much fun as when the crowd's hot and we're out there ripping it up.

MATT: The thing is, if you're in the wrestling business and you don't truly love it, then you won't last. There's way too much politics, and it takes too big a toll on your body and your mind for you to make it. That's a guarantee. Nobody makes it to the level we're at and stays there for any amount of time unless they truly love it.

Look at a guy like my good buddy Marty Garner. He's been losing money at it for eight years now, but he keeps going. Even when he was in ECW, he lost money. He'd drive from North Carolina to Philadelphia or wherever and get paid a big fifty dollars if he was lucky. By the time you pay for six meals on the road, the hotel and the gas, you're a hundred dollars in the hole.

We've been there. We've seen a lot of miles on the highway, doing the independent shows where we came home and were out more money than we'd made. But the reason you do it is because you have that goal, that tunnel vision that keeps you moving forward. The thing that keeps you motivated has got to be a genuine love for the business—it's hard work and you're losing money, but you're enjoying it every step of the way. I feel so fortunate that I was one of the ones that made it. There's so many people that should be making a good living in the business, but probably never will.

Looking past my days as an active competitor, I would love someday to be in a position where I can make decisions about talent relations and story lines and the overall booking of the product. I think I may be even stronger as a force behind the scenes, in terms of keeping people motivated and making the product grow. I'll always have something to offer to the professional wrestling business.

JEFF: As far as wrestling goes, I know I'm good at it. I'm *really* good at it. It's what I do better than anything else. But when it comes to talking about winning and losing matches, I simply do not care. When I quit wrestling altogether, I don't want to be remembered for how many matches I won or lost. I just want people to think, *Damn, I loved watching him.*

To win matches, you've got to play the game—fighting with the agents, kissing the booker's ass, whatever it takes. The love I have for wrestling comes from the performing part of it, from giving people a good show. Whether we win or lose, we get a standing ovation every time.

I think it's time to stop all the big highspots, like the hanging above the ring and the ridiculous falls off the ladder. They've gotten to the point like, "Where do you go from here?" It was great to be a part of that, but it's time for the next Hardy Boyz to step in and start doing new crazy shit. I'm twenty-five years old and I already feel like a veteran.

I admit it—I worry about the future. Jumping off the top and landing flat on your back night in and night out can't be a good thing. Because of my style, people always compare me to guys like Dynamite Kid, who's in a wheelchair, or Hayabusa, who's paralyzed. It makes me want to prove them wrong. There's so much more that I can do, and I'm ready to do it all.

MATT: Growing up, Jeff and I used to talk about how awesome it would be to have a T-shirt. Well, we've had a bunch of T-shirts, plus we've been in video games, we've had posters, we've had our own magazine, a home video/DVD, not to mention about thirty different action figures. We've been on a sitcom, we've been featured in commercials.

We've traveled all over the country and all over the world. We're six-time WWE Tag Team Champions, and we've both had singles titles. I'd say the Hardy Boyz have had a pretty good run. It's really amazing when you sit back and think about it.

With this book, we've done everything that we ever dreamed of doing in the wrestling business—except winning the WWE Championship.

That's the ultimate goal for both of us, becoming the WWE Champion. That's as high as you can go in our business. That's the biggest prize in our sport, as they say.

Now it's time for Jeff Hardy and Matt Hardy to go our separate ways and let the chips fall where they may. Team Extreme might have come to an end, but we'll always be brothers. Who knows? The Hardy Boyz will proba-bly get back together somewhere down the line, but for the time being, we need to develop our individual identities and take on a whole new set of challenges.

We've learned a lot through our experiences. We're smarter, more educated, and ready for anything. It's such an important thing to modify yourself as life goes on. Like our old football coach M. D. Guthrie used to say, "If you're not getting better, you're getting worse."

You've got to always work at being better. You should only stop because you've gone as far as you can go.

Jeff and me—we've still got a long way to go.

CAPTIONS

THE HARDY BOYZ

EXIST 2 INSPIRE